MINISTRY IN CONVERSATION

MINISTRY IN CONVERSATION

Essays in Honour of Paul Goodliff

Edited by
ANDY GOODLIFF *and* JOHN E. COLWELL

WIPF & STOCK · Eugene, Oregon

MINISTRY IN CONVERSATION
Essays in Honour of Paul Goodliff

Wipf & Stock
An Imprint of Wipf and Stock Publishers
199 W. 8th Ave., Suite 3
Eugene, OR 97401

www.wipfandstock.com

PAPERBACK ISBN: 978-1-6667-1926-0
HARDCOVER ISBN: 978-1-6667-1927-7
EBOOK ISBN: 978-1-6667-1928-4

MARCH 18, 2022 10:59 AM

Contents

Contributors

PAUL BEASLEY-MURRAY is an author, a minister to ministers, and an activist in his church and community.

MYRA BLYTH is a former Chaplain of Regent's Park College, Oxford.

RUTH BOTTOMS is a Baptist minister and head of Faith and Spirituality, West London Mission.

GEOFF COLMER is Regional Minister Team Leader, Central Baptist Association, and President of the Baptist Union of Great Britain, 2021–22.

JOHN COLWELL is a retired Baptist minister and former Tutor of Doctrine and Ethics, Spurgeon's College, London.

STEPHEN COPSON is Regional Minister, Central Baptist Association, and Secretary of the Baptist Historical Society.

ROBERT ELLIS was Principal, Regent's Park College, Oxford, until 2021 and is now a Senior Research Fellow.

PAUL FIDDES is Professor of Systematic Theology, University of Oxford, and a Senior Research Fellow, Regent's Park College, Oxford.

ANDY GOODLIFF is Minister of Belle Vue Baptist Church, Southend-on-Sea and Lecturer in Baptist History, Regent's Park College, Oxford.

RUTH GOULDBOURNE is Minister of Grove Lane Baptist Church, Cheadle Hulme.

WALE HUDSON-ROBERTS is Racial Justice Advisor, Baptist Union of Great Britain, and Minister of John Bunyan Baptist Church, Cowley, Oxford.

SALLY NELSON is Dean of Baptist Formation, St Hild College, Yorkshire.

ALISTAIR ROSS is Associate Professor in Psychotherapy, Department for Continuing Education, University of Oxford.

GRAHAM SPARKES is President of Luther King Centre, Manchester where he also teaches Christian Spirituality.

PAT TOOK is a retired Baptist minister and former Regional Minister Team Leader, London Baptist Association.

INTRODUCTION

IT MIGHT BE SAID of Paul Goodliff that, like his namesake, the apostle Paul, he was one "untimely born" (1 Cor 15:8). He was born around three weeks premature in Brighton on March 20, 1956. His survival was by no means certain, and yet survive he did; and perhaps this reflects that, unknown at the time, God had also set him, like Paul, apart and called him by grace to be one who preached among Gentiles (Gal 1:15–16).

Paul first felt a calling to Christian ministry as a teenager; at the time he was a confirmed member of the Church of England, attending All Saints, the parish church in Patcham, Brighton, where he grew up.[1] Any testing of that call was paused while he went to King's College London to study geography, and following that became a teacher at Tiffin's School for Boys in Kingston. Whilst at university, living in South London, he went to church at Lewin Road Baptist Church in Streatham, when Douglas McBain was minister, and there became a Baptist. Paul and Gill, following their marriage in 1977, settled at the church and in 1980 Paul was called to become an elder, and then in 1982 a full-time pastoral elder. For nine months Paul was the only pastor in a large church, between Douglas leaving and his replacement, Mike Wood, arriving.[2] A call to ministry was tested and supported and he began training for ministry in 1984 at Spurgeon's College, London.[3] He pioneered with another student, Martin Taylor, church-based training at Spurgeon's.[4] Paul was ordained in 1988 and remained at Lewin Road until 1992 when he was called to Bunyan Baptist Church, Stevenage. Between 1990 and 1992 he studied for a MTh

1. Goodliff, *Shaped for Service*, xi.

2. Goodliff, *Care in a Confused Climate*, 130–31.

3. Two of his fellow students were Alistair Ross and Geoff Colmer, who became good friends, and for one year Ruth Gouldbourne was also a fellow student.

4. Goodliff, "Anyone Still for Ordination?," 4.

in 20th Systematic Theology from King's College London, under Colin Gunton, with a dissertation on Eberhard Jüngel.

Paul's years in Stevenage were busy, not just with the church, but as a part-time chaplain at the local hospital (1993–98), as a Tutor in Pastoral Counselling at St. John's College, Nottingham (1994–2000), being chair of Swanwick Counselling (1994–96), and on the board of the Richard Baxter Institute for Ministry (1993–2005).[5] A sabbatical in 1997 saw him write his first book, *Care in a Confused Climate: Pastoral Care and Post-modern Culture*, published in 1998.[6]

In 1999, the post of General Superintendent for the Central Area (Herts, Beds, Bucks, Northants)[7] became available and Paul was appointed, having the distinction of being the last to be appointed,[8] for in 2002, following the changes to the Baptist Union's structures, General Superintendents were renamed as Regional Ministers, of which he became the Team Leader in the Central Baptist Association.[9]

In 2004 he was appointed as Head of Ministry for the Baptist Union and would remain in that position for ten years.[10] This was a demanding role, overseeing around two thousand ministers and with responsibility for their accreditation. Here he brought all his skills as a pastor, a counsellor, and a theologian to the different needs and challenges he faced. In these years he still found time to publish a second book in 2005, *With Unveiled Face: A Pastoral and Theological Exploration of Shame*; be a distance Tutor for the Open Theological College (1997–2009); and, as a Baptist representative of the Joint Consultative Group between the World Council of Churches and the Pentecostal churches (2001–), which has seen him most years, visit other parts of the world for their meetings. In 2009 he completed a DMin, again at King's College London, and his thesis on Baptist understandings of ministry and ordination in the late

5. This latter role was alongside his friend Paul Beasley-Murray.

6. He was especially pleased that Colin Gunton agreed to write the foreword.

7. For some reflections on his understanding of the task and role of Superintendency (and Regional Ministry), see Goodliff, "Contemporary Models." Sally Nelson was one of the ministers in the Central Area at that time, in Watford.

8. This role saw him join the Superintendent's Board alongside Pat Took, who was General Superintendent for the Metropolitan Area.

9. Stephen Copson was one of the other Regional Ministers appointed in the CBA at the same time, having being Secretary of the Hertfordshire Baptist Association. For a history of the changes, see Goodliff, *Renewing a Modern Denomination*.

10. At Baptist House he worked alongside Myra Blyth, Graham Sparkes, Wale Hudson-Roberts, and Ruth Bottoms.

twentieth century was published by Regent's Park College, Oxford, in 2010 as *Ministry, Sacrament and Representation*. In this book he argued for a sacramental turn in how Baptist ministers viewed ministry. Also in 2010 he realized a dream with several others as a founding member of the Order for Baptist Ministry.[11]

In 2014, he stepped down as Head of Ministry and returned to the local church, as a part-time pastor in Abingdon Baptist Church. Alongside this he was involved in teaching modules at Spurgeon's, Bristol Baptist College, and Regent's Park College.[12] It was in this period that he wrote a fourth book, *Shaped for Service: Ministerial Formation and Virtue Ethics*. Paul might have thought that he would end his ministry in the pastorate of a local church, but in 2017 he was encouraged to apply for the vacant position of General Secretary of Churches Together in England and found himself being appointed, a position he has held from 2018 until this year, 2022. This final role has once again been a demanding one and has required the virtues of patience, wisdom, and fortitude. In these four years, he has continued to write, contributing to and editing books on juridical law and ecumenism,[13] episcopacy,[14] and Baptist spirituality.[15]

As he retires from full-time ministry at sixty-six, we offer these essays on ministry in conversation with some of the particular loves in his life. What is missing is of course his love of Gill, his children and grandchildren, and wider family and friends. From a young age Paul was interested in art,[16] music,[17] literature, poetry,[18] geography, and history,[19]

---

11. For some of the story of the order and an engagement with its thought and practices, see Goodliff and Goodliff, *Rhythms of Faithfulness*. See also https://www. orderforbaptistministry.co.uk.

12. Rob Ellis was Principal at Regent's at the time and Paul Fiddes was still on staff. For several years Paul also worked alongside Rob during Rob's tenure as Moderator of the Baptist Union's Ministry Committee.

13. Goodliff, "Natural Law in the Baptist Tradition" and "Baptist Church Polity."

14. Goodliff and Standing, eds., *Episkope*.

15. Goodliff and Goodliff, eds., *Rhythms of Faithfulness*.

16. Paul is an occasional painter. One of his paintings graces the front cover of Blyth and Goodliff, *Gathering Disciples*. Other works have appeared at the Baptist Assembly, and many more can be found on the walls of his home.

17. Paul plays the guitar and was a choirboy in his youth. He loves classical music and jazz.

18. In 2018 two of his poems were published in the journal *Theology*.

19. Books of literature, poetry, geography, and history can be found scattered across his home; almost every room has shelving for books of some kind. He is an

and into adulthood he has added wine, gardening, travel,[20] and of course some of those activities associated with ministry: preaching, prayer, education, counselling, and ecumenism.

In seeking a title for this collection of essays, we pondered various possibilities; what is it that holds these chapters together? We eventually decided on "Ministry in Conversation." The choice of the word "conversation" points to a way of seeing ministry as one which is focused on enabling a people within and beyond the church to have an ongoing conversation about "the difference that Christ makes."[21] Ministers are those who know how to have a good conversation. In this book many of the chapters begin a conversation with a "partner" not usually had with ministry and this indicates a view that a ministry captivated with Christ is one also open to the world,[22] whether that be, for example, the world of poetry, wine, geography, or gardening. None of these conversations are designed to be the last word; rather they seek to engender new or fresh conversations.

We hope that these essays provide stimulation and further reflection on the particular calling of ministry that has been the joy of Paul's life for over forty years and to which others will also find helpful. As one of Paul's first theological teachers (John) and as one of Paul's sons (Andy), in different ways we have benefited from his example, his care, his encouragement, and many conversations, as have all those others who have contributed to this book. Festchrifts do not just honour achievement, but they are, we hope, also a testimony to friendship, and the joy of having companions on the way of Jesus.

---

unapologetic bibliophile.

20. Travel with the WCC has taken him around the world (Egypt, South Korea, Switzerland, Tanzania, USA), but he has enjoyed travelling on holidays and visiting different parts of Europe over the years.

21. I borrow this phrase from an essay by Sam Wells.

22. The phrasing here is borrowed from Brock, *Captive to Christ, Open to the World*.

1

MINISTRY AND ART

Graham Sparkes

ORIGINS

There is no doubt that a major influence on the early development of Baptist theology and identity was the magisterial reformer John Calvin. Other foundational influences can certainly be identified, including groupings such as the Anabaptists and Mennonites, who have come to be described as the radical wing of the Reformations taking place in Europe. But there is no denying the ways in which Calvin shaped the Baptist and the wider Puritan movement as it began to establish itself in England in the seventeenth century.

Calvin's systematic treatment of Christian doctrine and practice provided an invaluable guide for churches looking to follow a pathway that would offer reform rooted in the evangelical faith as revealed in Scripture. His *Institutes of the Christian Religion*, first published in 1536 and subsequently revised and expanded, became the normative expression of Reformed faith, and it was a manual that influenced the life and faith of all Baptists, but especially those who became part of the early network of "Particular" Baptist churches.[1] Yet with it came teachings that, I would suggest, have not always served Baptists well. One of these is

---

1. Though, of course, there were issues such as infant baptism where Baptists would offer a dissenting voice, the strong influence of Calvinist thought is present, for example, in the early 1644 Confession of Faith and in the developing Baptist understanding of the Lord's Supper (see Fiddes, *Tracks and Traces*, 157–92).

Calvin's deep suspicion of the potential of human imagination to open us to new understandings of God—and alongside it a reluctance to grant any theological place to the use of images themselves.

According to Calvin,

> when miserable men do seek after God, instead of ascending higher than themselves, as they ought to do, they measure him by their own carnal stupidity, and, neglecting solid inquiry, fly off to indulge their curiosity in vain speculation. Hence, they do not conceive of him in the character in which he is manifested, but imagine him to be whatever their own rashness has devised.[2]

Left to its own devices, the human heart inevitably relies on its own imagination, and this is inherently dangerous as it leads a person away from God. The only way, says Calvin, that we can come to right knowledge of God, of ourselves, and our world is through Scripture, and this knowledge is conveyed to us by the Spirit, who is present in its reading and preaching. What is needed is a method of "solid inquiry"—a method that will provide the necessary clear understanding that will correct our tendency to stray into superstition, speculation, and imaginative fantasy, and enable us truly to know God and offer God true worship. It is this method Calvin proceeds to set out in the *Institutes*.

In discussing Calvin's approach, Dyrness declares that "Calvin never makes any positive reference to what we would call the work of 'imagination.'"[3] It is a product of our fallen human nature and as such offers us a pathway to ignorance. In turn, images succeed only in leading to idolatry; it is true preaching of the Word alone that allows us to grasp Christ in our hearts through faith, and visual representations that derive from human imagination can have no place in worship. True, we have the visual presence of the sacraments. But even here Calvin is clear that the way we know Christ is inwardly by faith, and that the image must always be joined to the word.[4]

As a Baptist minister, there is no doubting Paul Goodliff's commitment to the kind of true preaching that Calvin would have wanted and expected. In his exploration of what it means to be formed as a preacher, Paul speaks of his own training as rooting him in "a careful attention to

---

2. Calvin, *Institutes*, I.iv.1.

3. Dyrness, *Reformed Theology*, 65.

4. Dyrness, *Reformed Theology*, 71.

the text of Scripture"[5] that has continued to serve him well throughout his long ministry. Indeed, Calvin's influence can be seen not only in Paul's conviction that preaching has to be rooted in the Word revealed in Scripture, but also in his wider explorations of the ministry and discipleship of the whole people of God.

Yet despite this very evident debt to Calvin's thinking, I would suggest that Paul—along with myself—would want to question the suspicion of images and the use of the imagination that is a notable part of Calvin's legacy to us. While serving as minister at Abingdon Baptist Church, Paul chose to offer a series of four ecumenical Lent lectures on the theme of "Let's Wait and See," and in doing so based his reflections on images of some of the key biblical stories. The chosen works of art became the source of careful, attentive exploration not unlike the practice of contemplative prayer. Such engagement with art and images is there, too, in Paul's writings and forms an integral part of his explorations of ministry, pastoral care, and our contemporary culture. We see the way in which images become an important way of understanding the human condition and developing key metaphors for ministerial formation.[6] And anyone who has visited Paul's home will know that its walls are rich with the presence of beautifully curated images!

As an acknowledgement of Paul's own imaginative creativity and his appreciation of the value of art, I want to examine one or two aspects of our nonconformist suspicion of imagination and argue for a greater intentionality amongst Baptists—and all Christians—in the use of images to enrich and nurture our faith.

IMAGINATION AND FANCY

In early English Protestantism the word often used for imagination is "fancy." The prevailing culture and literature of the time regarded imagination as a breeding ground for what had the potential to be unreliable, unstable, and chaotic. It opened the door for what was no better than human fancy, when what was needed for right thinking and practice was a church marked by order and decency. But while this was the prevailing attitude of the time, it is clear that the debates behind what was described

5. Goodliff, *Shaped for Service*, 245.

6. See, for example, Goodliff, *Care in a Confused Climate*, 39–40, 51–52; and *Shaped for Service*, 17–25, 196–208.

as human fancy were complex, reflecting both the context and the questions that were being asked within different Christian communities. The increasing availability of the Scriptures meant that Protestants—including Baptists—now had a freedom to read and interpret their meaning in ways that had not previously been possible, and with that freedom came questions about the limits, boundaries, and responsibilities that this entailed. How is a right understanding of doctrine to be decided? Who has authority to determine the meaning and message of Scripture? Where lies the boundary between divinely ordered reason and human fancy? And, in particular, how is the role of the Holy Spirit to be understood? These were challenging questions that even Calvin's *Institutes* could not fully settle.

Nuttall argues in his exploration of the role of the Spirit in Puritan life and faith that in periods when Christianity takes on a settled form, less attention tends to be given to the Spirit.[7] However, the impact of the Reformation in Europe together with the spread of the Scriptures and the growth of dissenting and nonconformist movements in England ensured that these were not settled times. It is therefore hardly surprising to find lively discussions taking place, not least regarding the extent to which human fantasy could be a source of the Spirit's guidance.

On the one hand, Nuttall identifies those radicals—particularly Quakers—who were convinced that the Spirit could be discerned through the use of human imagination. The Spirit, they believed, was present within every person, granting spiritual perception through experience. Thus, when the Quaker missionary James Parnell turned up at Fen Stanton, the Baptist records show that questions were asked as to whether he placed the Spirit above the Scriptures: "We then desired him, before he said any more, to prove what he had said . . . 'He found it by experience,' he said. We desired him to prove it by the Scriptures, for we would not be ruled by his fancy."[8] For Quakers, Scripture did matter, as did reason; yet the light offered by the Spirit provided a spiritual perception that went beyond such knowledge. Hence, even an uneducated person might experience God more deeply and fully than one who relied only on understanding.

On the other hand, the concerns expressed at Fen Stanton were illustrative of many who were far more resistant to granting any value

---

7. Nuttall, *Holy Spirit in Puritan Faith*.

8. Quoted by Nuttall, *Holy Spirit in Puritan Faith*, 35.

to imagination or fancy. They were deeply concerned about the dangers it posed, wanting to assert both the primacy of Scripture and the fact that the Spirit works through reason, this highest of human powers that grants knowledge of God. Nuttall draws on the writings of the prominent nonconformist Richard Baxter as an example of someone who brings together into a synthesis "the rational and the spiritual principles," and who criticized the Quakers for failing "to test the movings of the Spirit by Scripture and by reason."[9]

It is interesting to note that, as Barbour has shown in his wider study of literature and religious culture in seventeenth century England, there were a growing number of factions within Protestantism that frequently charged each other with falling into the trap of allowing too great a reliance on the imagination. No one wanted to be tainted by the suggestion that they gave credence to unreliable human invention in the search to know and worship God. The Laudian movement within the Church of England accused Puritans of encouraging an individualized faith that ignored the ordered, tried, and tested formal liturgy of the national church, and gave opportunity for the creation of fanciful idols; Puritans accused Laudians of clinging on to the trappings of Catholicism with their dangerous appeal to the imaginary senses at the expense of preaching that was rooted in Scripture; and both accused Baptists and other dissenters of allowing imagination to have far too much scope in worship through—for example—the use of extemporary prayer, which inevitably encouraged the worship of private idols created within the human mind.[10] Human fancy had all kinds of negative associations, and almost every church grouping wanted to distance itself from the suggestion that its life and worship was shaped by the imagination.

There were genuine fears and concerns here. In these early years, Baptists along with other dissenting congregations were wanting to establish their identity in opposition to the Church of England—a church they regarded as little better that the Church of Rome, and a church that regarded them as dangerous subversives. They saw within that church much that continued to echo the spiritual poverty and corruption that had initially prompted the great reforming movements, and in their eyes those failings had much to do with human fancy. Dissenters looked at the continuing ceremonies and rituals that formed part of the liturgy,

9. Nuttall, *Holy Spirit in Puritan Faith*, 47.

10. Barbour, *Literature and Religious Culture*, 91–117.

for example, and regarded these as a deliberate attempt to appeal to the senses in ways that undermined sound biblical doctrine and teaching.

At the same time, they could not ignore the internal challenges their developing sense of identity posed. A resistance to hierarchical and autocratic church structures inevitably led to the question of where authority was to be located, and how the activity of the Spirit amongst the people of God was to be recognized. An openness to Scripture and to its reading and interpretation by all who are called and gifted by the Spirit quickly leads to issues of how a congregation might distinguish the genuine prophetic voice in the midst over against the wild and fanciful imagination of a voice that should not be trusted.

Indeed, such questions still have resonance today. For Baptists, as for many other traditions, the strengths and weaknesses of different models of leadership continue to be debated, and there is a recognized need to be always vigilant to the questions raised by different interpretations of Scripture, and how we give proper place to liberty of conscience while still wanting to discern what is of the Spirit and what is not.

UNDERSTANDING IMAGINATION

At this point it is important to put in a word of defence on Calvin's behalf—which will also help make sense of the suspicion of imagination as merely fanciful, particularly amongst early Baptists and other nonconformists. It has to do with our changing and growing understanding of the nature of human imagination.

For the sixteenth-century reformers and their immediate heirs, imagination had a particular function. Drawing on Rossky's work on Renaissance approaches to the imagination, Barbour describes it as:

> a mediating agent in the human system of mental apprehension, which means that fancy's duties to receive, reshape, and transmit data from the senses to reason and from reason to the will are as crucial to thought as they are fallible and whimsical.[11]

In other words, it had a distinctive purpose having to do with memorizing and then transferring—rather like that of a digital camera. In the process, it was all too easy for the images to become corrupted, such that they failed to provide accurate information for reason to work

---

11. Barbour, *Literature and Religious Culture*, 105.

with. And hence the dangers of imagination becoming merely fanciful. It was fundamentally private and therefore untestable, and thus Puritans, dissenters, and nonconformists all struggled with its divisive potential and were very wary of those who claimed divine messages within their dreams. It is worth noting that in this explanation of how the imagination works there is no place given to any idea of creativity.[12] But that is not how we now understand imagination. Numerous philosophical—and theological—studies have taken place in recent years into aspects of the imagination, and it has been increasingly recognized as a pervasive feature of our humanity.[13] We no longer see it as a discrete human faculty that can be set alongside reason or will or conscience, each contributing something distinctive to the way our human minds operate. We cannot distinguish and separate off imagination. Rather, as Trevor Hart suggests, "Imagination is better thought of as *a way of thinking, responding and acting* across the whole spread of our experience, not some arcane 'thing' with a carefully specified and limited remit."[14] It is integral to our whole existence; being imaginative is at the core of our humanity, both in the engagement with fairly mundane and ordinary activities (such as planning, hoping, analyzing, loving) and in the performance of more self-consciously creative activities (such as writing, painting, composing).

Viewed in this way, we might declare that Calvin himself was an immensely imaginative theologian. Amongst early Baptists and nonconformists it is also possible to point to fine examples of those who used their imagination in ways that have had notable influence—though not without challenges due to the ways in which its workings used to be understood.

IMAGINATION IN BUNYAN AND BLAKE

John Bunyan's *The Pilgrim's Progress* has been one of the most widely read theological works of fiction. Born in 1628, Bunyan initially followed a path of Anglican conformity, but gradually he developed Puritan sympathies during the course of his life that led him to become part of an independent Separatist congregation in Bedford and a notable local preacher. His unlawful preaching resulted in imprisonment, during which it is

12. See Barbour, *Literature and Religious Culture*, 91–117.

13. A list of some of these is provided in Hart, *Between the Image and the Word*, 3.

14. Hart, *Between the Image and the Word*, 5.

likely he wrote much of the first part of *The Pilgrim's Progress*, published in 1678. The second part was completed and published in 1685.

It is an allegory, telling the story of Christian making his pilgrimage through this world to the Heavenly City, and exploring the cost involved in staying faithful on the journey and so finding salvation. As such, it is a piece of writing that grows out of Bunyan's imagination. In her fascinating article Bethany Joy Bear shows how conflicted Bunyan himself was over the use of the fancy, noting that "proffering a work of fancy is daring not only in the context of larger theological uncertainties but also within Bunyan's own oeuvre." She indicates that, "Throughout his own treatises and sermons, Bunyan consistently characterizes the relationship between the human fancy and true faith as problematic."[15] Yet he proceeds with his work in the recognition that though fancy is part of our fallen nature and particularly susceptible to satanic delusions, it can be redeemed. He shares with many other Protestant writers a deep concern about imaginative storytelling that serves no purpose, yet believes that if there is an intention that is good and true and faithful, then it can be justified. As Bear says, "Bunyan recognizes that the value of his allegories—direct products of the fancy—depend on whether they aim merely to entertain (as fables) or to edify (as parables), following Christ's habit of using narratives for spiritual instruction."[16]

Bear goes on to explore how the tension between Bunyan's deep convictions about fancy and his own work of the imagination play out within *The Pilgrim's Progress*. In Part I, the figure of Ignorance "represents the excesses of human fancy."[17] He walks alone, trusting to his own understandings and perceptions, and as a result he ends up being dragged down into hell. For Bunyan, the dangerous reliance of Ignorance on his own fancy to direct his faith mirrors that of the Quakers, who are content to trust the authority of individual revelations that claim the inspiration of the Spirit.

In Part II, however, Bear suggests that Bunyan takes a rather different approach. He develops a complex and careful defence of imagination, particularly through the figure of Christiana. She needs to be "recognized as an allegorical representation of the fancy itself" as she is so often associated in the text with dreams and the use of the imagination to interpret

15. Bear, "Fantastical Faith," 676.
16. Bear, "Fantastical Faith," 679.
17. Bear, "Fantastical Faith," 681.

them. Bunyan, says Bear, "wishes to demonstrate how fancy can play a key part in sanctification."[18]

There are potentially issues to do with gender surfacing here, which should not surprise us and are certainly noted by Bear in her article. Yet two things clearly emerge in Bunyan's writing of Part II. First, Christiana offers a model of faithful pilgrimage within which the Spirit is very evidently working to redeem the fancy. Stories, testimonies, and experiences all bear witness to the ability of the Spirit to use the imagination to enrich the journey of discipleship. Second, Christiana walks her pilgrimage in company with others, and it is this link with the Christian community that enables Christiana's spirituality to develop a depth and a richness that are lost to the person who walks alone. The pilgrim company, mirroring the practices of the early church, becomes the place where the guidance of the Spirit is discerned. It is not an institution established by the state, but a humble people who instruct one another, encourage each other, and walk together in faith and obedience. It is here, within the fellowship of God's people, that the testing and refining of the use of the fancy takes place through the guidance and inspiration of the Spirit. As Bear concludes, "For Bunyan, the Spirit redeems fancy not by enabling the human fancy to apprehend truth on its own but by bestowing dreams, sustaining love among Christians, and transforming the former enemy of faith into a faculty that guides all Spirit-led 'Fantastical Fools' to their home in the Celestial City."[19] We shall return to this community vision of Christian discernment in due course.

Working over a hundred years later, William Blake felt none of Bunyan's internal conflict over the use of the fancy. He was born in London into a family of dissenters, and though the rites of the Church of England marked the key moments of his life, Blake's influencers lay within the radical traditions.[20] His mother, Catherine Armitage, had been a member of the Moravian Church of Fetter Lane in London, and Blake's own name appears as a signatory of the minute book of the separatist Swedenborgian New Jerusalem Church in 1789. But though we know little of what active part Blake may or may not have played in the life of such dissenting congregations, the work he did as an engraver, poet, and

---

18. Bear, "Fantastical Faith," 684.

19. Bear, "Fantastical Faith," 701.

20. See Rix, *William Blake and the Cultures of Radical Christianity.*

artist is testimony to the way such radical expressions of the Christian faith shaped his life.

Most significant of all, Blake rooted himself very clearly in the Bible. He may not always have read it in an orthodox way, but it is the core inspiration for his work, not least because he believed that "he shared the 'Poetic Genius' with those who wrote the Bible."[21] Blake saw himself as standing firmly in the tradition of the prophets—including Christ himself—with their apocalyptic visions and insights, and he despised any suggestion that the Bible was a book of rules, a dead text from the past that merely had to be repeated and obeyed. Rather, he wanted to free people from such institutional approaches in order to rediscover the essential, dynamic faith of Christianity, and this required the use of the imagination.

Blake had no qualms about the central importance of the fancy. In his book *The Marriage of Heaven and Hell*, he offers one of several images that he describes as a "memorable fancy" of himself dining and conversing with Isaiah and Ezekiel, and in the process gaining new insight into the truth about both heaven and hell.[22] In the aphorisms he included on the *Laocoon* plate, Blake is more daring, describing Jesus as the archetypal artist and thus the model for all artistic activity. As Billingsley says, for Blake "Christ's identity is Imagination, and as such all his acts and all activity in him are art."[23] Put simply, for Blake word and image come together. The reader also becomes the viewer, sharing in the creative process. True art is seen as spiritual, with each individual called to pursue such creativity, and it is in this fusion of literary and visual elements that the Spirit is at work, enabling Scripture's meaning to be constantly reborn, thus maintaining its power to bring life.

Within the creative complexity of Blake's theological world, we are left in no doubt that imagination is essential to Christian vision. In the words of Christopher Rowland, Blake believed that "Allowing reason to triumph over imagination denies a wisdom 'Permanent in the Imagination,' through which one could open Eternal Worlds."[24] Yet it was perhaps inevitable that many in Blake's own day regarded him as suffering from madness for expressing such views. How could the imagination—the

21. Rowland, *Blake and the Bible*, 119.

22. Blake, *Marriage of Heaven and Hell*, xx–xxi.

23. See Billingsley, *Visionary Art of William Blake*, Introduction.

24. Rowland, "Christology, Controversy and Apocalypse," 369–70.

fancy—be regarded as a source of truth and wisdom? How could something so inherently unstable offer the kind of security that is only found in solid rational enquiry? Blake showed remarkable courage in breaking free from inherited suspicions of our human imagination.

NONCONFORMIST IMAGINATION FOR TODAY

Maybe Blake's daring insight into the importance of human imagination is something nonconformists, including we who are Baptists, would do well to reflect on with far greater seriousness. Even today I fear that our congregations tend to live with a cautious and fearful approach to the imagination, still concerned that it is much more likely to lead us to error rather than truth, and all too rarely giving attention to the potential significance of the visual for our shared life together. We can notice, for example, how little the imagination figures in our reflections on the congregational processes of discernment that lie close to the heart of our Baptist identity.

The general principles are clearly and effectively articulated. In his discussion of congregational government and the church meeting, Stephen Holmes reminds us that "an outworking of our commitment to congregational government of the church" is central to Baptist identity, alongside our claim that "every member of the congregation shares properly in the task of discerning the calling of Christ on the church."[25] Later on, in a helpfully argued chapter, he proposes that competency to discern is entirely dependent on the Spirit—it is the Spirit that must shape our practices as together we read and apply Scripture. The American Baptist Curtis Freeman develops the same convictions, arguing that the church meeting is the place where members together seek the purpose of Christ. He says that "discerning the mind of Christ relies on a corporate interpretation of Scripture."[26] It is this community reading of Scripture, guided by the Spirit, that allows more light and truth to be discovered.

I want to argue, however, that there is scope here to think rather more deeply about exactly how the processes of discernment might take shape. What might they look like? How does the Spirit work amongst us? What enables and supports the reading of Scripture together? Too often our answers to such questions are heavily prescribed by established

25. Holmes, "Knowing Together the Mind of Christ," 172.
26. Freeman, *Contesting Catholicity*, 276.

patterns of discussion, prayer, and the reading and interpreting of Scripture. The context is a meeting where words dominate and persuasive debate commands majority support. Such meetings tend to favour those whose voices offer clear-sighted reasoning, who can offer prudent arguments rooted in the careful exegesis of Scripture, and whose claims to Spirit-led insights can be supported by accepted theological truth. None of this is wrong—but it only enables certain voices to be heard and certain practices to be followed. It does not encourage proper communal discernment that might draw on processes that allow much greater space and opportunity to embrace our human imaginative capacities.

It is worth thinking further about how relationships shape our identity as human beings. Each of us is a particular individual occupying a space that is our own, and yet the identity of this self always emerges through the interactions that take place with those who become part of us. We develop our sense of who we are through a recognition of what is held in common, and also through a sense of otherness that challenges and even disturbs us at times. The point is that the two are inextricably interwoven. We learn what it is to be the same as the other and to agree with them; we learn what it means to be different from the other and so to disagree. And it is an unfolding process that goes on developing and changing over time.

Within the context of a community that has its own distinctive identity—such as a Baptist congregation—both acknowledging and understanding how this web of complex relationships shapes identity is crucial. For if we are to actually live as a community of God's people, not only do we have to recognize what draws us together and what makes us different, but we have to take steps to integrate that into a shared vision of who we are. That requires of us a willingness to step outside of our own horizon, to lose a sense of our own particular self, and engage in what has been described as "imaginative self-transcendence."[27] Only as we dare to try to imagine from the perspective of the other, however limited that attempt may be, will we be able to build genuine community.

So, what practices might we follow in order to see from the perspective of the other? There will certainly need to be disciplines that encourage attentive listening, such that we are able to properly attend to the life of the other and overcome our natural inclinations to label and categorize.

27. Hart, *Between the Image and the Word*, 103. For a fuller exploration of some of the issues and ideas raised in these paragraphs, see Hart, *Between the Image and the Word*, 97–118.

Such attentiveness invariably requires both time and effort, and might draw very deliberately on the practices of *lectio divina* and on the Ignatian processes of discernment, which have enriched the life of the church over many centuries. It may also be appropriate to find ways of enabling a community to occupy a different physical space and standpoint so as discern more clearly. To engage with language classes for those seeking asylum, or staff a foodbank, or simply walk the local neighbourhood can challenge us to see things in the way others see them, and so enable community to be built in new ways. But one of the most significant practices is a commitment to the use of images to support imaginative journeys of discernment. Images allow a seeing that encompasses mind, heart, and body; they allow perspectives of the other to be grasped by those who find it less easy to engage with words; and they open up space for renewed forms of reflection on Scripture and the life of faith.

Two brief illustrations might help make clear how and why the use of visual images might be important within the life of a community.

THE FACE OF THE OTHER

In his book *With Unveiled Face*, Goodliff explores the concept of shame. In doing so he recognizes its complex nature—the ways in which shame can be appropriate, but also the times when it can be deeply destructive—and uses the image of the hidden face to express the impact shame can have. "The face," he writes, "this object of wonder, loathing, window on the soul, revealer of emotions and significant aspect of our identity, is hidden with shame."[28]

Amongst the biblical stories Goodliff looks at in order to address the issue of shame is the encounter between Jesus and the woman caught in adultery (John 7:53—8:11). It is already a highly visual story as described by the gospel writer and it is not hard to imagine the scene as it plays out. Yet what an artist is able to draw attention to is precisely the feature that Goodliff identifies as crucial—that of the face: the face of the woman who is being shamed, the face of Jesus, and the faces of those who look on whether in accusation or sympathy. The painting by Pieter Brueghel the Younger *Christ and the Woman Taken in Adultery*, circa 1600, is one example.[29] In this painting we are confronted with a crowd of

---

28. Goodliff, *With Unveiled Face*, 94.

29. This painting can be found at https://commons.wikimedia.org/wiki/

faces, representing the whole range of responses to both the woman and to the attitudes and actions of Jesus. We are invited to read those faces— those who retain their spirit of condemnation, those who want to quietly disappear into the crowd, and those who look back with uncertainty and remorse. The faces reveal so much! Though there is less of a crowd, the close-up faces in the painting by Lucas Cranach the Younger *Christ and the Woman Taken in Adultery*, circa 1532, achieve a similar purpose.[30] The closeness with which the faces crowd in on the main protagonists convey the sense of a threatening mob, but in the individual features it is clear that there are very different dynamics at work. Again, we see the different ways the face betrays the responses of the heart.

One of the key functions of images such as these—and, indeed, of any kind of portrait showing someone's face—is that it freezes time. It has an "occasionality," as Hans-Georg Gadamer describes it. We look at a face at one particular moment, and that single freeze-frame exists in tension with the ongoing life of the person pictured, whether real or imaginary.[31] Thus, unlike the more extended and distant verbal telling of the gospel story, when we as individuals and as part of a community are invited to reflect using images such as these, there is given the opportunity to see and enter into the particular lives and experiences represented. The faces have an immediacy. The story can no longer be the source of an abstract discussion about shame; rather we engage directly with the human face of what happens when the compassionate message of Jesus is heard, and each of us is challenged to consider our own response. The pastoral implications that follow from this kind of imaginative engagement with the story might well be highly significant.

In a very different way, the face that is hidden with shame might well be regarded as a feature of much of the art of the African American Jacob Lawrence. During the twentieth century, Lawrence used his art to tell the stories of slavery, racism, and injustice that were a potent part of his own American experience, and *The Migration Series* is a deeply moving example of his work.[32] It is a series of sixty paintings each accompanied by a sparse piece of text that recounts the journey many thousands of African Americans made from the South to the North of the country in

---

File:Brueghel_II,_Pieter_-_Christ_and_the_Woman_Taken_in_Adultery_1600.jpg.

30. This painting can be found at https://commons.wikimedia.org/wiki/File:Lucas_Cranach_d._J._-_Christ_and_the_Woman_Taken_in_Adultery_-_WGA05733.jpg.

31. See West, *Portraiture*, 43–70.

32. This series can be viewed at https://lawrencemigration.phillipscollection.org.

search of improved social, economic, and political conditions. In essence it was a journey of escape from the realities of racism and oppression, in hope of new freedom and dignity.

In the majority of the paintings, it is notable that Lawrence paints the African Americans with few if any facial features. Panels 1 and 12 are examples of crowd scenes where every face is anonymized, with the exception of the two white men in the latter panel. Often we only see their backs, such as in Panels 14 and 22, so as to further enforce the sense that their dignity as human beings is under threat. This hiding of the face by Lawrence is surely a disturbing indication of both the external and internal consequences of racism. It shows us how constantly proclaimed messages of inferiority, of being less than fully human, together with actions by those in power that oppress and deny basic justice, can destroy dignity and self-esteem in ways that generate a deep sense of shame.

We should not think, however, that Lawrence's art merely reinforces the unjustified shame experienced within his community. Far from it! He remains brutally realistic about the consequences of racism, but he also uses his art to tell the stories of African Americans such that they can gain a sense of their own identity and the potential of a new future. Within *The Migration Series* we can see the ways in which, despite the hidden faces, there are signs of strength and hope. Panel 58, for example, offers us the image of children receiving education and so growing in dignity and confidence as a result.

I would hope, too, that Lawrence's art might have imaginative power to challenge our faith communities on this side of the Atlantic if we allow it. As Goodliff rightly says, we need to work at "creating non-shaming communities" that address "the struggle to be inclusive communities," and he names racism as a key issue to be addressed.[33] An opportunity to engage carefully with images such as the ones we have noted has the potential to allow a congregation to tell its own stories of discrimination, oppression, and exclusion, to recognize how shaming has taken place, and to find paths to repentance and renewal. These images are a way of seeing from the perspective of the other, such that we enter imaginatively into their situation and find ourselves transformed.

33. Goodliff, *With Unveiled Face*, 125.

CONCLUSIONS

In looking at Bunyan's *The Pilgrim's Progress*, we noted how the community can become a way of testing and refining the imagination such that the voice of the Spirit can be discerned. For Baptists in particular, and nonconformists more generally, this emphasis on the community as the place of discerning God's voice remains a feature of our identity, and yet over the course of our history we have never really given proper weight to the ways the Spirit leads us towards a deeper spirituality through our God-given human imagination. It has remained a source of suspicion, with our processes almost wholly dependent on the use of rational argument and propositional truth.

It would be entirely appropriate to develop a more comprehensive approach that argues not only for the importance of imagination, but for its necessity in the task of doing theology. There is a real sense in which it is impossible to speak of God without the use of poetry, metaphor, and story, and when it comes to offering our worship or even formulating our doctrine, such activities will always be the work of the imagination.

But I hope we can at least begin with the more modest task of embracing the value of images. As our Baptist theology and identity responds to new contexts, it is time to recognize the importance of a renewed imagination that enlarges our vision. We can describe it as an imaginative journey that takes us to different vantage points, such that we are more attentive to the perspective of the other and therefore what it means to be a diverse yet inclusive community. This is not an argument for rejecting words, nor our historic commitment to the texts of Scripture. Rather, it is a call to learn what it means to *paint* the text as well as to read it, and find within our images an imagination that allows the Spirit to lead us into yet more light and truth.

2

MINISTRY AND MUSIC

Geoff Colmer

I MET PAUL IN the spring of 1986 at Spurgeon's College in South London, where we were being interviewed for training for Baptist ministry. During the following year I became a Student Assistant at Lewin Road Baptist Church, where Paul was serving as a Church Worker, and it was the start of an enduring friendship. It soon became clear that not only were we both enthusiastic about the vocation to which we were being called, but we also shared a passion for music. I had just left the music profession, having played the bassoon in an orchestra, and Paul had a considerable knowledge and appreciation of classical music. Our friendship has embraced other mutual interests but these two have been central, and while many conversations have been about different aspects of pastoral ministry, a similar number have been about music. We have attended concerts together that range from Renaissance church music to minimalist jazz, and while Paul remains largely ambivalent about opera and unconvinced by the symphonies of Gustav Mahler, I live in hope that one day these might become part of our shared enjoyment!

Martin Luther, in the *Tischreden*—the record of his mealtime conversations—proclaimed, "I always loved music; whoso has skill in this art is of a good temperament, fitted for all things. We must teach music in schools: a schoolmaster ought to have skill in music or I would not regard him; neither should we ordain young men as preachers unless they have been well exercised in music." I think that Martin Luther would have approved of our friendship! My intention in this chapter is to honour this friendship through these shared enthusiasms and to make some connections between music and pastoral ministry.

ATTENTIVENESS

I am listening to Mozart's Serenade in C Minor for Wind Octet (K. 388), in a recording by The Music Serenade, in which I took part shortly before leaving the music profession to train for Baptist ministry. It's very good! What amazes me is not only its incredible beauty but the way that eight musicians play this piece, and three other similar works, with such precision and togetherness. How do we do this? By listening very carefully to each other—yet more than this: by being attentive to each other and watching for body language, sometimes the smallest inflection of the head, the eye, or the arm. This attentiveness is refined through hours of playing together; we were the wind section of the English Northern Philharmonia—the Orchestra of Opera North—and we knew each other's playing intimately. What is true of this particular ensemble is true of any good music group, be it string quartet, jazz quintet, or rock band, because—with or without conductor—attentiveness to the other performers is vital. The conductor plays an important role (although I still recall the advice of a seasoned professional who said, "Whatever you do, don't look at the conductor!") but playing with others, listening, watching, and intuiting, is how a performance comes together.

I wonder whether one of the tasks of pastoral ministry is to help the church become an attentive community. For the minister this requires a high degree of personal attentiveness in a number of areas, each one of them demanding. In the first instance the minister is to be attentive to God, through personal prayer; then to the individual members who make up the church community, in pastoral care; to the community itself as it comes together as a body, in the varied expressions of its life together; and to the wider community in which the church is set, as it seeks to reach out in service and mission.[1] While the minister will probably require varying levels of attentiveness across these aspects, and is certainly not the only community member to require it, they nonetheless carry a particular responsibility to be attentive.

---

1. For one account of Baptist spirituality that works with the concept of attentiveness, see Fiddes, "Spirituality as Attentiveness."

A popular metaphor for church leadership is the minister as conductor of the orchestra, with the understanding that the conductor facilitates the players to give of their best. While there is some truth in this, I struggle with it. Even today in some parts of the world the conductor is referred to by the old-fashioned term "Maestro," and therein is the clue. Although conductors do not wield the power they had one hundred years ago, or even not so long ago, they still exercise considerable control and perhaps could be described as a benign dictator. Undoubtedly, a good conductor will want to facilitate the players to give of their best, and players may have some say, but generally conductors do not work on the basis of consensus. And so I return to the analogy of the chamber music group, in which the minister is a significant player—listening, watching and intuiting, to help the church become an attentive community.

DISCIPLINE

I have often reflected that I don't know of any gifted musicians who are not dedicated musicians, and my observation is that the more gifted they are the more dedicated they are. I recall a friend at the Royal College of Music who would enter the canteen in which a number of us had congregated, leisurely eating breakfast and drinking tea, having already done an hour and a half of practice. She has occupied the principal flute seat in a number of significant orchestras. Musicians acquire the discipline of practice. I must have driven my family mad as a teenager: each day began with ten minutes of long-note practice, followed by scales, and then studies; at other points in the day I would practice pieces and orchestral repertoire. It became a way of life and probably has served me in other ways.

"Discipline" is an unpopular word; it has a resonance of punishment and restriction. But the way I am using it is as something which serves, rather than subdues. When it comes to our life in God, this is not on account of anything that we do but is entirely by grace; however, grace does not negate the need for discipline as we seek to live a grace-given life. It may be that the language of "spiritual disciplines" is better replaced by "spiritual practices," but whatever you call them, they require some discipline! In *Subversive Spirituality*, Eugene Peterson provides four "items of counsel" on spirituality. These are: "discover what Scripture says about spirituality and immerse yourself in it"; "embrace friends in the faith wherever you find them"; "but then return home and explore your own tradition." These are all pieces of wise counsel but none more so than the second item, "shun spirituality that does not require commitment."[2] Peterson elaborates on this:

> Personal commitment to the God personally revealed in Jesus is at the heart of spirituality. Faddish spiritualities, within and without the church, ignore or deny commitment. Evangelical counsel places the Lord's commands—believe, follow, endure— at the core of all spirituality. A lifelong faith commitment to God as revealed in Jesus Christ is essential to any true spiritual- ity . . . The ancestors we look to for encouragement in this busi- ness—Augustine of Hippo and Julian of Norwich, John Calvin and Amy Carmichael, John Bunyan and Teresa of Avila—didn't flit. They stayed.[3]

As someone who has a keen interest in spirituality, I need to heed these words lest I am swayed by the faddish. For me, a daily office provides the foundation, and over the past ten years the Order for Baptist Minis- try (OBM) has provided a rich resource.[4] This, together with Ignatian contemplative practices, especially the examen, contributes to my daily practice of disciplines. Different people with different personalities will adopt different habits but, in the light of Scripture and the history of the church, some form of spiritual practice cannot be avoided if we are "to be committed to the way of Christ" and "faithful to the call of Christ," to draw on words from the OBM Daily Office.

TENSION

As a regional minister, some of my ministry has been focused on the tensions that arise in churches. At its worst it has been "Christians behav- ing badly" but often it has been more nuanced. I have found the insights that come from family systems theory to be highly instructive and enor- mously helpful. But again, music has something to impart.

---

2. Peterson, *Subversive Spirituality*, 37–39. Peterson does include a fifth item: "look for mature guides, honor wise leaders" (40).

3. Peterson, *Subversive Spirituality*, 38.

4. See https://www.orderforbaptistministry.co.uk.

Music, or certainly most Western tonal music, works on the principle of ETR; that is, equilibrium, tension, and resolution.[5] Music starts from a place of equilibrium, from which tension is created, and then the tension is resolved. How composers manage the resolution of tension is what music is all about. Take a piece of music such as "Humpty Dumpty" and hear it in your head.

Humpty Dumpty sat on a wall
You're still more or less at home.
Humpty Dumpty had a great fall
You're at a point of tension and definitely away from home.
All the King's horses and all the King's men
The tension is intensified.
Couldn't put Humpty together again
Then comes resolution and you're back home again.

(It has to be acknowledged that there wasn't much resolution for Humpty Dumpty!)

I could provide countless other examples: Beethoven's "Für Elise," or the theme from *Schindler's List*; the slow movement of Brahms' 2nd Symphony; or if you've got five hours to spare, there's Wagner's opera *Tristan and Isolde*!

Great music contains tensions within tensions; how the tension is held, partly resolved, resolved only to open up another tension, and resolved completely, bringing closure, is the stuff of music—all Western tonal music. You might not be aware of this while you listen—and there's no reason why you should—but this is what's going on. Great composers and songwriters use tension to generate expectations, which are deliberately delayed through the diversions and digressions that the music takes. Regardless of the musical style, be it pop, soul, rock, electronic, country, classical, or jazz, particularly where music is "composed" in the instant, composers must learn to manage the space between tensions and delayed resolutions in ways that sustain both interest and expectation. It's what makes music so appealing.

What I've described is not limited to music but is a characteristic of much of life: you're asleep—equilibrium; the alarm goes off—tension; you turn the alarm off—resolution! It is equally true of church life. Admittedly, some tension can be destructive, but often it can be creative. Without an upset of the equilibrium, music would hold little interest and

---

5. This section owes much to Begbie, *Resounding Truth*, 278.

appear to be going nowhere, and the same goes for the life of the church. The more important issue is how the tension is managed. In the life of the church, tension expresses itself in anxiety, and that anxiety—like lightning to a lightning conductor—earths itself to the most responsible or the most vulnerable person in the community, who is frequently the minister. How that person manages the tension is critical. Family systems theory speaks about self-differentiation—about the need to define self—while continuing to stay in touch with those who are anxious. Most important in this process is for the self-differentiating person to be a non-anxious presence. Anxiety begets anxiety; tension begets tension. And it is by being a non-anxious presence that the anxiety is considerably lessened, enabling the issue to be viewed responsively and not reactively, with clarity and creativity.

To talk about tension in church life may simply be a euphemism for conflict! But again, conflict is a normal part of human interaction and need not always be a "blood on the carpet" issue. The Chinese character for "conflict" is a mixture of "danger" and "opportunity." Musically speaking, the word for conflict is "dissonance," and if music without tension is boring, music without dissonance is equally so. While much music of the twentieth century has reinvented musical language so that any talk of music being in a particular key is redundant, Western tonal music employs dissonance creatively: intensifying tension, creating surprise, and intentionally causing discomfort, though mostly reaching some resolution. In a presentation to some of our churches called "When Churches Disagree," I've explored how conflict can be positive, necessitating involvement, clarifying ideas, helping define identity, stimulating creativity, opening potential for new and deeper relationships, for binding people together.

WRONG NOTES

I recall an instance when I was at Opera North when my colleague was unwell and we had a deputy come in for a performance of the opera *Carmen* by Bizet. At the beginning of the second act is an *entr'acte*, an orchestral piece, that features two bassoons very prominently. At one point there is a trill from an E to an F#. Sadly, the deputy played a trill from an E to an F and the effect was cacophonous. Quickly he realized his mistake but the damage was done. It caused much hilarity among the rest of the orchestra and his obvious embarrassment was enough to own the mistake. One of the distinctives of playing music professionally is the high standard of consistency with which a musician performs. While mistakes, wrong notes, (or at least noticeable ones) don't happen often, they do happen. When they do, there are two responses. The first (and best) is not to bat an eyelid, but to appear as though this is how it should be. You certainly should not make any kind of fuss or gesture of regret. The second, if other people are playing at the same time, is to glare at someone else as if they are the person who made the mistake. While being utterly dishonourable, it works from an audience perspective! However infrequently, mistakes and wrong notes are a part of live music, and among the piano's eighty-eight keys, sadly there is no delete key.

It is fair to say that music demands a high degree of precision, if not perfection, but if this standard were applied to pastoral ministry, then we would all be in serious trouble. Wrong notes, mistakes, and failure, as we have observed already, are a reality within the Christian community of which the minister is a part. This is challenging in a culture that places a high premium on success. The church will desire to be effective in what it does, seeking to do "the utmost for his highest"[6] and be for the benefit of others, but faithfulness and fruitfulness are the goal—not success.

While acknowledging that Christians are those in whom Christ has made a home and who are being transformed into his likeness, the testimony of Scripture is full of flawed characters and those whose ministries do not realize their intended purpose. On the eve of Jesus's crucifixion, while Judas betrayed him, all of his disciples deserted him and Peter denied him. Timothy Radcliffe, in his book *Alive in God: A Christian Imagination*, speaks about "bifocal vision."[7] He reflects that in Acts 4:32 we see a community of perfect unity, but then comes the story of Ananias and Sapphire, followed in chapter 6 by divisions between the Greek-speaking and Hebrew-speaking Christians on the distribution of bread. He comments that "Luke's accounts are both true, but in different ways . . . The true nature of that earliest community, and our own, is caught in the interplay of these two accounts. Bifocal vision is needed to glimpse the victory and the failure that characterize the Christian life."[8] At a fundamental level this is portrayed in the cross of Christ, which to

6. This is the title of a book by Oswald Chambers, considered to be a classic of devotional literature.

7. Timothy Radcliffe, *Alive in God*, 302–3.

8. Radcliffe, *Alive in God*, 303.

the world was a symbol of failure, but came to symbolize the ultimate victory. This is played out in the rest of the New Testament: it seems that most of the New Testament epistles are written in response to the challenges that the churches were facing, often from within.

What of the wrong notes played by the minister? With serious wrong notes there are inevitable consequences, but the minister who seeks to be perfect will spend the whole of ministry seeking to be just that and not much else. Mistakes are inevitable—small ones and not-so-small ones. These need to be recognized and owned, and not concealed. In so doing we see not only openness and expression of regret, but also the important acknowledgment that none of us, including the minister, is perfect; that we are all fallible human beings, saints in the making.

IMPROVISATION

Working with the Newly Accredited Ministers' Programme, we have often explored issues that come up under "what they didn't teach me at theological college." Pastoral ministry, especially in the early years, presents us with issues and situations where we find ourselves needing to improvise. In music, improvisation is often associated with jazz and is indeed one of the key elements of that genre. But improvisation isn't the preserve of jazz alone, and has a long history in so-called serious music. J. S. Bach was a phenomenal improviser, as were Mozart and Beethoven, and soloists in the classical era would be expected to improvise the cadenza in a concerto. The cathedral organist, as well as many church organists, will have the ability to extemporize. But jazz, since its genesis in the music of African Americans in the Southern United States at the beginning of the twentieth century, and through all its different expressions (swing, Dixieland, European, bebop, cool, hard bop, Latin, fusion, smooth), has, as a key element, improvisation. It is one of its defining characteristics.

Improvisation isn't immediately associated with my instrument, the bassoon, although there are some very accomplished practitioners. However, I am fascinated by improvisation. First, because it's not within my gift and so remains something of a mystery. I have friends who are astonishing improvisers, and while I understand what's going on at one level, at another level I'm simply in awe. There is a fascinating TED Talk given by Charles Limb, a doctor and a musician, who has researched the way musical creativity works in the brain by putting jazz musicians and a rapper in a specially constructed MRI (not at the same time!).[9] It seems that there is a very specific part of the brain that functions during improvisation, and my conclusion is that either I don't have this bit of the brain or it has never been developed. I think the latter is true and my sense is that this needs to happen earlier in life rather than later. The second reason is because of the inherent nature of improvisation. As a jazz musician improvises, they conceive and perform music simultaneously. Good players are well schooled in jazz scales and chords; they will, critically, have learned their craft through listening and much practice; they will have evolved a style which is their own while owing much to the tradition. But when it happens and they improvise, all of this is drawn upon to produce something unique, in the moment, never to be captured in that way again.

As with the jazz musician, improvisation in the practice of pastoral ministry, while uncomfortable, should hold no terror provided that a number of things are in place. Is the practitioner well schooled in the basic pastoral skills, which will have been learned through attentiveness and practice? And, while they are unique persons, are they true to the tradition? These are the keys to facing the myriad issues that don't fit into the ministerial formation curriculum. I find helpful a construction based on the words "conscious" and "competence," and their opposites, "unconscious" and "incompetence." There are four combinations: unconscious incompetence, conscious incompetence, unconscious competence, and conscious competence. When I began my role as a regional minister, I was on an extremely steep learning curve and I could only play the "I'm new to this role" card for so long. At times I found myself doing what seemed to be "blagging" only to realize that what I was doing came from my unconscious competence. In short, I was improvising, effectively for the most part, on the basis of skills that I had learned and experience I had gained, and being rooted in my particular tradition.

REPETITION

Music is appreciated largely by way of repeated listening. A piece of music may make an instant impact, but if so, the immediate desire is to repeat the experience and listen again. Conversely, some pieces are

9. Charles Limb, "Your Brain on Improv," https://www.ted.com/talks/charles_limb_your_brain_on_improv/transcript?language=en.

less accessible but grow on us as we listen again and in due course may become favourites: in my own experience I think of the late Beethoven string quartets. In previous times this meant waiting for another performance or, as was the practice, playing the music at home in reductions for keyboard. Today, often the performance can be heard again online or, if not the performance itself, the piece, through various streaming services, or by purchasing the music as a CD or MP3. Repetition is the way that music gets into us, whether it is complex or very simple music. To fully appreciate music we need to listen to it again and again.

Within music there is much repetition. In the classical sonata, as well as in classical symphonies, after an "*exposition*" section comes the "development"; then, towards the end of the work, there is the "recapitulation," where, with some difference, the exposition is, as it were, reframed. Even within the exposition, often the whole section is repeated before moving on to the development section. Jeremy Begbie states that to some degree every piece of music "integrates 'sameness' with 'difference.'"[10] Music needs sameness to be *a* piece, but difference to avoid monotony. What is striking is that sameness appears to play a more crucial part than difference: "Repetition, whether small or large-scale, is the prime form-building agent of music. The 'repeat sign' on a score can prescribe the reiteration of long stretches of music, note for note."[11] It seems that music can never have enough of saying again and again what has already been said. Even within music, motifs are used repeatedly and Begbie gives the example of Beethoven's 6th Symphony, where the same rhythmic motif is repeated forty-eight times without a break. Over this is a melody which in its shape remains the same throughout. When this concludes, another section begins with the identical character to the first. What prevents this from becoming tedious in the extreme, and is the genius of Beethoven, is the slight change in the melody, the difference in the orchestration affecting the timbre, the shift in the background harmony, and the variation in volume.

Inevitably, much of church life is repetitive: the times and seasons of our gatherings, the liturgies or worship patterns we use, the prayers we use within these liturgies even when they are extempore, the issues that come round again and again. Much of this has a "thus and so"-ness about it, or maybe even the "same old." This can be challenging for many in our

---

10. This section owes much to Begbie, "Play It (Again)," 46–47.

11. Begbie, "Play It (Again)," 47.

contemporary culture, who are used to constant and often rapid change, with a desire for the new and the different. It raises important questions as to how we manage sameness so that it doesn't become stale, and how we welcome difference without the constant pursuit of that which is novel.

On closer examination, the same isn't actually the same because the church community itself is changing week by week, month by month. We are not the same as we were the last time we met. Our life experience has changed and our faith experience is being changed as we continue to follow Christ. The theme repeated at the end of Bach's Goldberg Variations, although exactly the same as the beginning, sounds different because we have become different people through having experienced all the variations on this theme. We hear it through different ears at the end than at the beginning. This sense of change in who we are is also expressed in the times and seasons in which we meet, following at least to some extent the church year when we journey from Advent through to Pentecost. The key word is "journey," something which is undertaken collectively, and results in difference as we progress together. As an aside, most of the church year through which we journey is in Ordinary Time. If, as has been previously observed, the church is constantly undergoing seasons of equilibrium, tension, and resolution, this too will produce some variation within the sameness of the community—those subtle (and sometimes not so subtle) changes in melody, harmony, timbre, and volume.

For repetition not to be experienced as monotonous or stale, a freshness is required from those responsible for the life of the church. This is a personal challenge to ensure that ministry in its various aspects does not become like a treadmill. It requires spiritual life and energy, which takes us back to the need for some kind of sustaining spiritual discipline. Acknowledging all of this, the counterpoint to repetition—difference—needs to be welcomed in more overt ways. There will be occasions when, attentive to what the Spirit is saying, the church will need to respond with difference and effect change through the renewal of its life and in seeking to reach out to the rapidly changing world in which we live.

SILENCE

Reading Daniel Barenboim's *Everything Is Connected: The Power of Music*,[12] I am reminded how music emerges out of silence and then retreats into silence. Music and silence are like the relationship between a physical object and the force of gravity. An object that is lifted from the ground demands a certain amount of energy to keep it raised. Unless the additional energy is provided, it will fall to the ground, obeying the laws of gravity. In the same way, unless sound is sustained, it is driven to silence. The musician who produces a sound brings it into the physical world. Unless she provides energy, the sound will die. Sustaining the sound is in any case an act of defiance against the pull of silence. At the beginning of a piece of music, music either interrupts the silence or evolves out of it; for example, Richard Strauss's *Ein Heldenleben* or Stravinsky's *The Rite of Spring*. At the end of a piece of music, silence can arrive after a tremendous build-up of tension, or after a gradual diminution of sound, where the music becomes so quiet that the next possible step can only be silence; for example, Beethoven's 9th Symphony or Mahler's 9th Symphony, respectively. That second or two of silence, for me, is a summation when the whole experience coalesces. In performing a piece of music I have often been struck by how it is the silence that makes sense of the notes; it is the rests that give the music the space to breathe. They are not to be rushed over. Silence helps music, which takes place in time, to take time.

What place does silence have within the life of the Christian community? "Not much" may be the reply from those within the Baptist tradition, and this has largely been my experience over eighteen years of trans-local ministry. So, how might silence be given greater place?

While training for Baptist ministry, I spent ten days in Taizé, the ecumenical Christian community in France. One of my most striking memories is the silence. The vast worship space was dark yet pin-pricked with numerous night-lights and candles. The worshippers gathered in silence. This was broken as one of the brothers sang "Alleluia!," to which the congregation responded with a chant. Later on, after the reading of Scripture, nine minutes of silence was held. This made a lasting impact on me. The silence wasn't a pure silence: with five thousand people gathered some noise was inevitable, but still it qualified as silence and had a special quality about it. It was neither empty or awkward but plentiful and life-giving—at least to me.

---

12. Barenboim, *Everything Is Connected.*

Baptist worship has always had a strong musical element to it but the contemporary worship style can lead to music being dominant, with each song bridged to the next and, when prayers are spoken, a background keyboard accompaniment. This can result in twenty minutes or longer of uninterrupted music. It is my desire for musical expressions of worship at some point to open onto some silence, where there is space apart from sound.[13] My experience has been that in such a space God may be encountered powerfully.

After the reading of Scripture, to pause and sit silently for a moment rather than to launch straight into further spoken words is to allow the passage to take root. The same applies following the sermon; instead of going straight into spoken prayer or a sung response, what of the potentially fertile space afforded by silence before such a response? In prayers of intercession, to intersperse prayers with short periods of silence invites the congregation into a deeper experience of prayer than just listening to someone else praying and adding an "Amen" at the end.

In any service of worship there will be those who are glad, sad, mad, or bad (I use "mad" in the sense of angry, and "bad" in the sense of not feeling good about themselves). To provide space and silence within the order of the service may be hugely helpful, if not healing, to many people, especially those who are sad. In pastoral engagement with those who are grieving or hurting, often the most appropriate response is to be fully present but with few, if any, words. Silence, within this held space, can be received as a gift. None of this is to suggest replicating monastic worship, but even small uses of silence can make a significant difference. It has been my practice in local church ministry and regional ministry to hold quiet days and also to encourage contemplative practices as ways of deepening an experience of God through more extended periods of silence.

SURPRISE

The slow movement of Haydn's Symphony no. 94 in G Major begins with a very quiet, simple, almost simplistic melody. This is repeated, but at the end of the repeat there is a very loud chord. This accounts for the symphony being known as *The Surprise*. At that time, during the classical period, audiences weren't very well behaved and there would be much talking and general hubbub, especially after a meal, which was

13. For a similar argument, see Shaw, "God of Love We Praise You," 53–55.

often when music was performed. Slow movements were occasions when maybe more of a silence would descend and you can imagine some of the patrons of the arts dropping off to sleep, only to be woken up by the loud crash at the end of the repeat. Following this, the music has no other surprises, and is actually a beautiful, gentle theme with variations. Haydn uses what is called "the principle of expectancy violation." In other words, you expect the music to play in a certain way, but then you're taken completely by surprise; your expectation is violated. This is a common technique in many kinds of music. Having reflected upon repetition and the dominance of sameness over difference—the example above is a prime example of repetition, albeit with a sting in the tail—we see also that music often has this element of surprise. And while the full impact of the surprise cannot be repeated, something of it continues to live on in the music, just as a really good joke can still be funny the next time, even if it doesn't have quite the same impact.

Gerard Hughes, a Jesuit, wrote a hugely influential book with the title *God of Surprises.*[14] It is an exploration of Ignatian spirituality in which a fundamental conviction is that as we engage imaginatively with Scripture, God inevitably surprises us with encounter. This is true in my experience, and it is not limited to the Ignatian approach. The God of grace, whose nature is to give, is not predictable and constantly violates our expectancy, as Scripture and church history show. This is particularly true of pastoral ministry. Despite the familiarity of much of what we do and the expectations that we hold, ministry is full of surprises. Some of these may be unwelcome, but many are a cause for rejoicing. In the process can come a heightened sense of encounter with God, a renewed sense of mission, and also a timely reminder that however much we might think we have it sorted and are in control, we do not and are not. With this comes an important realignment as we acknowledge that this is not my ministry, or my church, but God's. In my training as a spiritual director there was a fundamental recognition that however large the part that I play in the process, God is the spiritual director, not me; and the same goes for ministry.

We cannot be constantly on the lookout for surprises. The violation of expectancy does not work that way, but we can live with the expectation that from time to time God will interrupt the familiarity, cause a

14. Hughes, *God of Surprises.*

sharp intake of breath, make us ask, "Where did that come from?," and in so doing remind us that ministry itself, despite its challenges, is a gift.

UNITY

In drawing to a close I am mindful of the significant contribution that Paul has made as a committed ecumenist over many years. While the apostle Paul writes about the church as the body of Christ, I find myself musing about what he might have made of the symphony orchestra had this been available as a metaphor.

One of the pieces of classical music that many people at a young age first hear is Benjamin Britten's *Young Person's Guide to the Orchestra: A Theme with Variations*. It can be played with narration as an introduction to the different instruments of the orchestra, or without, as a performance. It concludes with a fugue that never ceases to raise the hairs on the back of my neck, especially at the very end, when the stately theme is reintroduced amidst all the business of the fugue's conclusion.

The orchestra is made up of an assortment of string instruments, woodwind, brass, and percussion. Within the orchestra some instruments tend to have more prominence, such as the first violins, the flute and clarinet, and the trumpet and the timpani, for example. But actually every instrument is necessary: take away one particular instrument and the piece will not sound the same. I am always struck by the very significant part the modest triangle has in Vaughan Williams's *The Lark Ascending*, or the thud of the bass drum just before the tenor sings his heart out at the end of the first act of Puccini's *La Bohème*—remove it, and something is decidedly lacking at that certain point in the music.

In our Baptist understanding of the local church, every church is wholly the church, but every church is not the *whole church*.[15] As Baptists we have made much of the independence of the local church and, at least in our theology if not always in our practice, our interdependence with other Baptist churches. In most places Baptist churches enjoy relationship with other churches, to a greater or lesser degree, and for me this has been a significant part of my experience of ministry. But this is comparatively recent: I can remember growing up in an atmosphere of suspicion between the different churches, if not hostility. To see and experience churches together thriving is a major cause of rejoicing. I have

15. See "Statement from the Baptist World Alliance."

often reflected with my Roman Catholic bishop friends that not so long ago we wouldn't have even talked together. We have come a long way in recognising our unity and that we are better together.

Unity is, on one hand, a given. But it also needs to be worked on. As for the dream of organic unity—of the disappearance of our different denominations—I am not confident this side of the Parousia. But to play as one orchestra with all of the instruments making their unique contribution remains something to aspire to and work towards. Jesus prayed "that they may all be one" (John 17:21) and while that prayer has not yet been answered, it is not to be dismissed. As Jesus goes on to say, this unity is "that the world may believe." However gratifying it might be for the orchestra to perform, it does not exist for itself but for those who listen to it. As Archbishop William Temple said, "The Church is the only organisation which exists for the benefit of its non-members."[16] And, as J. S. Bach understood as paramount, writing it on the pages of his manuscripts, *Deo Gloria*, to the glory of God.

16. Spencer, in *Christ in All Things: William Temple and His Writings*, ix, can find no record in Temple's published work of this sentence.

3

MINISTRY AND POETRY

Paul S. Fiddes

GEORGE HERBERT, GERARD MANLEY HOPKINS, AND R. S. THOMAS were all priest-poets, and their vocation to Christian ministry has often been commented upon, even occasionally compared.[1] The point of this essay, however, is to focus on the way that their experience of the practice of pastoral care is reflected in their poetry, and to ask how their poetic speech might relate to their pastoral practice. Herbert was actually a practising pastor for only three years before his death at age thirty-nine, Hopkins similarly spent about three years in parish ministry before university teaching and death at forty-four, while Thomas's ministry lasted forty-two years before retirement and eventual death at age eighty-seven. I hope that this exercise might honour Paul Goodliff, whose years of pastoral practice correspond more closely to those of Thomas among the three poets, who has given exceptional service to the formation of pastors as well as being one himself, and who is both a poetry lover and a published poet. Herbert was ordained in the seventeenth-century Church of England, Hopkins was a Jesuit priest in the nineteenth-century Roman Catholic Church in England, and Thomas was a priest of the twentieth-century Anglican Church in Wales. I am glad to bring them into virtual company in this essay with Paul, a minister in the Baptist Union of Great Britain in the twentieth and twenty-first centuries, and an ecumenical leader.

---

1. See, for example, McGill, "Calling"; McKenzie, "Torn in Two."

HERBERT: IN CONVERSATION WITH GOD

Herbert was remembered by his parishioners as "little less than sainted,"[2] but his parish ministry at Bemerton (with Fugglestone) in Wiltshire was a short one. It followed years of uncertainty about calling to priesthood while he was a don and public orator in the University of Cambridge, and notably brought to an end in 1630 a seven-year period of hesitation after he had left Cambridge and had "drifted about"[3] as a guest in houses of wealthier friends and relatives, in search of something to give meaning to his life. His ordination as a deacon in 1624, with a canonry of Salisbury Cathedral attached and a prebend at Leighton Bromswold in Huntingdonshire to follow, offered income but only very nominal pastoral duties. He put effort into the restoration of the church building at Leighton Bromswold rather than into the cure of souls, and all this might be seen as a way of putting off the larger decision about the vocation of priest with its sacramental as well as pastoral office. His life as a pastor began at Bemerton, after ordination as a priest in September 1630, and he immediately began to write a handbook for other country parsons, finishing it halfway through what was to be a three-year ministry.

This manual, called on publication in 1652 *The Priest to the Temple, or, A Country Parson*, might be thought a precocious undertaking for a new minister in his first charge, but he made clear that he intended it to be "a Mark to aim at" for himself. Significantly, he does not see it as essentially a set of instructions, but, in striking accord with our modern mood about "formation" rather than "training," he describes it as "set[ting] down the Form and Character of a true Pastour."[4] We also perceive that it draws upon some two decades of his personal struggle with God, charting his experiences of divine demands and divine grace, expressed in poetry written over that period. His collected poems, which his friend Nicholas Ferrar named *The Temple*, were to be published after his death (1633), and contain either transcriptions or revisions of his earlier poems, together with new ones written at Bemerton.

In effect he has left us, then, two spiritual autobiographies—his handbook to pastoral care and his poetry—and there are fascinating links between the two which illuminate the way that a poet might go about the sacred business of pastoral practice, both of them spheres of

2. Edward Herbert, *Autobiography*, 11.

3. Drury, *Music at Midnight*, 162.

4. Herbert, *Priest to the Temple*, 224.

a holy imagination. "Business" in fact is an apt word, since in his poem "Employment (I)," probably written early on but revised during his seven years "adrift," he laments that he has no satisfying employment given him by God:

> All things are busie; onely I
> Neither bring hony with the bees,
> Nor flowres to make that, nor the husbandrie
> To water these.[5]

In this poem the text he makes on the page as a poet and the textuality of his life merge, as media for devotion to God. He laments "A life as barren to thy praise," but when he prays in his last lines, "Lord place me in thy consort; give one strain/ To my poore reed," he is thinking of divine music-making in his poetry as much as in his daily life. Helen Wilcox comments that "The 'reed' can also be understood as the poet's pen, and as the 'bruised reed'—a biblical metaphor for vulnerability . . . see Isaiah xlii: 3."[6]

In his period of relative contentment at Bemerton, when he felt that God had at last given him satisfying work to do, he approaches pastoral practice as a kind of "business." He describes, exuberantly, his labour on a Sunday, comparing it to that of tradesmen:

> The Country Parson, as soon as he awakes on Sunday morning, presently falls to work, and seems to himself so as a Market-man is, when the Market day comes, or a shopkeeper, when customers use to come in . . . Then having read divine Service twice fully, and preached in the morning and catechized in the afternoon, he thinks he hath in some measure, discharged the public duties of the Congregation. The rest of the day he spends either in reconciling neighbours that are at variance, or in visiting the sick, or in exhortations to some of his flock by themselves, whom his Sermons cannot, or do not reach.[7]

The work of public worship, private reconciliation, sick-visiting, and personal teaching is then concluded by offering hospitality to neighbours in the rectory. Typically, Herbert celebrates Sunday, "a day of mirth," in a poem of that name, and—according to Izaak Walton—he sung it to

---

5. Herbert, *English Poems*, 204–5.
6. Herbert, *English Poems*, 206.
7. Herbert, *Priest*, 235–36.

his lute on his sickbed shortly before his death.[8] The fruitful labour of pastoral practice is not, of course, confined to a Sunday, and Herbert describes how the pastor is to be involved as counsellor, visitor, reconciler, catechizer, local legal officer, and herbal physician throughout the "worky-daies."[9] Advising his readers to do hard work on the Fathers and other commentators on the Bible to gather resources for future sermons, he comments that it will be "an honest joy ever after to looke upon his well-spent hours,"[10] though he adds immediately that this material must be shaped by the "library" of life and personal experience.

In "Constancie," he asks "Who is the honest man?" and replies that he is the one whose "words and works" are "all of a piece, and all are cleare and straight," whose good works can still "runne" in the darkness, and who calmly continues in his duties despite the obstacles of pastoral experience (at least as he sees them):

> Who, when he is to treat
> With sick folks, women, those whom passions sway,
> Allows for that, and keeps his constant way.[11]

The advice is often given to modern ministers young in their profession to treat their pastoral work as being like the daily employment of the members of their congregation, with similar demands and routine. There is much of this in Herbert, but he also opens up an intersection with his experience of creativity as a poet. This too, he finds, is a work, a craft. In his dedication to *The Temple*, Herbert names the ensuing poems as the "first fruits" of his labour. The heart of his poem "The Elixer," in a verse which remains unchanged over its many revisions, is:

> A man that looks on glasse,
> On it may stay his eye;
> Or if he pleaseth, through it passe.
> And then the heav'n espie.[12]

Taking the image of a telescope (glasse), or perhaps a stained-glass window, *through* which one can look to celestial things, this evidently applies to the way we look upon our daily work: "A servant with this clause/ Makes

---

8. Herbert, *English Poems*, 270–73; Walton, *Lives*, 324.

9. Phrase from "Sunday," in Herbert, *English Poems*, 271.

10. Herbert, *Priest*, 230.

11. Herbert, *English Poems*, 65.

12. Herbert, *English Poems*, 641.

drudgerie divine." We are being urged to "see" God through all things and so to "do" all things "for thee." But at the same time, the "glasse" is a metaphor in a poem through which the poet is viewing the divine. The poet is using images to "see" God, just as he uses daily activity to see God; indeed, "if he pleaseth" means "if his life is acceptable to God."[13] The text of life and the poem fuse, and so does the craft of both. For Herbert this leads to a crucial perception: as a poet he is aware that he can work too intensively on a poem with his "metaphysical" method, that he has "sought out quaint words, and trim invention," "curling with metaphors a plain intention" ("Jordan (II)"). He has "bustled" or been overly busy, as if he were making an ornate article to "sell," and he imagines he can hear a friend

> Whisper, *How wide is all this long pretence!*
> *There is in love a sweetnesse readie penn'd:*
> *Copie out onely that, and save expense.*[14]

That Herbert perceives there can be a similar artificiality or exaggerated effort in being busy in pastoral practice is surely indicated by the verse that he adds to "The Elixer" in his Bemerton period. Now, following from "to do it as for thee," he continues:

> Not rudely, as a beast,
>   To runne into an action;
> But still to make thee prepossest,
>   And give it his perfection.[15]

In his manual, Herbert observes of his parishioners that "some labour anxiously, when they overdo it, to the loss of their quiet and health," so that "they labour profanely, when they set themselves to work like brute beasts, never raising their thoughts to God."[16] Now he appears to recognize that he himself is in danger of this kind of over-activity like "a beast" ("what I do"), admonishing himself that he should regard every action as "prepossest" by God—that is, owned by God, with God's holding the responsibility for it. This is the parallel in practice to the "love" which is "readie penn'd" by God and can be discovered in the making of a poem.

---

13. So Wilcox, in Herbert, *English Poems*, 642.

14. Herbert, *English Poems*, 367.

15. Herbert, *English Poems*, 640.

16. Herbert, *Priest*, 247–48.

The overlap between creativity as a poet with imaginative pastoral work is deepened by the experience of dialogue. Herbert's poetry is suffused and transfigured by conversations—between parts of himself, between himself and an imagined other, and above all between himself and God. In "The Collar," for instance, we have a glimpse into a mood of the poet that breaks out occasionally to disturb the generally serene contentment of the Bemerton idyll: "I struck the board and cry'd, No more."[17] The "board" here is probably that of the wooden altar, and so dates the poem to the period of Herbert's office as priest.[18] But we are back in the temper of protest against God that marked the time before Bemerton, the complaint about a life which is unsatisfying and lacks meaning: "have I no harvest but a thorn?"; "Is the yeare onely lost to me?"; "No flowers, no garlands gay? All blasted? All wasted?" The iron "collar" of the title which the poet feels he is wearing is a pun with "choler," and Herbert's brother Edmund records that, for all his legendary saintliness, even at Bemerton George "was not exempt from passion and choler."[19] The irregularity, even the chaos, of the poetic form reflects the choleric outburst, but it is brought to order, in one of Herbert's wonderfully quiet closes, with a snatch of conversation:

> But as I rav'd and grew more fierce and wilde
> At every word,
> Me thoughts I heard one calling, *Childe:*
> And I reply'd, *My Lord.*[20]

The character of prayer as dialogue with God is reflected in the poem "Prayer (I)," with its images of reciprocal speech: "God's breath in man returning to his birth," "Engine against th' Almightie," "reversed thunder."[21] Herbert carries this dialogical spiritual experience, and his conversational poetic form, into his pastoral practice: the divine conversation can be heard best when public prayer is in the form of dialogue between priest and people. In *The Country Parson* he requires everyone in the congregation to

> answer[. . .] aloud both Amen and all the other answers, which
> are on the Clerks and peoples part to answer; which answers

17. Herbert, *English Poems*, 526

18. Drury, *Music at Midnight*, 45, dates it at that period, but for other reasons.

19. Edward Herbert, *Autobiography*, 11.

20. Herbert, *English Poems*, 526.

21. Herbert, *English Poems*, 178.

are also to be done not in a hudling, or slubbering fashion, gap-
ing, or scratching the head, or spitting even in the midst of their
answer, but gently and pausably, thinking what they say; so that
while they answer, *As it was in the beginning*, &c. they meditate
as they speak . . .[22]

That Herbert believes that the human dialogue is open to the divine is
clear from his reference to meditating "as they speak," and to offering
of a "reasonable service" to God (Rom 12:1) in responses, "when we
speak not as Parrats, without reason." Izaak Walton records that Herbert
was so enthusiastic about responsorial worship that he even invited the
congregation to join with him in the collects, where these are assigned
in the Prayer Book to the minister.[23] The dialogical method is also basic
to Herbert's teaching, as he prefers the two-way speech of catechizing
to the one-way direction of the sermon, and recommends turning the
formal question and answer of the catechism into a Socratic conversation
by extending and varying the questions and drawing out what is of value
and truth in the mind of "silly [i.e., rustic or homely] Trades-men."[24]
Converse with others is at the heart of pastoral care for Herbert, who
urges that together with specifically religious exhortation, the parson
"mingles other discourses for conversation sake,"[25] listening to the other
and picking up his language, such as "knowledge of tillage."[26]

These various kinds of speech are to be marked not only by dialogue,
but by other features with which Herbert experiments in his poetry, and
finds to be the means of devotion, "when the soul unto the lines accords."[27]
Metaphor and story move into the sermon, and also into more informal
pastoral conversation. The preacher is to "tell them stories . . . for them
also men heed, and remember better then exhortations; which though
earnest, yet often dy with the Sermon."[28] In his poem "Redemption"
Herbert communicates the doctrine of atonement by telling a story of
his seeking to find a "rich lord" to whom he wants to present a petition;
failing to find him in "great resorts,"

---

22. Herbert, *Priest*, 231.

23. Walton, *Lives*, 303–4.

24. Herbert, *Priest*, 256.

25. Herbert, *Priest*, 249

26. Herbert, *Priest*, 228.

27. Herbert, "A true Hymne," line 10, in *English Poems*, 576.

28. Herbert, *Priest*, 233.

> At length I heard a ragged noise and mirth
> Of theeves and murderers: there I him espied,
> Who straight, *Your suit is granted,* said, & died.[29]

We can imagine this translating into a sermon, as with many of Herbert's poetic images, which he reminds us are to be found in Scripture. Expanding his reference in "The Elixer" to the "glasse," he recommends the use of imagery and illustration in the questions of his modified catechism:

> This is the skill, and doubtlesse the Holy Scripture intends thus much, when it condescends to the naming of a plough, a hatchet, a bushell, leaven, boyes piping and dancing; shewing that things of ordinary use are not only to serve in the way of drudgery, but to be washed, and cleansed, and serve for lights even of Heavenly Truths. This is the Practice . . .[30]

We might continue the sentence as "the Practice of the pastor and the poet." Another practice exceeds the verbal: that of hospitality. Herbert tells us that the pastor is to entertain at his table every person in the parish by turn over the year, is to encourage each parishioner to offer hospitality regularly to the other, and that when Communion is celebrated in the church the poor are to receive a good meal.[31] He observes that if people are not invited, they are quickly persuaded that they are "hated," and the the pastor "by all means avoids" giving such an impression; in offering such welcome, the parson is a "tracker of God's wayes."[32] In his poem "Love (III)," the poet presents himself—in a dialogue—as feeling an unworthy guest when "Love bade me welcome," but

> You must sit down, sayes Love, and taste my meat;
> So I did sit and eat.[33]

The divine hospitality is clearly associated here with Communion, and in Herbert's arrangement of *The Temple* this poem forms the climax to the collection. In his latest revision (compared with the earlier Williams manuscript) he makes the eucharistic association explicit by adding at the end the opening lines of the *Gloria* sung at the end of the Anglican Communion service. It is poignant then that Love insists that the poet

29. Herbert, *English Poems*, 132

30. Herbert, *Priest*, 256.

31. Herbert, *Priest*, 236, 243, 284.

32. Herbert, *Priest*, 244.

33. Herbert, *English Poems*, 661.

should "sit and eat"; Herbert admits that sitting is natural at Communion since it is a meal, but that it is not properly reverent:

> The Feast indeed requires sitting, because it is a Feast; but man's unpreparedness asks kneeling. Hee that comes to the Sacrament, hath the confidence of a Guest, and hee that kneels, confesseth himself an unworthy one . . . but hee that sits, or lies, puts up to [presumes to claim to be] an Apostle.[34]

It has been suggested that Herbert envisages himself sitting because he is thinking of the eschatological banquet at the end of the earthly pilgrimage,[35] but the point is surely that there is a merging here of Communion, daily hospitality, and the event of encounter with God through the poem itself. There is not just a *parallel* between the imagination of poetry and an imaginative pastoral practice; each *enables* the other. In the very writing of the poem there is an experience of divine hospitality, which can only be described in such scriptural images as in the Song of Songs: "I sat down . . . He brought me to the banqueting house, and his banner over me was love" (2:3–4). The text of Herbert's poem is eucharistic, the words a sacrament of the presence of God, a place where God comes to dwell. Such an encounter cannot be separated from pastoral practice of encounter, and so "sitting," with others.

HOPKINS: THE PARTICULARITY OF THINGS

It seems that Herbert's poetry was much admired by Gerard Manley Hopkins for its "fragrant sweetness,"[36] and it has been suggested that the "casual conversational entrance" into a poem such as "The Windhover," leading to more intense content, is "Herbertian" in style.[37] The apostrophe in the last line of this poem addressed to Christ—"ah my dear"—is certainly borrowed from Herbert's cry to love, "Ah my deare/ I cannot look on thee" ("Love III").[38] As far as I can ascertain, however, a direct

---

34. Herbert, *Priest*, 259.

35. Williams, "Gracious Accommodations," 18.

36. Hopkins to Richard Watson Dixon, 27 February 1879, in Hopkins, *Correspondence*, vol. 1, 346.

37. White, *Hopkins*, 283.

38. Hopkins's choice of a text for a sermon in front of his fellow Jesuit students, "Make the men sit down" (John 6:10), whose repetition drove them into hysterics, may have been prompted by his half-remembering Herbert's "and I did sit and eat";

parallel with Herbert's poem "Employment (I)" has been totally over-looked. Herbert, as we have seen, laments that:

> All things are busie; onely I
> Neither bring hony with the bees,
> Nor flowres to make that, nor the husbandrie
> To water these.

In "Thou art indeed just, Lord," a poem of uncomfortable conversation with God, Hopkins asks—reminscent of Herbert's complaint about his "barren" life—why disappointment must end all his endeavours, and laments:

> . . . birds build—but not I build; no, but strain,
> Time's eunuch, and not breed one work that wakes,
> Mine, O thou lord of life, send my roots rain.[39]

Herbert's "onely I/ Neither bring" is echoed in Hopkins "but not I build," and where Herbert appeals to the busy bees, Hopkins contrasts his state with the building birds. Flowers appear in both as flourishing where the poet is not (see Hopkins's "fretty chervil"), and there is need for refreshing water in both poems. The word "strain" appears towards the close of both as an end-line rhyme, though Herbert's "strain" is the music that he wants God to give him, whereas Hopkins's "strain" is futile exertion. More germane to the theme of this chapter, in both poets the experience of lack of creativity in poetry is fused with a sense of lack of creative employment in practical life. We cannot distinguish whether the poet is talking about frustration in writing poetry or in lack of meaningful activity more generally. For Herbert, this was a period before the happy employment at Bemerton, while Hopkins is reflecting the exhaustion and lack of purpose he finds in his role as Professor of Greek in the newly established Catholic university in Dublin. In another poem of the time, addressed to Robert Bridges, Hopkins refers to himself as being in a "winter world," complains that he lacks "the one rapture of an inspiration," and thinks that Bridges will miss "the roll, the rise, the carol, the creation" in his "lagging lines."[40]

In both poets, the experience of being a poet and the experience of vocation in everyday life are deeply related, and we find this to be

---

see Hopkins, *Sermons*, 233.

39. Hopkins, *Poems*, 106–7.

40. Hopkins, "To R. B.," in *Poems*, 108.

the case in Hopkins's earlier poems, where there is a happier integration between poetry and his pastoral ministry in a congregation. After seven years' formation as a Jesuit, Hopkins was ordained priest in 1877 and then served five short curacies over some three years, in London, Oxford, Bedford Leigh (Lancashire), Liverpool, and Glasgow.[41] A cast of characters from what was to be his only experience of pastoral practice appears in poems written at the time[42]—the anonymous "Jessy or Jack," a bugler boy to whom he gave his first Communion, a boy who helped him in Holy Week, a beggar on the street, a young couple at whose marriage he had assisted, a farrier with whom he sat while he was dying, a young girl sorrowing over the loss of trees' leaves in autumn, a brother watching another perform in a play,[43] and a ploughman guiding his plough.[44] Hopkins's biographer, Norman White, may well be right that Hopkins had to "assert positive feelings in order to carry on work for which he had no talent or inclination,"[45] especially among the poor in industrial Liverpool, and Hopkins was also unsuccessful as a preacher. But he had a persistence in duty, to God and his order, which was no less sustained than Herbert's, who had found his inclination at Bemerton. Nor are the parishioners who make their appearance just subjects of poems. As with Herbert, we can detect how observation of them merged with his handling of words and rhythms as a poet and so how practice and poesy informed each other. In Hopkins's case this process centred on his vision of "inscape," and this is acutely expressed in a poem whose present form probably dates to the end of his period of curacies (1880–1881).

The poem "As Kingfishers Catch Fire" seems to belong with his earlier profusion of poetry about finding Christ at the heart of the natural world (1877),[46] written before his ordination as priest, but the difference

41. Subsequently, after a short period as a teacher in a Catholic school, he was appointed Professor of Greek at University College, Dublin, where he died in 1888 of typhoid.

42. The poems from which the examples are taken are: "The Candle Indoors," "The Bugler's First Communion," "The Handsome Heart," "Cheery Beggar" (fragment), "At the Wedding March," "Felix Randall," "Spring and Fall," "Brothers," "Harry Ploughman."

43. "Brothers" refers to an incident Hopkins observed in 1878 before his curacies, but it was written in 1880.

44. The autograph of "Harry Ploughman" dates to 1887 (Dublin) but is the revision of an earlier poem.

45. White, Hopkins, 320.

46. The autograph is undated and is a draft with corrections and variants. White,

from these—deriving, perhaps, from his pastoral experience—is in the climax of the poem, where Christ is also to be found in human faces.

> As kingfishers catch fire, dragonflies draw flame;
> As tumbled over rim in roundy wells
> Stones ring; like each tucked string tells, each hung bell's
> Bow swung finds tongue to fling out broad its name;
> Each mortal thing does one thing and the same:
> Deals out that being indoors each one dwells;
> Selves—goes itself; *myself* it speaks and spells;
> Crying *What I do is me: for that I came.*
>
> I say more: the just man justices;
> Keeps grace: that keeps all his goings graces;
> Acts in God's eye what in God's eye he is—
> Christ—for Christ plays in ten thousand places,
> Lovely in limbs, and lovely in eyes not his
> To the Father through the features of men's faces.[47]

For Hopkins, everything has a unique "self" or its own characteristic form, which he characterized with Duns Scotus's term *haecceitas* or "thisness."[48] The universe is full of individual forms like notes in a musical scale or separate fractions in scales of light. Hopkins calls the form of these myriad selves their "inscape," denoting that they have an outer shape (scape) which expresses an inner nature; so, everything "deals out that being each one dwells/ . . . myself it speaks and spells." So, for instance, creatures reflect sunlight in different ways—"As kingfishers catch fire, dragonflies draw flame." Each stone makes its own kind of splash when thrown into a well; each bell makes its own ring, "finds tongue to fling out broad its name." Hopkins finds inscapes to be sustained by a charge of energy which he calls "stress," and this also makes a bridge of communication between them. One inscape delivers a surge of stress out of itself to another, and, linked to the inscape, this energy becomes "instress." In an early essay, Hopkins writes that "I have often felt . . . the depth of an instress or how fast the inscape holds a thing."[49] For the "stress" that holds everything together is nothing less than the grace of God, and this

---

Hopkins, 275–76, dates it to 1877; but Gardner and MacKenzie, in Hopkins, *Poems*, 280–81, place the present version in about 1881.

47. Hopkins, *Poems*, 90.

48. Hopkins, *Sermons*, 151, 341–43.

49. Hopkins, *Journals*, 127.

grace depends on an eternal act of sacrifice, which is God's gift of Christ in creation and redemption. In a badly received sermon in his Liverpool curacy, Hopkins declares that "It is as if the blissful agony of stress or selving in God has forced out drops of sweat and blood, which drops were the world."[50] Christ, then, is incarnate in all the inscapes of the world, and Hopkins sees him in the flight of a kestrel, the eucharistic grain of the clouds, and the bright light of the stars. By the time of this poem, Hopkins is also seeing Christ in the human inscape, as when a just person "justices"—expresses what he truly is as just.

It is sensitivity to the particularity of other things that motivates Hopkins's own astonishing use of language, stretching its capacities in a way that had not happened since Shakespeare. To grasp the uniqueness of the objects he observes, he creates compound words, shifts adjectives to surprising places, chimes the sounds of words in the middle of lines, uses unexpected alliterations, and interrupts the expected syntax, often wildly separating subject from verb. He himself speaks of poetry as "the current language heightened . . . and unlike itself."[51] His language reflects the pent-up energy of stress within the inscapes of the world, observing, for example, of a candle-beam that "to-fro tender trambeams truckle at the eye," and of a ploughman: "See his wind-lilylocks-laced;/ Churlsgrace, too, child of Amansstrength, how it hangs or hurls . . ."[52] This complexity of language corresponds to Hopkins's special delight in inscapes that are "dappled and freckled," or which combine shapes and colours in odd combinations. In "Pied Beauty" he celebrates:

> All things counter, original, spare, strange;
> Whatever is fickle, freckled (who knows how?)
> With swift, slow; sweet, sour; adazzle, dim . . .[53]

Now, there are implications of this vision of inscape for the fusing of poetic imagination and language with pastoral practice, as the poems which have traces of his parishioners within them show. Hopkins observes their particularity, recording it with a poetic language that reflects their "thisness" or their uniqueness. As he then allows this impression to develop in the imagination, he plays with embedding it

50. Hopkins, *Sermons*, 197.

51. Hopkins to Robert Bridges, August 14, 1870, in *Correspondence I*, 363.

52. Hopkins, "The Candle Indoors," in *Poems*, 81; "Harry Ploughman," in *Poems*, 104. Both examples come from poems that reflect pastoral experience.

53. Hopkins, *Poems*, 69.

in his "heightened" language, and so arrives at new insights. One can suppose that these perceptions would in turn have an effect on the way that Hopkins makes pastoral relations, either with those mentioned or with others; they certainly form at once a means of prayer for those whom he has met.

For example, Hopkins records the gracious response of a boy who had helped him in church services; Hopkins had asked him what gift he would like, and he had replied at first that he wanted nothing, and then—on being pressed—that he would be happy to receive anything Hopkins himself chose. Hopkins finds in his manner a particular inscape and instress, and expresses it in a distinctive alliteration: "He swung to his first poised purport of reply."[54] Now, in reflection, the language becomes more broken and yet intense, comparing the boy's "wild and self-stressed" heart to a carrier pigeon finding its way through a dark night to its home in the grace of God:

> What the heart is! Which, like carriers let fly—
> Doff darkness, homing nature knows the rest—
> To its own fine function, wild and self-instressed . . .

The result of this poetic meditation is to pray, "On that path you pace/ Run all your race . . ." In an earlier poem, he had observed the same of himself: "My heart, but you were dovewinged, I can tell/ Carrier-witted, I am bold to boast."[55]

Similarly, though with more obvious Victorian sentimentality, Hopkins recalls granting a bugler boy's request ("boon") to give him his first Communion.[56] Perhaps Hopkins goes too far in rhyming the grammatically fragmented phrase "a boon he on" with "communion," and is more successful in his daring rhyming of "consolation" with "royal ration." The last phrase catches something of the particularity of this event and the boy's inscape (a "self-wise self-will"): a military youngster ("fresh youth fretted in a bloomfall") is kneeling in regimental red to receive the ration of Christ himself, which Hopkins describes as a "his treat . . . low-latched in leaf-light housel his too huge godhead." Hopkins is struck by the "thisness" of the event; "Nothing else is like it." W. H. Gardner acutely comments that as Hopkins continues to meditate, "the starts and involutions of syntax . . . express tortuously the tortuous turns

54. Hopkins, "The Handsome Heart: at a Gracious Answer," in *Poems*, 81–82.
55. Hopkins, "The Wreck of the Deutschland," stanza 5, in *Poems*, 53.
56. Hopkins, "The Bugler's First Communion," in *Poems*, 82–83.

and recoils of living thought and genuine emotion."[57] The fear of disappointment about how the boy will develop is mixed with hope, expressed in the tangled:

Let me though see no more of him, and not disappointment

Those sweet hopes quell whose least me quickenings lift
In scarlet or somewhere of some day seeing
    That brow and bead of being
An our day's God's own Galahad.

We can disentangle this thought into something like an anxiety lest "disappointment quell those sweet hopes, whose least quickenings lift me, of some day seeing that brow and bead of being as God's own Galahad in our day, whether in scarlet or somewhere [else]." But then we would miss the extraordinary and spontaneous mixture of emotions that are generated in Hopkins's mind, assisted by the play of words. Recognizing this reaction, even facing the unhealthy thought "let me see no more of him"[58] will develop Hopkins's own pastoral sensitivity. In another prayer of broken syntax he asks a

Frowning and forefending angel-warder
Squander the hell-rook ranks sally to molest him;
    March, kind comrade, abreast him;
Dress his days to a dexterous and starlight order.

Hopkins perceives that there are many in the army ("hell-rook ranks") who will want to deter this young disciple from his moral course, hopes they may be dispelled by a guardian angel, and prays for a steady promotion (regimental "dress") in Christ's own army ("starlight order").

Beginning another poem conversationally, "Felix Randal the farrier, O is he dead then?,"[59] Hopkins catches the distinctive quality of Felix's last illness with two different sets of alliteration, "m"s, "b"s, and "h"s representing his strength—"mould of man, big-boned, and hardy-handsome"— and the softer "r"s and "f"s recording his descent into weakness: "reason rambled and some / Fatal four disorders, fleshed there." Hopkins recalls sitting with him and giving him Communion ("our sweet reprieve

---

57. Gardner, *Gerard Manley Hopkins*, vol. 2, 296.

58. Hopkins notoriously wrote to Robert Bridges on October 8, 1879, "I am half inclined to hope the Hero of [the poem] may be killed in Afghanistan," i.e., so as not to lose his youthful goodness. *Correspondence I*, 368.

59. "Felix Randall," in Hopkins, *Poems*, 86.

and ransom") and Last Unction ("anointed and all"). As a priest, Hopkins recognizes that this confession may not have been complete, but with generosity prays, "Ah well, God rest him all road ever he offended!" This particular event, its uniqueness caught in the net of Hopkins's language, now becomes the source of meditation and further poetic transformation. While the fatal illness, described in the octet of the sonnet, followed the course from strength to weakness, in the sextet Hopkins's thoughts now move in the opposite direction. There is transition from the weakness of tears Hopkins had experienced ("Thy tears that touched my heart, child") to the hope of resurrection glory. For the poem ends with an apparent recollection of Felix's active days making horseshoes at his forge, but the language has something apocalyptic about it, the horse and the shoe being more magnificent than could have been the case in life; in "powerful among peers" we catch an echo of the communion of the saints:

> . . . poor Felix Randal;
> How far from then forethought of, all thy more boisterous years,
> When thou at the random grim forge, powerful amidst peers,
> Didst fettle for the great drayhorse his bright and battering sandal!

There is a perception here about the relation between weakness and strength that Hopkins could have taken into other pastoral relations. Whether he did we cannot know, but we find something similar in his meditation on the wedding of a young couple. Moved to tears at their procession, and apparently feeling vulnerable in his own state of celibacy, his playfulness with language creates in his mind another progression, from the "wonder wedlock" of any Christian with Christ to an eternity of bliss:

> Then let the March tread our ears:
> I to him turn with tears
> Who to wedlock, his wonder wedlock,
> Deals triumph and immortal years.[60]

---

60. "At the Wedding March," in Hopkins, *Poems*, 86.

THOMAS: GOD IN THE SILENCE

Our third priest-poet, R. S. Thomas, makes a significant reference to both Herbert and Hopkins in a late poem, "Resurrections":[61]

> Easier for them, God
> only at the beginning
> of his recession. Blandish him
> said the times and they did so,
> Herbert, Traherne, walking
> in a garden not yet
> polluted . . .
>
> The corners of the spirit waiting
> to be developed, Hopkins
> renewed the endearments
> taming the lion-like presence
> lying against him. What
> happened? Suddenly he was
> gone. Leaving love guttering
> in his withdrawal.

Unlike Herbert and Hopkins in their time, Thomas is dealing in his own time with what is felt to be the withdrawal of God. In his selection of Herbert's poetry, Thomas notes that Herbert is continually engaged in "dialogue, encounter, confrontation" with God, a conversation which could become an argument, but which "God always won."[62] The reference in this poem to Hopkins is to his sonnet "Carrion Comfort," which was written in the same period of desolation as "Thou art indeed just, Lord," whose similarity to Herbert's "Employment (I)" I have already commented on. For Hopkins, the desolation is deeper because he can no longer find Christ "at home" in the inscapes of the world.[63] In "Carrion Comfort" Hopkins writes of his experience as a wrestling with God by night (like Jacob), and protests that God has laid "a lionlimb against me."[64] Thomas's comment is that Hopkins was able to "renew endearments/ taming the lion-like presence," or come back into loving conversation with God; we might find evidence of this in "Patience" and "My own heart let me more

61. Thomas, *No Truce*, 47.

62. Thomas, *Choice*, 12, 16.

63. So, in the poem beginning "I wake and feel the fell of dark," Hopkins laments the absence of "dearest him that lives alas! Away"; *Poems*, 101.

64. Hopkins, *Poems*, 99–100.

have pity on." We might even say that the earlier "terrible sonnet" itself
bears witness to it, ending:

> That night, that year
> Of now done darkness I wretch lay wrestling with (my God!) my God.

The darkness is apparently over, and Hopkins's version of Christ's cry of
abandonment on the cross has something of the tone of Herbert's "ah, my
dear" about it.

For Thomas, there are no such "renewed endearments," as experienced by Herbert and Hopkins, since "Suddenly he was/ gone." In "Via
Negativa" he writes,

> I never thought other than
> That God is that great absence
> In our lives, the empty silence
> Within, the place where we go
> Seeking, not in hope to
> Arrive or find.[65]

Thomas is well aware of the relation between his poetic imagination
and pastoral practice, writing of "the obligation which I feel upon me—to
try to experience life in all its richness, wonder and strangeness, and to
use the best language which I possess to describe that experience."[66] A
key element of that requirement, I suggest, is linking the silence that he
finds among people in his pastoral practice and the silence of God that
he finds among the words of his poetry. One silence is not just a record of
the other; as we find in both Herbert and Hopkins, practice and poetry
each illuminate the other. In "Petition" Thomas conjoins silence in poetry
with his silent "witnessing" in his pastoral work, with "eyes merely":

> Seeking the poem
> In the pain, I have learned
> Silence is best, paying for it
> With my conscience. I am eyes
> Merely, witnessing virtue's
> Defeat: seeing the young born
> Fair, knowing the cancer
> Awaits them.[67]

---

65. Thomas, *Collected Poems*, 220

66. Thomas, "Making of a Poem," 113.

67. Thomas, "Petition," in *Collected Poems*, 209.

We have the impression that he is driven by the human and divine silence he meets in his pastoral life into an interior silence of poetry, from which he returns to find silence again in new ways.

Thomas's pastoral practice was far more extensive than either Herbert's or Hopkins's. Six years of curacy in two churches (Chirk and Hanmer), beginning in 1936, were followed by a total of thirty-six years as a vicar in three places (Manafon, Eglwys-fach, and Aberdaron). He chose to spend his whole ministry in small rural parishes of Wales, while publishing some fifteen volumes of poetry. In a late poem called "Words" he bids his reader, "Accuse me of sincerity . . . art is my necessity."[68] And one strong impression that emerges from his unsentimental, often brutal, accounts of parish ministry is that people are silent to him—in the sense that they are either unable or reluctant to open their feelings to him. He does not accuse them of being superficial, but their depths are hidden to him; an image that appears consistently is that of a cold wind blowing from empty places, and this is an experience that is associated for him with the silence of God, or the Word of God falling into a deep abyss.[69]

Thomas reflects that his parishioners may want to communicate with him, but somehow their bodies stand in the way; as "The priest picks his way/ Through the parish," he finds "Hearts wanting him to come near./ The flesh rejects him."[70] There is a "dark filling" even in "their smiling sandwich."

He discerns that it is loneliness that locks people into themselves. In "The Word" he tells of being commanded by "the god" to write what it is to be human; he spells out

> the word 'lonely'. And my hand moved
> to erase it; but the voices
> of all those waiting at life's
> window cried out loud: 'It is true'.[71]

The wind that blows from the empty places is associated with this loneliness, and so with silence. In "The Calling" he records receiving a commission from God to go to a "lean parish," where he is to learn the silence that is wisdom, and to be as alone with himself as his parishioners

---

68. Thomas, *No Truce*, 85.

69. See Thomas, *Echoes*, 25.

70. Thomas, "The Priest," in *Collected Poems*, 196.

71. Thomas, *Collected Poems*, 265.

are alone in their rooms which are chilled by the wind.[72] In "Country Cures" he records that "life is bare/ Of all but the cold fact of the wind," and he knows the "lean men, / Whose collars fasten them by the neck/ To loneliness."[73] Thomas appears to have an ironic theory about the making of human persons: when two people meet, they produce a "darkness" in which their very relationship forces them apart:

> I learn there are two beings
> so that, when one is present, the other
> is far off. There is no room
> for them both.[74]

Thomas now places this silence of the people to whom he is ministering alongside the silence of God which he knows both as a priest and as a poet. Despite his life-long love of his wife, he muses, "this one, had he ever been anything but solitary?"[75] Yet he affirms that prayer is still possible, though it is prayer to a silent God. He does not find a voice, or the sense of a presence, but he believes he is making a kind of relation with God. Unlike Elijah in the windy cave, there is "no still, small/ voice" (1 Kgs 19:12), and yet he affirms that "the prayer formed." Like Herbert and Hopkins, he prays, "Deliver me from the long drought/ of the mind."[76]

While Thomas often witnesses to the *feeling* that God is absent, and uses a language of absence,[77] he is convinced that there is still a *relationship* between himself and God. God then is not actually absent, but silent, and so hidden: God is "a power/ in hiding . . . waiting to be christened [named]."[78] He writes:

> After all, there is nothing more important than the relationship between man and God. Nor anything more difficult than establishing that relationship. Who is it that ever saw God? Who ever heard him speak? We have to live virtually the whole of our lives

---

72. Thomas, "The Calling," in *Laboratories of the Spirit*, 50.

73. Thomas, *Collected Poems*, 124.

74. Thomas, "Revision," in *Collected Poems*, 492.

75. Thomas, *Echoes*, 118 (prose).

76. Thomas, "The Prayer," in *Collected Poems*, 270. Cf. Herbert's "Employment (I)" and Hopkins's "Thou art indeed just, Lord" compared earlier in this chapter.

77. E.g. Thomas, "The Absence," in *Collected Poems*, 361.

78. Thomas, "The Waiting," in *No Truce*, 64; emphasis added.

in the presence of an invisible and mute God. But that was never a bar to anyone seeking to come into contact with Him.[79]

He goes on to say, "That is what prayer is." In Thomas's case, it is also what *poetry* is. "Forming" a prayer and forming poetry are inseparable, and the very craft of words in both is a work that makes contact with the silent God who overhears us.[80] In "Revision" he asks, "How many/of man's prayers assume/ an eavesdropping God?," and tells us that "I . . . play my recording/ of his silence over/ and over to myself only."[81] His poetry is surely one way of recording the silence, as he writes:

> Seeking the poem
> In the pain, I have learned
> Silence is best.[82]

In "Revision" he particularly associates the silence of God with the celebration of Communion in bread and wine, and this may be why Thomas prefers the wordless eucharist of the natural world, with the sand crumbling like bread, and the wine "the light quietly lying/ in its own chalice."[83] Just as the meeting of two people results in one being "far off," so is the meeting between a person and God:

> "know this gulf you have created
> can be crossed by prayer" . . .

> "It is called silence, and it is a rope
>   over an unfathomable
> abyss, which goes on and on
> never arriving."[84]

There is a "grace given to maintain/ your balance," an "unseen/ current between two points, coming/ to song in the nerves."[85] The "song" is evidently prayer, but it is no less poetry, so that Thomas declares, "you have no words yet vibrate/ in me."[86]

79. Davies, R. S. *Thomas: Autobiographies*, 104.
80. See Thomas, *Echoes*, 113.
81. Thomas, *Collected Poems*, 492.
82. Thomas, "Petition," in *Collected Poems*, 209.
83. Thomas, "In Great Waters," in *Collected Poems*, 351.
84. Thomas, "Revision," in *Collected Poems*, 492–93.
85. Thomas, "Revision," in *Collected Poems*, 493.
86. Thomas, "Near and Far," in *No Truce*, 46.

When Thomas turns from the silence of prayer and poetry back to his silent flock, who leave through the door of the church with the "crumpled ticket" of the prayers he has uttered in their hands,[87] he has learnt to practise the same kind of making of contact and relationship whatever the response, or lack of it. The work of poetry and the work of prayer, bearing with the divine silence, can be continued in the work of the people's liturgy, the offices of birth, marriage, death, and "the visitation of the sick! A ministry more credible because more noticeable than the cure of souls."[88] He recalls visiting old ladies in bed who cannot find the words to speak to him, unable, it seems, to move their tongues to make a sound; yet he witnesses that visiting them gives his life a structure and a shape, keeping him from excesses of either joy or sorrow.[89]

Writing with appreciation of Herbert's poetry, he similarly finds "reason, not so much tinged with, as warmed by, emotion, and solidly based on order and discipline, the soul's good form."[90] So Thomas accepts the discipline to "stay here" with, for example, the sickly daughter of the village grocer, "blowing/ On the small soul in my/ Keeping with such breath as I have."[91] The fruit of this discipline in both poetry and pastoral office is love, and looking back on his ministry, he reflects that "Everywhere he went, despite his round collar and his licence, he was there to learn rather than teach love."[92] Beneath the silent surface there are not only the empty depths from where the cold wind blows, but love and "the holiness of the heart's affections." In the last prose piece of *The Echoes Return Slow*, he celebrates his two great loves, the sea and his wife, "both female," and feels that even here it has been a lifetime's apprenticeship in only navigating their surface, which covers the "unstable fathoms" of love's depths.[93]

87. Thomas, "The Calling," in *Laboratories of the Spirit*, 50.

88. Thomas, *Echoes*, 62 (prose).

89. Thomas, *Echoes*, 63.

90. Thomas, *Choice*, 17.

91. Thomas, "Invitation," in *Collected Poems*, 212.

92. Thomas, *Echoes*, 92 (prose).

93. Thomas, *Echoes*, 120 (prose).

CONCLUSION: THE MINISTER IN CONVERSATION, SOLILOQUY, AND SILENCE

Addressing God as "anonymous presence," Thomas writes:

> Conversation, soliloquy,
> silence—a descending or an ascending
> scale? That you are there
> to be found, the disciplines
> agree.[94]

If we apply his three stages of "conversation, soliloquy, silence" to the poetry and spirituality of Herbert, Hopkins, and himself, we find significant differences of emphasis. In Herbert, soliloquy and occasional silence is always moving into conversation. In Hopkins, soliloquy and a terrible period of silence could, we feel, always *become* conversation. In Thomas, soliloquy is always in the *face* of silence, and threatens to *become* silent. In each of them, however, we can find pastoral experience in interaction with poetry. Herbert's conversation with God is worked out in his pastoral method of dialogue. Hopkins offers a soliloquy in which he catches—or, in his desolation, feels that he fails to express—the God-given particularities of people in the peculiarities of his poetic diction. Thomas breaks silence in his poetry only to record the silence of God, and to gain courage to persist with the silence of people, surprised to find love beneath the surface. His God and his parishioners are "there to be found."

To all pastors Thomas poses the question in his poem above: are the three modes to be experienced and practised in "a descending or ascending scale"? Is silence (and listening) the necessary prelude for inner soliloquy and outward conversation with others? Or does all talk, whether inner or outer, necessarily lead to silence? To know when one or other sequence is appropriate calls for the pastor to have the imagination of a poet.

---

94. Thomas, *Echoes*, 115.

4

MINISTRY AND GEOGRAPHY

Andy Goodliff

WHAT HAS GEOGRAPHY GOT to do with ministry? Paul Goodliff knows a lot about geography. His first degree was in geography and he spent four years teaching the subject to secondary-age children. He is always paying attention to the weather, collects ordinance survey maps, and has a keen interest in rivers, coasts, and hills. Paul Goodliff also knows a lot about ministry, both as a minister in practice for over thirty years and one who has reflected theologically on its nature. In this chapter I want to explore how geography might be a helpful way of reflecting on ministry. As far as I can tell, my father has never brought the study of geography and the study of ministry into conversation with one another.

We do not think a lot about geography, although of course we cannot escape it: we are always located, placed somewhere, in relation to land and people. "Geography matters. Place matters to God,"[1] says Willie James Jennings[2] in his commentary on the book of Acts. I want in this chapter to reflect on what I have learned from reading Willie Jennings and Timothy Gorringe. Jennings's theological project is in part a geographical project. In his study of theology and the origins of

---

1. Jennings, *Acts*, 16. Eugene Peterson says something similar: "geography and theology are biblical bedfellows"; "Foreword," in Jacobsen, *Sidewalks in the Kingdom*, 9.

2. Jennings is a fellow ordained Baptist minister and theologian. For many years, alongside his academic roles, he was associate minister at Mount Level Missionary Baptist Church, Durham, North Carolina.

race, *The Christian Imagination*, he highlights the way that colonialism introduced a separation of identity from land and the creation of racial identity, one of the results of which is a doctrine of creation that has had nothing to say about people and place. Jennings states, "I want Christians to recognize the grotesque nature of a social performance of Christianity that imagines Christian identity floating above land, landscape, animals, place, and space, leaving such realities to the machinations of capitalistic calculations and the commodity chains of private property."[3] In his Acts commentary this is rephrased as "the church has often failed to see the geographic dimensions of discipleship."[4] Following Jesus, and for the purposes of this essay, being ministers of Jesus is also to be geographers, that is, those who take seriously place and space.

Jennings is interested in how physical geography has been, and continues to be, for some people integral to identity, where ways of life "are patterned not after, but actually with space, with land, trees, water, animals."[5] He asks, "what if your skin was inextricably bound to 'the skin of the world'"?[6] He goes on to explore how a "sense of particular places anchors community building,"[7] drawing on the work of Keith Basso's book *Wisdom Sits in Places*.[8] The idea of wisdom residing in places immediately jars with our sense of wisdom being found in people.[9] Geography is linked to stories that cultivate formation; it is to understand "places as moral agents."[10] His argument is to listen and receive more openly the theologies of creation from indigenous peoples. Jennings demonstrates that there are other ways of seeing places than those of private property, where land is given only an "economic logic."[11] The possessing of land, claiming it as property, transformed geography.

3. Jennings, *Christian Imagination*, 293.

4. Jennings, *Acts*, 249.

5. Jennings, *Christian Imagination*, 50.

6. Jennings, *Christian Imagination*, 39 quoting Martin, *Way of the Human Being*, 40.

7. Jennings, *Christian Imagination*, 55.

8. Basso's book is a study of the *ndee*, commonly known as Western Apache, and "how native peoples remember, learn, and perpetuate moral vision"; Jennings, *Christian Imagination*, 54.

9. Jennings is critical of a whole approach to education and learning associated with how we think of knowledge and wisdom; see Jennings, *After Whiteness*.

10. Jennings, *Christian Imagination*, 57.

11. Jennings suggests this was how the merchant came to see the land; Jennings, "Disfigurations of Christian Identity," 70.

Land could be "purchase[d] by measurement and location."[12] In addition it transformed identity, as lines and circles enclosed both land and bodies, so that "racial existence came into being at the site of geographic enclosure."[13] This is the colonial legacy.[14] There is, he claims, within Christian faith and theology "the possibility of knowing and renarrating identity with geography," but it has never been "fully realized" or "truly explored."[15] This explains his wider project to "reframe" and "recast" the doctrine of creation.[16] Jennings argues that "a Christian doctrine of creation is first a doctrine of place and people."[17] In another place he writes, "a Christian doctrine of creation must intervene in in the formation of geographic life or it is not a Christian doctrine of creation."[18]

Jennings adds a second way that colonialism impacted geography was through translation. He takes as an example the hymns of Isaac Watts, who translated the Psalms so that Great Britain replaced Israel.[19] Great Britain becomes God's elect people. In 1889 the Baptist John Clifford published *God's Greater Britain*.[20] In its colonial context, this "became a mangled and diseased thing" because the Bible becomes an "engine of cultural nationalism."[21] The merchant, the soldier, and the missionary end up sharing the same goal of "geographic and literary supremacy."[22] This remains the largely unconscious "diseased social imagination"[23] we live with. It was then not just the geography of the "new world" that changed, but also Great Britain, and this became most apparent in the

---

12. Jennings, *Christian Imagination*, 226. Michael Northcott explores some of this from a different perspective in *Place, Ecology and the Sacred*.

13. Jennings, "Reframing the World," 391.

14. In his book *The Book of Trespass*, Nick Hayes shows how the legacy of enclosure in England has a much longer history. Hayes makes an argument with regards the effect of people on being dispossessed from access and use of land.

15. Jennings, *Christian Imagination*, 42.

16. Jennings is completing a book project entitled *Unfolding the World: Recasting a Christian Doctrine of Creation*.

17. Jennings, *Christian Imagination*, 248.

18. Jennings, "Reframing the World," 405.

19. Jennings, *Christian Imagination*, 210–20. See also Jennings, "Protestantism," 251–52.

20. See Carey, *God's Empire*, 3-4.

21. Jennings, "Protestantism," 252.

22. Jennings, "Protestantism," 252. See here also Stanley, *Bible and the Flag*.

23. Jennings, *Christian Imagination*, 6.

immigration from the colonies in the latter half of the twentieth century.[24] Our colonial past continues historically, theologically, economically, and geographically to impact our present, and is something we have not fully reckoned with.[25] Reading Jennings, who writes as an African American firstly to America, invites British readers to look at the impact in our own context of the "colonial wound."[26]

If the emphasis in *The Christian Imagination* is on displacement— how we became displaced from peoples and place—Jennings's commentary on the book of Acts is an account of the divine desire of God in the Holy Spirit to join us together in the face of segregation.[27] Segregation, says Jennings, "teaches us to see the world in slices, fragmented pieces of geographic space that we may own or control."[28] Segregation is a seduction; it keeps people at a distance; it separates people spatially, culturally, and sometimes desperately.[29] Instead of communion and joining, the world and the church live with the "legacy of segregation."[30] Jennings argues that "life in cultural, economic, and social silos, performed in multiple parallel lines, is the inner logic of too many communities, and such configurations accepted by Christians confront the church with its deepest sin: it denies the power of the living Spirit."[31]

For Jennings geography and theology need to come into conversation because the Spirit "presses us into an alternative life . . . to deep and abiding connections with all that surrounds us, not only the people but also the land, not only the land, not only the land but also the animals, not only the animals but also the rhythms of particular, local life."[32] This leads him to contend that Christians do not have an adequate doctrine of creation beyond saying God created the world. To pay attention to geography is to find a much more real doctrine of creation in which "we are creatures with other creatures."[33] The implication of this, for the

24. See Panayi, "Immigration, Multiculturalism and Racism."

25. For one example that seeks to address it, see Reddie, *Theologising Brexit*.

26. The language of "colonial wound" comes from Mignolo, *Idea of Latin America*, 8; cited in Jennings, *Christian Imagination*, 114.

27. Jennings, *Acts*, 10-12.

28. Jennings, *Acts*, 12.

29. Jennings, *Acts*, 145–49.

30. Jennings, *Acts*, 146.

31. Jennings, *Acts*, 148.

32. Jennings, *Acts*, 249.

33. Jennings, "Eco-Theology and Zoning Meetings," https://reflections.yale.edu/article/

church and for ministry, is to engage, says Jennings, in two struggles. The first struggle is take seriously the "geographic formations of life"[34] where we live. The shaping and developing of land is something for the church in which to participate as part of our love of neighbour and neighbourhood. "We fight against the segregation that shapes or worlds, and we work to weave lives together."[35] The church is called to be a contrast community,[36] that looks different, not in theory but in actuality.

The second struggle Jennings identifies is one of "yield[ing] to the Spirit's leading,"[37] that is, towards how the Spirit is concerned with joining and the communal. This, he sees, is the concern of the book of Acts: "the Spirit offers us God's own fantasy of desire for people, of joining and life together and of shared stories bound to a new destiny in God."[38] The word "joining" is the key word in how Jennings understands the work of God and the life of the church.[39] His vision of the church is one that seeks joining, which "involves entering into the lives of peoples to build actual life together, lives enfolded and kinship networks established through the worship of and service to God of Israel in Jesus Christ."[40] Ministry and church are an "incarnational participation" where "we follow the Spirit into places and spaces, extending our lives into those sites as acts of love and desire."[41]

For Jennings, Christians needs to be prepared to meet these two struggles by starting with communities that have been left behind: "we join them, we move to them, or we stay in them, or we form them, or

---

crucified-creation-green-faith-rising/eco-theology-and-zoning-meetings-interview-willie.

34. Jennings, *Acts*, 250.

35. Jennings, "Can White People Be Saved?," 43.

36. Jennings, "Can White People Be Saved?," 43. The language of "contrast community" comes from Lohfink, *Jesus and Community*.

37. Jennings, *Acts*, 250.

38. Jennings, *Acts*, 11.

39. Jennings in *The Christian Imagination* unpacks joining as "the incarnate life of the Son of God, who took on . . . a life of joining, belonging, connection, and intimacy" (7); "a faith that understands its own deep wisdom and power of joining, mixing, merging, and changed by multiple ways of life to witness a God who surprises us by love of differences" (9); "the Spirit descended on the disciples and drove them into the languages of the world to enact the joining desired by the Father of Jesus for all people" (267).

40. Jennings, *Christian Imagination*, 287.

41. Jennings, "Overcoming Racial Faith," 9.

we advocate for them, or we protect them."[42] Jennings helps us see that ministry is geographical—it is located in places with people and wider surroundings—because it is theological. In reading John Colwell I learned that the church is summoned to indwell the gospel story;[43] what Jennings wants to add to that is that the church also indwells a place, and therefore ministry becomes a conversation between gospel and place, between theology and geography. It leads him to ask two questions:

> What if we lived as though the well-being of those around us, including our surroundings, was as important to us as our own lives? What if for the first time I felt the absolute depths of God's love and concern not only for the one God has drawn into my life and me into theirs but also for the place I inhabit, the streets I traverse, the animals I see, and the plants I touch with all my senses every day?[44]

At the end of *The Christian Imagination*, Jennings says, "by attending to the spatial dynamics at play in the formation of social existence, we would be able to imagine reconfigurations of living spaces that might promote more just societies."[45] This offers a means to introduce the work of Timothy Gorringe. In article entitled "Salvation by Bricks: Theological Reflections on the Planning Process," Gorringe argues that "Christians have a clear ethical duty to involve themselves in the planning process."[46] This article should be read in the context of Gorringe's more detailed engagements in his two monographs *A Theology of the Built Environment* and *The Common Good and the Global Emergency*, which both seek to address questions of geography and in particular the built environment of cities, towns, and villages. Like Jennings, Gorringe wants to make a theological argument that Christian should care about the well-being of our places. He is concerned that theology has been too silent on what he considers a theological ethical issue. In his words, "buildings are 'the third human skin.'"[47]

42. Jennings, "Can White People Be Saved?," 43.

43. Colwell, *Living the Story*.

44. Jennings, *Acts*, 251.

45. Jennings, *Christian Imagination*, 294. A few pages earlier he says, "we must enter the struggle of land acquisition, space and place design, targeted housing development, buying, and selling which constantly re-establishes and strengthens segregationist mentalities and racial identities" (287).

46. Gorringe, "Salvation by Bricks," 111.

47. Gorringe, "Salvation by Bricks," 101. The idea of "third human skin" comes

Gorringe presents seven marks of the church that he believes have "implications for the shaping of the homeliness of the world, for our cities and other settlements."[48] The first mark is that the "church is local, but globally networked."[49] The church is a community of people who know one another, but who also look outwards. The church is thus concerned for itself and for the wider place in which it is located. The second mark is that the church "lives by memory and tradition,"[50] or, to use other language, it is apostolic. The church is connected to the life of Jesus of Nazareth two thousand years ago, and by virtue of this it is also connected to the life of Israel and to that of the early church. This living memory shapes the church's life. Together with that tradition is the memory of the place where the church found. The history and stories of a place are important. The third mark that Gorringe offers is that church "exists by virtue of a common story and common hope."[51] The church understands itself as those "called to one hope"; that is, it looks forward as well as back. Gorringe quotes Raymond Williams, who sees that the "making of a society is the finding of common meanings . . . *writing themselves into the land*."[52] The planned geography of a place needs to share a story, a hope—common meanings—that embedded themselves into people's lives and living. The fourth mark acknowledges that the church is "a community where sin is recognized and forgiveness asked for." The church is not perfect. Elsewhere Gorringe states that "all forms of the Church have involved themselves in structures of deceit and very often systematic coercion."[53] The planning of places will also not be perfect; the phrase "salvation by bricks" was Reinhold Niebuhr's "sneer at those who put too much faith in the possibility of change through planning."[54] The fifth mark is "a sense of justice at the heart of [the church's] narrative."[55]

---

from Day, *Places of the Soul*, 10, 42; cited in Gorringe, *Theology of the Built Environment*, 82.

48. Gorringe, "Salvation by Bricks," 111. He presents a version of these marks in *Theology of the Built Environment*, 185–92.

49. Gorringe, "Salvation by Bricks," 111.

50. Gorringe, "Salvation by Bricks," 111.

51. Gorringe, "Salvation by Bricks," 112.

52. Gorringe, "Salvation by Bricks," 112. The quote comes from Williams, "Culture in Ordinary," 4; cited in Gorringe, *Theology of the Built Environment*, 243.

53. Gorringe, *Theology of the Built Environment*, 246.

54. Gorringe, "Salvation by Bricks," 113.

55. Gorringe, "Salvation by Bricks," 113.

This sense of justice is present throughout Scripture, but perhaps most clearly sensed in the prophets of Israel. People and places must seek social justice, which in the prophets was understood as "ensur[ing] that all Israelites had their rightful share in the land which was gifted to all," and wherein christologically all are viewed as sisters and brothers of and in Christ.[56] Gorringe's sixth mark is a concern for beauty, which he says has been present among Christians since at least the fourth century.[57] "God is beautiful, and all creation shares to some extent in that beauty";[58] therefore our places and buildings should give some "sensory delight"[59] and in this there is what Gorringe calls "an expression of grace."[60] The last mark is that the "church is *semper reformanda*, always in the process of re-creation and re-discovery."[61] The church is always developing, always a pilgrim community, always having a sense of fragility about it. Likewise, people and places—cities, towns, and villages—will not be static, but growing and changing, and the church should be supportive of that, without letting go of the mark of memory and tradition.[62]

These seven criteria and Gorringe's wider argument have the potential to find some overlap with Jennings's vision of "ecclesial joining." Gorringe recognizes, at least in part, that church and society have something of what Jennings calls a "diseased social imagination," although he does not make a direct link to colonialism. Jennings would argue, I think, that there is more that needs to be untangled within the church if Gorringe's vision of the task of the church is to fruitful.

For the church and its minister, Gorringe offers a call to be involved in its place, its local geography, like Jennings, as a contrast community, where "all the Lord's peoples are prophets."[63] Involvement in decisions

56. Gorringe, *Theology of the Built Environment*, 189.

57. Gorringe, "Salvation by Bricks," 113–14.

58. Gorringe, *Theology of the Built Environment*, 197.

59. This phrase is borrowed from Nicholas Wolterstorff, whom Gorringe quotes in "Salvation by Bricks," 114. The full sentence form Wolterstorff says, "the tragedy of modern urban life is not only that so many of our cities are oppressed and powerless, but also that so many have nothing surrounding them in which any human being could possibly take sensory delight"; Wolterstorff, *Act in Action*, 82.

60. Gorringe, *Theology of the Built Environment*, 221.

61. Gorringe, "Salvation by Bricks," 114.

62. For an interesting and helpful account of tradition, see Medley, "Stewards, Interrogators, and Inventors."

63. These words from Numbers 11:29 feature as the epigraph to *Theology of the Built Environment* and are repeated several times through the book. Gorringe's

about places requires a greater democracy and active participation than is often the case. It requires the practice of congregational government. In his words, he sees that as "a question of re-learning that the so-called secular is not outside our remit, that the High Street is still more of a Christian task than the repair of the church tower."[64]

The impact of reading Jennings and Gorringe for those of us who are ministers of the gospel is that we take place and geography more seriously. Ministry in the local church is discovering that we inhabit not only a congregation, but a wider community and its land, and encouraging our congregations to do the same. It is to pay more attention to the landscape, the histories and development of a place. As Eugene Peterson says, "every church is located someplace. There are no churches in general, no generic churches, no one-size-fits-all churches."[65] Ministry is learning to love not just a congregation but a people, not just a church but a place.[66] While for those of us who are Baptists we might resist the rigidity of the Anglican parish, we nonetheless work with a sense of place, even if informally—"this is our patch," "this is our mission field." Our sense of patch and mission field of course needs to recognize that any and every place is first that which belongs to God, that over which the Holy Spirit hovers.

When ministers join a church we go usually as one called to teach. Jennings says that "being a disciple of Jesus and following Jesus requires that we become radically adaptive learners."[67] Ministers are often outsiders to a place; we should therefore come, learning to be "second readers,"[68] taking a different posture of listening and learning. Of course, we already do this to some degree; moving to a new place means having to become orientated to where everything is and how best to get there (that is, learning the shortcuts). This description of second readers is part of Jennings's argument that as Gentiles we were joined to Israel—we read after them—but this also goes the other way as Jews had to learn

attention to them appears to have come from William Blake, where the verse is suffix to his poem "Jerusalem"; Gorringe, *Theology of the Built Environment*, 19.

64. Gorringe, *Theology of the Built Environment*, 260.

65. Peterson, *Under the Unpredictable Plant*, 123.

66. In becoming attentive to people and place, this will introduce questions of class and race.

67. Jennings, "Overcoming Racial Faith," 9.

68. Jennings, "Reframing the World," 394.

to be joined to Gentiles and their world (Acts 10 and 15).[69] Jennings warns against any "pedagogical imperialism," a sense that the minister (because of their ordination and education) knows best. As ministers we are listening and looking for the places of new joining, of common meaning, of beauty, of the Holy Spirit's prompting.[70] Some of this becomes helping a congregation and community appreciate its location and so discover together what a life rooted with creation might look like. One of the strange gifts of the COVID pandemic was that many people began to walk locally and value the place in which they live and its wildlife.[71] Here then is the beginning of an opportunity to relearn our creatureliness, to see that discipleship is about "being with creation."[72] Ministry so often takes place indoors that we might need to consider finding ways for ministry to happen outdoors.[73]

To speak of ministry outdoors leads to speaking of an attention not only to land, but also to the climate. We live in a "global emergency"[74] and a "planetary ecological crisis."[75] Both Jennings and Gorringe bring us to a new focus on place, and in the context of an anthropocene world climate change should be now "a confessional issue"[76] for Christians. Christian ministers who learn to think geographically can no longer ignore or be silent on the climate crisis and its effects; our relation to climate and land is a matter of the gospel. A geographic doctrine of creation highlights how the whole world is a balancing act, where all things are interconnected and so in terms of climate national borders are a fiction. Following

69. Jennings, "Reframing the World," 394.

70. In Peterson's words, "Long before I arrive on the scene, the Spirit is at work. I must fit into what is going on. I have no idea yet what is taking place here; I must study the contours, understand the weather, know what kind of crops grow in this climate, be in awe of the complex intricacies between past and present, between the people in the parish and those outside"; *Under the Unpredictable Plant*, 133.

71. See the report from the Office of National Statistics: https://www.ons.gov.uk/economy/environmentalaccounts/articles/howhaslockdownchanged ourrelationshipwithnature/2021-04-26.

72. Wells, *Incarnational Ministry*, 63–79. For more on creatureliness, see Wirzba, *From Nature to Creation* and *This Sacred Life*.

73. So perhaps exploring those who have pioneered things like Forest Church or Wild Church.

74. Gorringe, *Common Good and the Global Emergency*.

75. Jennings, "Christian Story of God's Work," 474.

76. Gorringe, "Climate Change."

Stanley Hauerwas's claim that we can only act in a world we see,[77] perhaps what is needed first in response to the ecological crisis is to see (once again) the world and ourselves as creation. A church that learns to see the world and ourselves as creation learns humility, recognizes the need for solidarity with our neighbours around the world, seeks to example appropriate ways of living with creation, holds ourselves and those in power to account, and finally discovers hope not in ourselves but in God.[78] With regards to hope, Charles Campbell says, "in the context of climate change, hope cannot serve as the nice, neat resolution"; instead, "hope will remain an unresolved resolution."[79]

This highlighting of place and land needs also to be grounded in the worship of a congregation. While worship often is shaped by time—the seasons and festivals—there is an opportunity to see worship emerging with and from place. Ashley Lovett sees possibilities in the leading of the Lord's Supper to address the "local context."[80] He finds an example in a Baptist congregation in Openshaw, Manchester and their book of prayers and liturgies which is described as "coming 'out of a particular time and place.'"[81] John Weaver also tells the story of the congregation of El Cordero de Dios Baptist Church in San Salvador, which created a mural to hang behind the Communion table of images that "represented their life as a church."[82] These included "scenes from the urban and rural communities that surrounded the church, the work activities of church members, and depictions of home life and worship."[83] On one occasion Jennings expresses something similar: "I want you to think about both sermon and song, but also dirt and grass and pavement. I want you to think about what happens at an altar with the breaking of a body and the shedding of blood for you, but I also want you to think about broken earth,

---

77. Hauerwas, *Peaceable Kingdom*, 29.

78. These five responses come from Wells, "Changing the Moral Climate," a sermon preached at St Martin-in-the-Fields, London, August 8, 2021.

79. Campbell, *Scandal of the Gospel*, 68.

80. Lovett, "To Become the Future Now," 169.

81. Lovett, "To Become the Future Now," 169; citing McBeath and Presswood, *Crumbs of Hope*, 2.

82. Weaver, "Spirituality in Everyday Life," 147. John Bunyan Baptist Church in Cowley, Oxford, under the ministry of James Grote, did something similar in creating several special crosses depicting the local places.

83. Weaver, "Spirituality in Everyday Life," 148.

rearranged landscapes and neighbourhoods."[84] Too often worship can be abstract or universal so that it has no connection to the particularity of a people and place. Ministry is an invitation to enable the congregation to see God and faith embodied in places, without slipping into a nationalism or parochialism in which God is tied only to this place.[85] Having said that, Jennings is critical of a simple turn to practices without recognising their "demonic deployment in the formation of the New World."[86] For Jennings, "faithful Christian practices today that follow Jesus" are those "done in and among diverse communities where the histories of colonial wounds are addressed."[87] This leans in the direction of Gorringe's mark of confessing sin and being forgiven.

This attending to place lends itself to the wider societal moves of reconnecting with the local, the recognition that we are creatures of somewhere and not just anywhere.[88] This is perhaps a challenge to embrace longer ministries. If to be called to a church is also to be called to a place, ministry and church in this place will take time; it will require stability and patience.[89] Short ministries in a place leave us potentially being simply like tourists, holidaying in people's lives, taking pictures, putting them in our scrapbooks, and moving on.[90] What if the norm of ministry in one place was closer to fifteen years rather than six or seven? I'm struck by Kyle Childress, a Baptist minister in Texas, who has been pastor of Austin Heights Baptist Church (which is considered in the USA as small (!) with a membership of less than two hundred) for over thirty years. In the past he has been asked, "When are you going to a bigger church? Why do you stay?" He responds, "Because I read too much Wendell Berry."[91] Berry, a highly acclaimed writer and poet, has been a farmer in one place.[92] Childress says, "Just as Berry committed to

84. Jennings, "Place of Redemption."

85. On nationalism see Jennings, *Acts*, 20–24.

86. Jennings, "Being Baptized: Race," 285.

87. Jennings, "Foreword," 5.

88. On somewheres and anywheres see Goodhart, *Road to Somewhere*.

89. This is close to the ethics of slow church as described by Smith and Pattison, *Slow Church*.

90. I am here anglicising the words of Ron Swanson from the US sitcom *Parks and Recreation*, referenced in Smith and Pattison, *Slow Church*, 64.

91. Childress, "Proper Work," 71.

92. There is a fair amount of joining of vision between Berry, Jennings and Gorringe. For more on Berry, see his *The Art of the Common Place*.

staying on the farm, somewhere along the way I decided that I needed to do the same—commit to a particular congregation of people over the long haul."[93] This argument for long-haul ministry in one place is also made by Peterson, who comments that "the congregation is not a job site to be abandoned when a better offer comes along."[94] I wonder whether ministers would approach the task of ministry in a place differently if they expected to be there a long time.[95]

Longer ministries will give the opportunity for minister and church to be involved in their community and engage with planning processes for the built environment as Jennings and Gorringe suggest. Gorringe himself has been involved in the "Transition Towns" movement.[96] In my own context in Southend-on-Sea, the church and I are at the beginnings of getting involved with a new community organisation named Project Southchurch, which aims to "improve the area we live, learn, work and trade in."[97] One of its plans is around the environment, with a desire to create a twenty-minute neighbourhood, as well as seeing civic gardening and urban agriculture develop. As a local minister of a local church in Southchurch, becoming part of this community organising is one concrete way of ministry and geography being fused together and seeing whether the theological vision of Jennings and Gorringe might have a part to play in the community's conversations and actions that will develop going forward.

This chapter has sought to demonstrate that ministry and geography have something to say to each other. Thinking geographically is an essential lens for ministry; more so, it is unavoidable if we recognize that every congregation is rooted in some place. The Baptist theology of the local church has rich potential to foster a geographical ministry. As two Baptist theologians have said: "whether located in the hills or meadows of a rural county, or somewhere in the concrete maze of a large city, or on the edge of suburbia surrounded by housing developments and [retail

93. Childress, "Proper Work," 73.

94. Peterson, *Under the Unpredictable Plant,* 133. See also Copenhaver, "Vow of Stability."

95. Many in the congregation, of course, is committed to being there for a long time, and some will have seen a number of ministers come and go.

96. Gorringe and Beckham, *Transition Movement for Churches.* See here an interview with Gorringe about his research focused on the Transition Town Movement: https://www.paccsresearch.org.uk/blog/transition-town-movement.

97. https://www.projectsouthchurch.org.uk.

parks], local congregations are places that can embody, express, and witness to the church's local catholicity as they minister to the people who inhabit a local place."[98] I offer this essay to my father as an invitation to him to bring these twin loves in his life into conversation himself.

98. Essick and Medley, "Local Catholicity," 58.

5

MINISTRY AND HISTORY

Stephen Copson

IT WAS A PLEASURE to be asked to contribute to this collection of essays to mark a significant milestone in the life of Paul Goodliff, whom I have known as a valued colleague and friend for a quarter of a century. Why should Christians be interested in history? Because we may trace, albeit obliquely at times, the ways of God with individuals and groups. By choosing the diary of one minister, I hope the reader will, despite the wide difference in context, be able to recognise some familiar patterns and concerns that connect the present and the past in images of ministry.

This article offers a snapshot of the life of Cornelius Elven, early-nineteenth-century provincial Baptist minister. In the Suffolk Record Office in Bury St Edmunds are diaries covering 1823–1843. This essay will consider one volume in that series, covering 1829 to 1832, not because it holds anything of greater significance than the others, but because it is illustrative of one Baptist minister of the period.[1]

Cornelius Elven was born in Bury St Edmunds in 1797 and educated in the town. He was probably a tanner or factor or otherwise engaged in the leather industry and occasionally noted how his work took him to London on business (perhaps using the efficient coaching service). At first attending the Independent (Congregational) chapel in Bury, his

---

1. Suffolk Archives, Bury St Edmunds branch, Ref: 739/73, Diary of Cornelius Elven, marked "No 6," from October 4, 1829 to December 31, 1833. This essay was prepared during pandemic restrictions in 2021, when the manuscript of one diary was available to me at a time when archives were not accessible.

search of the Scriptures led him to Baptist views and in 1822 he became a member of the Ebenezer Chapel in Nether Baxter Street. When the minister, Barnabas Beddow, resigned in 1823, Elven was called to succeed him, indicating the trust the church had speedily placed in him. During the first decade of his ministry, the old building was enlarged and then a new chapel erected in Garland Street to house the growing congregation, even after members had left to found a new cause at Glemsford. His ministry at Bury St Edmunds stretched over fifty years and he became a highly respected pastor, preacher, and influential person in Baptist circles in East Anglia and beyond. Elven died in 1873.[2]

Bury St Edmunds in the 1820s had a population around ten thousand. Its main industries were related to the malting and brewing trades, whilst the traditional woollen industry was in decline and the silk industry was in crisis. Rural poverty was commonplace, although the town itself was not directly affected by the Poor Law Reform Act (1834) which did so much to strip away traditional protections, as the workhouse had already been incorporated. Politically, the town corporation had previously been dominated by two local aristocratic families—the Fitzroys and the Herveys—and their supporters, although a shift began in the 1830s.[3]

What sort of literature is the diary? Many entries simply list biblical texts for sermons, others give more information, and yet others are longer reflections on events or experiences. From one point of view, it is a diary of events, with elements of a commonplace book. One strand connects to Puritan journals of self-examination, identifying the providences of God in the life of the believer, and there is ample evidence of Cornelius Elven opening his heart to God and acknowledging his own shortcomings, whilst still confident that God will not abandon him. He expresses great joys and deep sorrows with interjections and exhortations to the Almighty. But there is also another reader that is Cornelius reflecting on himself through the authored text as he writes. It becomes a spirit-level of his life. He records all of his sermon texts. He also listed the names of those he baptized, although these were also recorded in the church book.[4] Some cameos of family life squeezed in. It is intriguing that other facets of his life and ministry which would have been thought significant have

2. See Tyrell, *History of Garland Street Baptist church.*

3. https://www.historyofparliamentonline.org/volume/1820-1832/constituencies/bury-st-edmunds.

4. "Church book belonging to the Baptist Church Bury St Edmunds." Suffolk Archives, Bury St Edmunds branch, ref: RO 739/17.

barely a mention. Cornelius was not writing for posterity, nor to inform or educate others. He wrote for himself, with an eye and ear for the divine audience. So the diary weaves a tapestry of personal spirituality, psychology and daily experience, theological reflection and factual information. It is a place where he can bare his heart to God and to himself—and he knows he cannot deceive God. The journal was not intended for any other readership—an irony that is not lost on this author as he offers a commentary in writing for publication.

The diary covers the time when the national Baptist Union was relaunched in 1832, after an initial initiative in 1813 had not gained sustained support, but there is no mention of it in the diary. Elven was a solid supporter of the local network of Baptist churches. In 1827 he had become Secretary of the Suffolk and Norfolk Association of Baptist churches.[5] Two years later there was a division and seven churches formed an association on strict Communion principles.[6] Fourteen churches were left in the old association. Three churches remained unassociated for the time. The diary does not make any reference to the division, but in 1830 at Otley Elven preached at the association meetings "in a waggon to an immense Concourse of persons in a field" on "Charity never faileth," taking the theme of Christian unity, and again at Wortwell in June 1831, where his message was "Spiritual Reform."[7] Elven's report on association life in the 1832 *Baptist Magazine* struck a conscious note of optimism, for at the annual meeting "No idle controversies, no jarring discords marred our union, but all was peace and love," but also made a positive reference to the other newly fledged association.[8] As Elven shared meetings with some of the ministers who had left, it seems at some level there was a lack of active animosity. In September 1833 the members renewed the commitment of the church to closed Communion, refusing to share the Lord's Supper with unbaptized believers.

References to worship and preaching figured strongly in the account, making up the majority of entries, but not the majority of the word count. Elven was a faithful chronicler of his pulpit ministry. In the diary, he recorded nearly 780 preaching occasions. There was a little inconsistency

5. For a general account of Suffolk Baptists, see Klaiber *Story of the Suffolk Baptists*.

6. A pictorial record of many of the churches that formed the new Association or subsequently joined can be found in Grass, *"There My Friends and kindred Dwell"*.

7. Elven, *Report of the Associated Churches* (1831).

8. *Baptist Magazine* 24 (1832) 366 (a pagination error means two pages are numbered 366).

in recording details, and he sometimes misquoted or forgot to add bibli-cal references. His Sunday ministry included two or sometimes three services,[9] plus midweek meetings and lectures, and services at other churches or special occasions. Of these sermons, 439 were from texts in the Old Testament and 338 from the New. In the period the diary covers, he preached on a text from at least one of every book in the Old Testa-ment, excepting Leviticus and Ezra, plus Joel, Obadiah, Jonah, Habba-kuk, and Haggai from the Minor Prophets. He preached at least once from every book in the New Testament except Titus, Philemon, and the last two Catholic Epistles.

The most chosen texts in the Old Testament were from Psalms (97) and Isaiah (76)—nearly 40 percent of the total—and in the New Testa-ment the Gospels scored 219 (65 percent), with Matthew (71) and John (87) preferred to Mark and Luke. Some favourite stories or texts were revisited over the four years; for example, John 4 and the Samaritan woman seven times, Proverbs 8:17 five times, and Deuteronomy 33 nine times. The texts from Revelation all came from the letters to the seven churches and not the apocalyptic section of the book. It is noticeable that some texts were revisited, and even if the script was not rehearsed or repeated, nonetheless there must have been a strong resemblance in sermons delivered on the same text and preached within weeks of each other—albeit to different congregations. On rare occasions a verse was expounded over more than one sermon but generally Elven did not follow a series, although on August 18, 1833 he preached three sermons on Mark 4:28.

Primarily these sermons were delivered to the congregation in Bury St Edmunds, or to one of its midweek meetings. Some were preached at Glemsford before it became a separate church. Elven's connections and his standing among the churches saw him attending and preaching at special events in the life of churches, as well as often being one of the association preachers. A one-off was a series of meetings in a boarding school in Aldeburgh, where the headmaster was John Swindell, who was also the Baptist minister.[10]

---

9. Although on January 9, 1832 the church book records that the afternoon ser-vices including the Lord's Supper would not be a preaching occasion.

10. Swindell later founded Mill Hill Academy in Newmarket, where a young Charles Haddon Spurgeon was an articled teacher in 1850. Elven was an encourager of Spurgeon in his early ministry.

In the period of the diary, he preached at the ordination of Mr Crate at Eye and Brother Harvey at Bildeston, one at Attleborough and another at Clare; at services related to new or extended buildings at Hadleigh, Sudbury, Bures, Clare, Stoke-by-Clare, and Brockley; and for anniversaries at Chelmsford, Lowestoft, Sudbury, and Bardswell. Indeed, at Lowestoft he was implored to preach a second time and spoke the next day to a larger congregation, as he noted with a hint of satisfaction.

One particular feature of the day was for preachers to be invited to raise funds for Sunday schools, which sometimes had almost a distinct organisation from the church. Joseph Kinghorn preached at Bury in 1830 and Mr Smith of Ilford came in 1831, whilst in 1830 Elven visited Isleham, [Kings] Lynn ("near 300 children"), Mildenhall, Laxfield ("the immediate object of my visit the collection amounting to upward of Ten pounds. This I think one of the finest schools in the county containing 278 children and conducted in such an excellent manner so much that at a Parish meeting £5 was voted unanimously to the funds of the school and paid by the Churchwardens"), and Rattlesden. In 1831 it was Newmarket and 1832 it was Battesford, Laxfield (with 46 teachers), and in 1833 Kenninghall, West Row, and Clare. In 1832 he took the risk of preaching himself at Bury ("by the unanimous request of the teachers") whilst anxious that this would raise fewer funds, but it was not so and he repeated the experiment in 1833. In 1828 the Bury Sunday school had 450 children.

The opportunities to preach to local congregations, along with similar efforts by other ministers, provided the practical and personal links of fellowship to those churches associated by church order as Baptist. The number of churches within Suffolk in the period was not large, and not all were linked with the association, even before the division. As ever, links between ministers assumed greater importance as the connecting point for the congregations, reinforcing a sense of shared identity in gospel fellowship and order. References to fellow ministers are scattered through the journal pages.[11]

11. Within Norfolk and Suffolk there were Goldsmith of Stradbroke, Joseph Green of Attleborough, Joshua Cooper of Stoke Ash, Collins of Grundisburgh, James Cole of Otley, James Tottman of Glemford and then Laxfield, Heath of Ipswich, William Payne of Aldringham, George Thredgold of Waldringham, Philip Dickenson of Rattlesden (and subsequently Lt Alie Street in Whitechapel), James Sprigg of Stoke Green Ipswich, Leonard Ellington of West Row, Mildenhall, Robert Harvey of Wortwell (and then Bildeston), William Hoddy of Bildeston, T Hoddy of Clare, James Puntis in St Clement's Norwich, Joseph Kinghorn of Norwich and Richard Clarke of Worstead.

Elven also held evening meetings in the town in houses belonging to congregation members to lecture—Cannon Place, Prospect Row, Eastgate Street, Field Lane, and Southgate Street. Another venue was the Bury workhouse, where Elven delivered a series of talks each week for much of the diary period. Whilst his sermons were intended to be expository and to inform, they were also designed with an evangelistic edge to challenge and convert. Before the split in the association, Elven and George Wright, who subsequently led the breakaway group, had been commissioned to encourage village evangelism and this is reflected in the number of rural locations where Elven visited.

On October 25, 1829 at Glemsford he held an open-air baptism in the village, where it was "supposed upwards of 2,000 persons were assembled." With echoes of the baptisms in the River Jordan, "I am sure we felt a conviction which the sprinklers of infants never can feel" and Elven preached to the crowds from a farm wagon. After praying, singing, and preaching, he baptized ten women and men, the onlookers behaving with appropriate decorum, "except a few boys laughing just at the time of baptizing." But on November 7 he attended a meeting of the people at Glemsford—there were around fifty Bury members meeting in the village—as there had been discontent among them and accusations aimed at their leader, Tottman. Elven discerned an antinomian feeling among them, dismissed the complaints as quibbles, affirmed the leadership of brother Tottmann—with payment—and told them the matter was closed—"mutually buried"—at the risk of invoking church discipline.

Encouraging to see that on April 18, 1830 he held a service to launch the people at Glemsford as a separate church of forty-four members, being assured of agreement to the articles of faith of the Bury church and having recognized the deacons chosen. He also attended the reformation on April 25, 1831 of the church under Brother Tottman at Laxfield, which had long previously been the "seat of division, discord & heresy" marked by "Antinomianism—Sabellianism—Socinianism." He shared the service with John Fisher, minister of the Independent church at Harleston.

Special services were tailored to discrete audiences: Christmas Day 1832 was directed at young people; an invitation to the builders of the new building was made (where Elven spoke on "He is like a man which built his house Luke 6:47") and handbills prepared to welcome the Yeomanry

---

Further afield were Benjamin Fuller of Harston, James Smith of Ilford, George Wesley of Tillingham. A brief account of the churches and ministers can be found in Browne, *History of Congregationalism.*

from Western Suffolk when stationed in the town, where on March 1, 1831 he preached on "Fear God and honour the King" with more than a hundred in the chapel in full military dress. On March 8 when they left he offered a farewell sermon on "A good soldier of Jesus Christ (2 Tim 2:3). On September 8, 1833 he used news of the unusual number of sudden local deaths to preach an improving sermon on being prepared. He also used a sermon during the cholera epidemic to warn his hearers.

Whilst often feeling inadequate to the task, Elven relished worship at the chapel. In May 1831 "I enjoyed much liberty and comfort in all the offices of the day—singing, Praying and Preaching." There was an expectation about Elven's confidence in the gospel to convince and save. He yearned to see people converted and baptized and brought into membership of the church. In March 1830 he confidently foresaw a harvest of thirty-, sixty-, and a hundred-fold. He felt disappointed in his annual end-of-year assessment when baptisms were few, but always attributed this to his own failings and weakness of faith. This anxiety was more than countered by the growing congregation as the congregation grew in members, requiring a new building to seat up to 1,200 in pews and gallery.

Not that everything was theologically unclouded. On October 29, 1829 he hoped that the church people would not dwell so much on "the minute detail of controversial doctrine but be of a missionary spirit." On November 6, 1829 he challenged the "antinomian" spirit in some of the people in the Glemsford branch. There had already been a division in Bury over doctrine that had led some with Joseph Clutton to leave.

There are seventeen references in eleven entries to "revival" in the journal. The church held meetings specifically to pray for revival. Elven found these meetings deeply satisfying and a weather vane of church fellowship.[12] On January 24, 1830 he talked of the experience of the prayer meeting as being an "Earnest" (arrhabon) of revival. On January 1, 1831 he prayed that "a glorious revival may be felt and seen in the Communion of Sinners the restoration of Backsliding and the increasing life & Zeal & Love of the Church." God alone brings revival; the church receives the blessings.

His self-examination took a well-worn path from complaint to consolation, owning his own failings and extolling the greatness of a

12. Church book, September 12, 1831: "Mr Elven submitted to the Church that he considered the establishment of Experience meetings for the members of the church to speak freely to each other of the state of their souls and their Religious experience."

merciful God. He begged for humility. He disregarded his successes. On January 8, 1832 he was tempted to despair:

> Satan did attempt to harrass me but he was able mercifully restrained by the chain of omnipotence which—adored be the Church's king—can never be either stretched or broken. One night indeed he was permitted to harrass my poor soul and a dreadful night it was. He suggested that "the Lord had forsaken me" and for a time I believed him and when raising from my bed & tossing about in mental agony. My dear wife endeavoured to compose me I cried out—refusing to be comforted "Oh no it is of no use your talking the Lord has forsaken me and I am lost" and deservedly so.

Whilst appearing somewhat formulaic, these outpourings were nonetheless a genuine expression of Calvinistic Baptist spirituality. Several times he referred to his "experimental" faith or experience, one that was tested in the doing. It was not an emotional response, although he did get emotional. He often experienced "melting" in prayer or devotions or preaching. Tears sometimes flowed. On June 17, 1830 he wished for a Pentecostal power to make his preaching effective.

A key feature of congregational church life was the relationship between pastor and people. Elven made sundry references to the warmth of this link. "But I fear for them still. Oh that the Enemy of souls may be thwarted in his designs to worry the little flock dear Jesus! Heavens Shepherd watch & keep & bless them!!!" He did not see them as simply souls to be saved but as people. January 16, 1832 "I looked upon some of the chosen family that I knew were sorely tried and thought of others that were on a bed of affliction for whom I shed tears of sympathy." He noted in his journal the name of every person that he had baptized. People entered the church through baptism and shortly after, usually at the next Lord's Supper, were received into membership with the symbolic right hand of fellowship. On December 23, 1832 he noted the church folk were a "praying band." They were fervent in prayer for his recovery from illness. On August 10, 1832, when he was due to leave for a week, they were earnest in urging his soon return. On New Year 1830 he was greatly moved to receive a New Year's gift from the women of the church, "an elegant Pulpit Bible with 2 vols Watts Ps and Hym and one of Rippon's Selection also Elegant and Expensively bound" [13] Plus on New Year's morning 1833 he

13. Church book, January 11, 1833 noted that only Rippon's *New Selection* and Watts were to be used but then compromised with no new hymns from Rippon to be

was given "a handsome" present by his "Juvenile Friends expressive of their affectionate regards."

It is not that this sense of fellowship was unique, but that Elven chose to record these and other instances. He did not take his people for granted. He said more than once that he felt "at home" with his people on Sunday and missed them when he had been away preaching. More than once they moved him to tears. He recorded funeral services that he had conducted, often noting how people made a good death in confessing their faith in Jesus and resting in their confidence of God for their salvation. The pastoral concern extended further on occasion. On October 7, 1832 the list of baptismal candidates included Sarah Moss of Barton Mills, who "was baptized here on account of the violent persecution of her husband who it was feared would have used violent means had she attempted to observe this ordinance in her own neighbourhood."

He recorded on April 9, 1830 how he and the church had been greatly distressed by the suicide by hanging of one Houghton, a respected member of the church. He identified the cause to an episode of depressive illness ("deranged") but pastorally and theologically it was a huge challenge. This was not a good Christian death. Elven was unable to verbalize that in the theology of the church the man's actions would have seen him consigned to hell—"it appeared to me most wise to be silent, 'God is his own interpreter and he will make it plain.'"

The week of January 15, 1830 saw him confront Amos Peck, who had left the church and joined a secession ("antinomian") group under Joseph Clutton. The young man had remained adamant about not returning despite Elven's one last attempt to reclaim him, and "I saw how hyper-sentiment had filled him with pride and obstinacy." In sadness he penned the next morning a poem of sad farewell which succeeded where theological arguments had failed, and the prodigal returned.

There are several instances of a special providence, Brother Peck's reclamation being one. January 1, 1833 one Cutting, husband of a church member who beat her and threatened Elven, was convinced of his sinfulness and "wept like a Magdalene at the feet of Jesus." July 2, 1833 Elven visited one Braine, "a drunken sabbath breaking wretch" who had heard Elven preach and asked to see him. At 4:30 a.m., before Braine started work, Elven found him in tears and holding a Bible, and spent time with

---

sung for twelve months.

him in prayer and conversation. Elven also noted the conversion of more than one "Magdalene" who had committed every sin except murder.

Elven commented that he thought he would not enjoy a long life. There is ample evidence of the longing for release from this life to enter the superior life in the next world. Death was an ever-present reality—Cornelius and Mary lost two children in the period of the journal. Episodes of ill health, minor and serious, are scattered through his writings. There is something of the prosaic in his litany of colds, sore throats, headaches, toothaches, migraine, indigestion, and general tiredness. On October 19, 1832, riding home in the cold evening air after the warmth of the meeting house at Risby, he caught a fever, with consequent delirium, and missed two Sundays' services. He usually confided to his diary his bodily weakness and infirmity, accompanied by an affirmation of the comfort and support of God: "November 15 1829. This morning I arose very ill having suffered all night from a most acute headache and was much afraid I should not be able to go up to the house of God. However I went up and I trust leaning on my beloved, and although much indisposed in body was graciously supported 'When I am weak, then am I strong.'"

Several times he expressed his sheer exhaustion at the exertions of the preaching ministry. Here was a man engaged in business who also travelled extensively on Sundays and midweek. His travelling and preaching tired him and adversely affected his health. January 31, 1830: "During this week I have been seriously ill having taken cold during the past week from being so much exposed to the weather and being completely exhausted in attendance upon so many of my Dear people that were afflicted that at length from waiting on them I have worn out my own strength so as this week to need nursing myself." He severally comforted himself by confiding his reliance "As thy days, so shall thy strength be."

Elven was a firm believer that God used the medium of illness to instruct. He talked of "Transfiguration Seasons." Each bout of illness offered the opportunity for spiritual examination, where he assured himself that God was with him in his suffering. In the week of October 4 1831 he wrote, "I have been so ill as to be prevented from attending any public service but have been favoured with a blessed tranquility of soul. I thought when pain was very acute [sic] what a rich mercy it was I had not then to enquire about my souls salvation feeling a humble yet immeasurable confidence that Jesus was mine and that all was well."

The most serious episode was in 1831 when he contracted typhus fever. For twelve whole weeks he was unable to minister, often felt confused, and at times was unconscious. When the fever abated, he discovered that two of his children had been infected, and one had died. Sharing his grief with the diary, he affirmed again his confidence in the ways of God, who had taken his daughter to a better place.

Family matters rarely appeared in the diary, confined largely to moments of great joy, worry, or sadness, although there was a single reference to family prayers. Elven noted the birth of daughter Elizabeth Sophia (January 1830): "I have been up almost all night—and was running from place to place after nurse, attendants &c," accepting his responsibility for bringing up this new life in the knowledge of God.

Then Hannah was born (January 1831) and Julia (April 1833). Times of delivery were recorded. With sadness he noted the death (August 1833) of the "dear little infant" Julia. Another (Elizabeth) died of typhus fever (January 1833). His sadness and grief at the loss of a child (always "it") is set alongside his unswerving confidence in the goodness and mercy of God; "nature cannot endure these separating strokes without feeling yet I hope I have felt a measure of sweet acquiescence with divine will & could say 'It is the Lord'" (August 1833). It is symptomatic of the period and the theology that he can genuinely hold together his grief for his children with the acceptance that God had taken them to a better place.

Childbirth carried ever-present risks of death for women. After Hannah's birth, Mary Elven suffered from pleurisy and continued to be very ill for several weeks, her husband fearing she would die—not that it kept him from leading worship. In March 1831 Mary "had been very bad on the Lords day during my absence, her friends and even the Medical attendant despairing of her life." But a prayer meeting organized by a church member specifically for Mary's welfare was the turning point to renewed health—another instance of the providence of God.

In 1830 he recalled the sixth anniversary of the death of his brother, who was much missed, and quoted from a hymn by Charles Wesley ("Ah lovely appearance of death"). Indeed, in the journal there were eighteen quotations (unattributed) from hymns, of which ten are in Rippon's selection and others in Watts. His favourite was Watts, and then Charles Wesley, but also hymns by Robert Robinson, Samuel Medley, William Hammond, as well as Edward Perronet and two from the Olney hymns of Cowper and Newton. One may even be hymn-writing of his own hand. He appreciated the generous gift of Rippon and Watts's collections, the books used in worship. They were a singing church. Hymns had been internalized for him by use in worship and reflection, and so they came naturally to mind as much as Scripture for him to express the response of religious experience.

Elven was a supporter of the overseas Baptist mission. Funds for the mission were raised by the practice of missionaries and home supporters itinerating the churches. On October 11, 1829, when Mr Davis of Walworth preached, the collection was £5.10, including "One Pound of Mr Bigg of Glemsford the product of the nuts in his garden which were devoted to the cause." In August 1830 and September 1833, Eustace Carey, son of the William of Serampore, preached in the chapel. In October 1831 £16 was raised when Mr Cantlow from Jamaica came, and in September Mr Flood from Jamaica visited. Elven heard a preacher from the Moravian missions, and he himself preached in Norwich on behalf of the Baptist Irish mission.

There seems to have been a positive attitude between the Nonconformists in the town. When the Methodist building needed refurbishment in 1830, Elven invited the congregation to use the Baptist building. When in 1831 Matthew Jeula, the minister of the Northgate Independent church, required larger premises for a funeral, Elven welcomed him too. Elven preached in Jeula's chapel on Good Friday 1831 and the Wesleyan chapel in October 1831. And during Elven's prolonged absence with typhus fever in 1832, Wesleyans and Independents supplied the pulpit. On another occasion the church closed to attend the meeting at Charles Dewhirst's Independent chapel in Whiting Street, where a Mr Chapman from Greenwich preached on behalf of the Moravian missions. The shared prayer meeting was launched in the Quaker meeting house.

Outside of Bury, Elven led services in the Independent chapels at Bocking, Harleston, and Stowmarket. When the church at Laxfield was reformed after having apparently been much reduced in a dispute over heterodox views, the launch service was conducted by Elven and John Fisher, the Independent minister from Harleston.

Elven attended the inaugural meeting of the local non-denominational Religious Tract Society in Bury. Mr. Webb, who was the secretary and agent of the British & Foreign Seamen & Soldiers Friends Society, preached in the Baptist church in Bury in November 1830 and December 1831. A singular preaching occasion was for the North East Cambridge Theological Institute meeting at Barton Mills.

An ecumenical encounter of a decidedly different temper was the controversy in September 1832 with the incumbent of Rougham, "the young stripling of a clergyman in that parish having recently undertaken to defend & prove Infant Sprinkling from these words [Ezek 36:25], and the poor baptists were handled it seems very unsparingly," where Elven preached to "a crowded audience." Subsequently a domestic servant returning to the family home from domestic service in Somerset encouraged Elven to preach there, and a church was formed at neighbouring Bradfield in 1834.[14]

In September 1831 Elven preached a sermon on the occasion of the Coronation of William IV. In June 1831 he used his association address to urge spiritual reform as well as political. In December 1831 he arranged a prayer meeting focussed on the imminent general election. With the echoes of civil unrest and rioting caused by the issue of franchise reform—"Tumults, poverty and incendiaries in prevailing in almost all parts of the Kingdom"—the dissenting ministers agreed to hold a Union prayer meeting—a fervent desire that "the nation is not destroyed." There was celebration at the passing of the Great Reform Act, which Bury dissenters welcomed and for which the Baptists organized a prayer meeting in thanksgiving. "An excellent meal" was provided in the vestry free for poor church members. And he noted with satisfaction how one church member who had joined the celebratory town revels instead had sheepishly confessed the errors of his ways a couple of days later.

Elven was also a supporter of the abolitionist movement. In October 1830 he gave an evening lecture from Luke 2:14, "Slavery incompatible with Christianity." And in September 1831 Mr Preston, "a man of colour from Nova Scotia," was invited to preach a midweek sermon for the church.[15] The Bury Nonconformists also supported abolition and organized meetings but their support, and in particular Elven's, did not go unnoticed by Benjamin Greene, a slaveholder in the West Indies and leading brewer in Bury, who used his newspaper as a vehicle to denounce abolitionists.[16]

14. https://www.brbaptistchurch.com/history1.

15. This was Richard Preston, a key organiser and minister in the black churches of Nova Scotia, who had arrived in Liverpool in 1831, and became part of abolitionist circles until his return to Nova Scotia in 1833. http://www.biographi.ca/en/bio.php?id_nbr=4138.

16. https://www.greeneking.co.uk/newsroom/latest-news/new-partnership-announced-between-greene-king-and-the-international-slavery-museum.

There was precious little reference to alcohol—only one note of a temperance meeting in December 1833. And yet Bury St Edmunds was heavily dependent on the brewing industry for employment, and temperance would not have been a popular cause, especially with Greene already prejudiced against the dissenters because of their abolitionist convictions.[17]

In 1830s England the spectre of cholera stalked the land. The outbreak provided the theme of a sermon and prayer meetings were held in the town to implore the Almighty that Bury be saved from the scourge. In fact, it was, although whether the fervour of the prayers affected the advance of the fever defies analysis.

Small details of interest are also recorded, although Elven is no Gilbert White or Francis Kilvert. He noted how low the thermometer mercury had sunk at 4 a.m. on the morning his daughter Elizabeth was born; he recorded colouring and washing at the chapel, and how on January 2, 1830 the weather was so poor he expected a low turnout but was greatly surprised at attendance. On May 23, 1830 he gave a lively description of how a violent thunderstorm during service so frightened a woman who suffered from "striving fits" that eight men were scarcely able to restrain her from throwing herself from the gallery. In January 1831 he recorded the death of a church member working in London who had been run over by a waggon, and on December 11 how one Crawley, a celebrated prizefighter-turned-evangelist, had visited Bury. On June 30, 1833 he recorded that Moses Gourland, a Jew with "a beautiful honesty" and not uninterested in the Christian faith but unable to recognize Jesus as Messiah, visited Bury. Little nuggets that he chose to record.

A broader and deeper appreciation of Cornelius Elven would be gained by study of the other diaries held at the Suffolk Record Office in conjunction with the account of his life prepared by Ridley, his assistant and successor in the pastorate.[18] He was one of those nineteenth-century provincial Baptist pastors who had a ministry in a single church for a long period in changing times. This piece has attempted to offer a reflection on his journal to reveal something of his church life and spiritual wrestling. In particulars, it is unique and yet in generalities it could have been written by any number of English Particular Baptist pastors in the first half of the nineteenth century.

17. The church book noted in January 1834 censured a member for opening a beer shop.

18. Ridley, "*In memoriam*".

This essay is offered in friendship to Paul Goodliff as a marker of a new chapter in his life. It seems almost incidental that (some) issues arising from the text reflect some of Paul's passions: a lively evangelical spirituality, a passion for the well-being of the local congregation, involvement in fostering good relationships among Baptists, an ecumenical breadth, and a concern for the growth of the kingdom of God in the local church and in society. So may it be. *Laus Deo*.

6

MINISTRY AS IMPROVISATION

Ruth Gouldbourne

THOUGH PAUL AND I attended Spurgeon's College at the same time, my main memory of him—as it is for so many, I suspect—is of his sterling service in the Ministry Office for the Baptist Union. And there was a moment when I had to phone him for advice, which he graciously and wisely gave. I remember ending that conversation with the comment that I was grateful because so often I felt like "I was making it up as I went along." His gentle comment then was, "Most of us feel the same."

I have no idea if that is true, but it is definitely a phrase I have heard people use as they have tried to make sense of being a minister, and offering their skills, gifts, and selves in response to a call to serve the people of God in a particular way—indeed, one might say, in a particular role.

And it is on the nature of role, and of making it up as we go along, that I want to reflect in this essay. The original request to write this essay pointed me towards ministry and literature, which can cover novels, poetry, or dramatic writing. At the heart of each of these is the creative act of doing something new, something that has not been done before.

For those of us who are ministers, the act of writing is one that takes up quite a bit of our attention and energy. However, for most of us it is a secondary activity; it is supportive of or expressive of our main endeavour, which is much more to do with who we are and how we present that to those around us—our congregation, our neighbourhood, perhaps those who read what we write. Therefore, in this essay I am concentrating on "performance," drawing on insights from drama.

It is clear that when we speak of the "role" of a minister, we are describing a place, status, function, and presence within a community. However, it is also true that the term applies to performance, and to the presentation of a persona as part of a drama or equivalent. I suggest that this can also be a part of what it is to be a minister—not in the sense that we are not fulfilling our "role" with integrity, or that we are pretending to be something we are not, but rather that to play a certain role is to adopt, portray, and indeed embody particular actions and behaviours that enable others to take part.

It is regularly noted that for such a public role, which involves standing up in front of others and speaking as well as so many other highly visible activities, there are a surprising number of ministers who would identify as introverts. One of the suggested reasons for this is that many of us, when we are finding our place within a congregation (particularly in adolescence and young adulthood), and especially if we find small talk hard, or are not particularly at ease in social situations, will often take on "jobs" to give us a context and something to talk about, and to do, all of which makes it easier to function. And the doing of such tasks and taking on of various responsibilities can often predispose others around us to begin to talk to us of service and ministry. This is clearly a broad-brush generalisation, and is obviously not an entire account of the nature of calling, but I suggest there is enough truth in it for it to be recognisable to some of us at least. What the jobs and responsibilities give us are scripts—things to do, ways of behaving, things to say, methods of interacting—that help us through what can often be challenging or awkward situations, when our own resources feel inadequate.

This being the case, many of us, as we begin to explore ministry, are well adapted to perceiving a script, adopting it, and playing the role that it shapes for us. That pattern serves us and our communities well. I do not wish to suggest that there is anything untrue in these ways of exploring and expressing ministry, nor that such a path is to be denigrated in any way. But then there are these moments when we do not have a script, when the role that we normally play does not meet the matter at hand or fit the situation in which we find ourselves, and when we find ourselves "making it up as we go along."

This can be experienced as very uncomfortable, and even more as some kind of, if not failure, at least lack. We can feel as if we *ought* to know what we are doing, *should* have at least an internal script, and *would*, if we were properly prepared, spiritual enough, or wise enough, be able to fulfil the role that is thrust upon us with complete certainty (ours and other peoples') that we are getting it right.

For those of us who find ourselves using this phrase of "making it up as we go along," how often is it at least in part experienced or even intended as a confession that we are not skilled enough to have the answers? (Even as I write this, I am wondering, "Maybe this is just me." But I hope not. If you recognize this, please read on, and I hope this will be a conversation to which you can bring something. If you don't recognize this, please read on, and discover how at least one minister feels about this impossible privilege which is ours.) "Making it up as we go along" is offered, very often, as a confession—albeit wry—that we are not able to do this task with the certainty, skill, and confidence that we and others expect.

But what would happen if we embraced "making it up as we go along" as a realistic response to a call on our lives that will constantly be taking us into places, outer and inner, where we have not been before. More than that, this "making it up as we go along" is not failure but actually a faithful, Christ-centred, indeed Christlike response of faith and obedience. What if we were to reframe "making it up as we go along" as *improvisation*, and to celebrate it as the creativity which is part of our God-given identity?

The notion of improvisation as a way of thinking about what it is to live as a faithful follower of Jesus and of how to read and accept the authority of Scripture has gained a great deal of traction in recent years. For example, N. T. Wright developed the notion of improvisation as he discussed the way in which the scriptural story is authoritative for us. He takes the image of a play where a missing final act assumes the capacity of those who know the play very well to improvise the continuing story in line with the previous acts. He develops this as a way of thinking about how the church takes the story given in Scripture and continues it.

> The church would then live under the 'authority' of the extant story, being required to offer something between an improvisa-tion and an actual performance of the final act. Appeal could always be made to the inconsistency of what was being offered with a major theme or characterization in the earlier material. Such an appeal—and such an offering!—would of course require sensitivity of a high order to the whole nature of the story and to the ways in which it would be (of course) inappropriate simply to repeat verbatim passages from earlier sections. Such sensitivity

(cashing out the model in terms of church life) is precisely what one would have expected to be required; did we ever imagine that the application of biblical authority ought to be something that could be done by a well-programmed computer?[1]

Sam Wells has also written using this model and has argued that Christian ethics are best understood as improvising on the Christian tradition.

> The Bible is not so much a script to rehearse, as it is a 'training school' that shapes the habits and practices of a community in action.[2]

Indeed, he is so convinced of this that he has written an entire book on the theme.[3]

Also considering ethics, Richard Holloway has developed the theme of improvisation by using a different metaphor. He writes:

> We can opt for a series of fixed texts that wear out and have to be constantly changed, or we choose the metaphor of the jazz session that constantly makes new music by listening to what's happening around it and applying what is left of the tradition to the current context . . . God invites us to join in the music, to listen and to adapt to one another, to keep the melody flowing.[4]

Improvisation as a form of dramatic presentation has enjoyed great vogue in the last years; the presence of improvised comedy, live and on radio and television, is now well established, and filmmakers such as Mike Leigh have used improvisation as a method of developing scripts and devising performances that are powerful and memorable.

For improvisation to be effective, those taking part do have to develop particular skills and practices. It is not simply a case of standing up onstage and saying the first thing that comes into one's head. It is a communal activity, in which the interaction between the participants is important, and works best when everybody is working with the same intentions and assumptions. At its heart, it is the capacity to respond creatively to what has been said by others on the stage, in the context of a scene that is given. The energy and the life of an improvised sketch,

---

1. Wright, "How Can the Bible Be Authoritative?," 19.
2. https://www.nomadpodcast.co.uk/sam-wells-improvising-faith-n223/.
3. Wells, *Improvisation*.
4. Holloway, *Godless Morality*, 33–34.

for example, comes from the interactions of all those involved, and the choices of each affects the choices of the others. In any scene that is being improvised, effectiveness depends on the nature of the responses offered to and fro. There are several rules to being effective: respond, take forward, don't block, take risks, trust that there are no mistakes but only new possibilities. To take part in this involves paying attention to what the other(s) are doing and shaping words and action in response, rather than coming in with a preprepared script about what should happen and forcing the action to take that shape. Above all, what makes an improvisation work is the saying of "yes" to whatever is offered by others, by the scene, by the audience.[5]

But simple response is not enough—for improvisation actually to go anywhere, it requires a response that moves the scene forward, rather than blocking it. So, for example, if in an improvised scene the first actor starts with "Can you help me? I've lost my way. How do I get to 33 Danube St," there are a whole variety of possible responses. "I'm lost too" is a response, but it does not immediately move the scene forward (though, one could think of developments from such an interaction; the first actor might produce a map and suggest they look at it together, for example.) A response along the lines of "I'm going that way; would you like to walk with me?" offers a way forward that can be developed, as does "That's where my great uncle lives; why are you going to see him?" or even, "Not 33? Haven't you heard that the police are staking it out today?"

A response of "Can't help, sorry" or "no" is not impossible to work with, but is effectively a blocking response, and certainly diminishes the participatory nature of improvisation, leaving the first actor with a great deal to do, and not much to do it with.

"I'm lost too," while not closing things down, is a very safe response, and leaves the first actor with a great deal to do, and not a lot to work with; quite a lot of energy needs to be put into finding a response to that which actually moves the scene forward rather than round in circles.

Rather than having a safe response of "I'm lost too" or a blocking response of "no," a risky response such as "Haven't you heard about the police stakeout?" can open up possibilities that the first actor had not envisaged; and if such a person is really willing to take risk, "Yes, I had heard; but I've got new information" can begin a scene that takes

---

5. For a fuller discussion of this, listen to *The Rule of Three* podcast, "Cariad Lloyd on *Whose Line Is It Anyway?*," season 1, episode 11 (July 4, 2018), https://www.ruleofthreepod.com/blog/new-episode-cariad-lloyd-on-whose-line-is-it-anyway.

on an energy that might lead somewhere very interesting. Improvised responses that actually respond to what is on offer and make an offer in return create possibility, energy, and change.

I suggest that the basic assumptions for successful improvisation are present in the teaching of Jesus. For example, when Jesus is explaining to his disciples what it is to live in a non-retaliatory way, he takes the previous script and explores it for them in new contexts, offering improvisational responses and inviting them to do the same. Thus, we could analyse the verses in Matthew 5:38–42 in this way, using the ideas of NT Wright:

> *You have heard that it was said, "An eye for an eye and a tooth for a tooth."*
>
> **The existing script — the text from which our direction is taken and with which we need to be congruent.**
>
> *But I say to you, do not resist an evildoer. But if anyone strikes you on the right cheek,*
>
> **a specific and new scene**
>
> *turn the other also;*
>
> **a risky and improvised response**
>
> *and if anyone wants to sue you and take your coat, give your cloak as well; and if anyone forces you to go one mile, go also the second mile. Give to everyone who begs from you, and do not refuse anyone who wants to borrow from you.*

Different scenes offer possibilities of different responses congruent with, but not predetermined by, the preceding script. The responses take what is offered—violence and rejection—and instead of blocking it, or finding a safe and protective response, open up new possibilities.

The creativity of the responses to these new scenes then offers not just new possibilities in particular circumstances, but a methodology of responding that takes the old script—"You have heard it said"—and derives new, congruent but different scenarios. The responses are flexible, open, and not pre-*script*-ive. In fact, Jesus often uses the model of "You have heard it said . . . but I say to you." We could call this taking an earlier script ("you have heard it said") and improvising on the theme ("but I say to you"), as he takes the earlier script and develops it. Thus, we could argue that in adopting a form of ministry that is improvisational, rather than prescriptive, we are following Jesus's own model. An understanding of ministry which embraces improvisation as a positive and creative approach, rather than fears or apologies that "making it up as I go along" is the not-very-good best we can offer, offers us a freedom and an affirmation of creativity which could be profoundly liberating.

Such a form of ministry is of course not simply a getting up there and saying or doing the first thing that comes into my head. It is one that demands significant discipline. It requires firstly a deep, heart knowledge of the scriptural script—not simply a familiarity with the text as an academic exercise, but a dwelling in Scripture rooted in prayerful, contemplative, ongoing reading and conversation. It will also be deepened by an understanding of the story of the people of God in other places and in other times. This will call us to a study not only of the history of the church, but an awareness of the church in other cultures and contexts— not in a superficial way, but with deep engagement of listening, receiving, and real encounter and relationship.

It will also call us to engage with a wide-ranging study of theological thinking—going beyond our own normal borders and reaching into ideas and assumptions that we do not share. Doing this deepens not just our awareness of other ideas, but expands our sympathies, and therefore our capacity to respond creatively to situations that are new to us. As anybody who takes part in improvisation on stage regularly knows, much can be learned from watching others who are good and practiced; new possibilities can be seen in others' skills and innovations. This is not simply a matter of observation of course; it requires that degree of humility which is necessary to go on learning.

However, so far, if this argument holds, it could be maintained that it is true for anyone who seeks to be a faithful follower of Jesus. We do need to ask what it might mean to be an improvisational minister.

I want to start by suggesting a couple of things I believe it does not mean—or at least what it is not limited to. I am not here primarily talking about preaching from minimal notes, and allowing ourselves to develop an improvised sermon. This is a gift to be cultivated (and it is a skill to be worked at for most of us, so that we are not simply rambling) but it is not the focus of this discussion. Nor yet am I considering extempore prayer; again, both a gift to be honoured and a skill to be reflected on and practiced, but not what I want to discuss. Rather, I want to ask, in those moments when we do find ourselves saying, "I'm making it up as I go along," what might developed skills in improvisation bring?

It is a phrase that, for me at least, is often used when I find myself facing those things which "they didn't train me for in college" (another phrase that trips off the tongue!). Writing this as I am in the wake of (and indeed continuing impact of) the coronavirus pandemic of 2020, there have been a lot of situations that everybody has faced which have been new, challenging, and, in the very overused term from the beginning of this experience, unprecedented. We have all been "making it up as we go along" because we had no script, and no idea what was coming next. Such a circumstance has, I believe, offered us the chance to see certain aspects of improvisational ministry being explored.

To start with, there needs to be a willingness to say, when faced with something unknown, "Let's try . . ." This can be risky because there is no certainty of outcome, and indeed, inevitably, there will be failures. But the failures have themselves can often lead to other possibilities that might not have been noticed unless the risk had been taken. Improvisational ministry requires a "Let's try" approach. This is necessarily an approach which is non-controlling. "Let's try" at its best is always open to the possibility of failure. This where the affirmation that "there is no such thing as failure" needs to be heard.

Now, of course, as a statement, this is patently untrue. There are things we do that fail—for all sorts of reasons. Some of these failures might be trivial, disappointing, frustrating, and these can be relatively easily sloughed off and treated as learning opportunities. But there are failures that are more serious—failures of nerve, of morals, of integrity. It is clearly important that such failures are recognized and named for what they are.

However, there is also a truth in the affirmation—for it is, surely, a statement to do with resurrection—that whatever disaster happens, up to and including the execution of the Son of God as a criminal, none of it is unredeemable in the mercy and grace of God. If we live in the light of resurrection promise, and offer our ministry in that conviction, might we find that even our worst failures, if accepted as such and offered as scenes for improvisation, become scenes in which newness we had not expected can be created? We will come back to this below.

For now, I want to stay with the improvisational skill of "Let's try." It is possible to "try" in a controlling way—but that can prove less than creative and is not a practice that can be truly said to be improvising. "Let's try" offered as disguise for "I'll let you go ahead, and when you fail, I'll step in and rescue things" or "We can try, but my level of commitment to the experiment is so low that I have sabotaged it before we begin" are both approaches that a minister can easily adopt (even from apparently good motives), and they are approaches that, while not guaranteeing failure, build it in as a likelihood from the beginning. If we are going to adopt a "Let's try" approach, it has to be with an openness to either success or failure, recognising that there are possibilities for development available through either outcome. In an improvised sketch, an attempt may or may not come off—but from either result something else can be improvised, and things can be moved forward. Such an approach liberates us from having to succeed by some external metric, and allows for continual experimentation, improvisation, and arrival at possibilities that could not have been envisaged had we not started down the "Let's try" path.

Another feature of improvisational ministry is clearly participation. Improvisation can be done alone, but it is at its more creative as a communal activity, as the reactions by each to are central to the creation of new possibilities and the opportunities to follow where they might lead. An improvisational minister is one who works with rather than for—or even more, at—the congregation. This might appear so obvious and indeed trivial that it does not need saying. But there are times when it does need to be said. We work with those who are other members; improvisational ministry is not about doing it all, either because only we can do it properly or because a congregation expects us or leaves us to do it. Working improvisationally involves enabling others to take part—which may at times require us to challenge people who have become passive, or to challenge our own sense of omnipotence.

An improvisational ministry is one that says "yes." This needs to be carefully unpacked of course. It is possible to become the kind of minister who never says "no" to any request or requirement and ends up burned out and destroyed. But the willingness to say yes to ideas, to suggestions, to offers, to insights and challenges is central to improvisation. It is a skill that requires wisdom and confidence—sometimes it is about saying "yes" in a way that is straightforwardly affirming and letting the idea or possibility develop and go in its own way. Sometimes it is about saying "yes" in a way that takes a measure of control of what is offered so that it can be held within the overall direction of the controlling script. This kind of ministry therefore depends on us knowing our script deeply—not simply being able to quote lines from it, but inhabiting it, and allowing it to form our intuitive and instinctive responses. It also has as a corollary the invitation to be one who enables others to dwell in the script equally deeply. An improvisational minister who practices saying "yes" can also play the role of a coach, enabling others to encounter the script in ways that mean that their own capacity to improvise will also be deepened. Saying "yes" is also to model a form of improvisation than allows others to take on new roles and builds mutual community rather than a dependent group with an overwhelmed leader.

Next, an improvisational ministry is one that is attentive to the context—the scene, as it were. Good improvisation on stage involves paying very close attention to what others are doing, and to what is going on in the audience, so that the actor can draw in and respond to reactions, making them part of the whole scene, and using them as ways to move the scene on. Similarly, an improvisational ministry is deeply attentive to the congregation; to things said and unsaid, to perceptions, assumptions, anxieties and hopes, and to the setting—the context in which the congregation functions. Again, this may involve a certain letting go of control, but it is not about being passive. Rather, it is about being responsive to what is there, not necessarily to what we want to be there, or even think ought to be there. A skilful improviser can move a scene on quite considerably, not by bringing in something from outside, but by working with what is offered by others on stage and those in the audience, both explicitly and implicitly.

Knowing your audience is not just about putting on an appropriate performance to them "out there," but rather about connecting, reacting, and involving all who are present. Expert improvisers are good at dealing with hecklers, for example—and, at their best, not by destroying them or shouting them down, but by including what they are saying into the whole. There will be times when our context consists of those who heckle us, either in fact or metaphorically. But even when it is not active heckling, we are *performing* church, doing the stuff, in a context in which we are seen and heard. Being open to involve what is around us is a skill that can provide all sorts of unexpected openings. It requires attentiveness, the willingness to take risks, and—again—allowing the possibility of failure. But when we are open and responsive to our context in this improvisational way, rather than a programmatic one, we discover that there is an Actor there before us. Again, we will return to this.

An improvisational ministry is one that is non-anxious—or, let us be accurate, less anxious. There are times and places when ministers are expected to offer what is in the jargon referred to as a "non-anxious presence," and it is a wonderful gift to give. But there are times when a *less anxious presence* is more realistic to who we are, and more appropriate to the scene. A minister who can hold a situation, especially one which others around are finding threatening or overwhelming, even in the midst of their own anxiety about not knowing what to do next, and hold themselves ready to respond as authentically and script-urally as possible, can be a means by which a community or an individual is able to find the next necessary step. Improvisation is, by its nature, a practice that generates a certain amount of anxiety, since it is without the certainty of answers, and is always just one step away from not working. An improvisational ministry therefore is unlikely to be one completely without anxiety. Consequently, an improvisational minister must needs understand her or his own anxiety—its shape, its effect, and its triggers—as much as possible. Knowing how to recognize and live with anxiety in ways that mean it is not overwhelming but might in fact offer a resource for growth and attention can be a huge means of enabling a congregation to embrace uncertainty and risk in healthy ways.

The one thing an improvisational ministry is not is unprepared. The model of ministry I am trying to explore here is by no means undemanding. It requires a deep and continuing commitment to reflective practice. Anybody who watches an actor regularly improvise will soon come to recognize signature patterns, skills, and means of expression. Clearly there is nothing wrong with that. Doing things in the way that is appropriate to who we are and that expresses ourselves is part of the integrity we bring to ministry. But watching an actor in this situation, we may also recognize signature tricks—ways of getting a laugh, of getting out of a difficult situation, of protecting themselves from too much exposure. This may or may not be good practice for a performer, but the danger of such tricks in ministry can be significant. It can be as particular as regularly using the same phrases and cadences in extempore prayer, without much thought, or as fundamental and wide-ranging as our deep and unreflective responses to challenges or difficulties. An improvisational ministry requires knowing our own reactions as fully as we can and being aware that there is a limit to self-knowledge and self-awareness, and therefore also taking advantage of possibilities, such as 360-degree reviews, to understand more fully how others encounter us, and what patterns exist that might need changed. An improvisational ministry must never be unreflective and that takes time, energy, and a willingness to allow others to comment on one's ministry.

Preparation also includes the effort that is put into knowing the situation—in the congregation and in the context. Good improvisers take the time to pay attention to what is going on elsewhere on the stage and don't give all their attention to planning their own next move. They also pay attention to the audience and modulate the performance to meet the responses—and to avoid the non-response! If our ministry is creative, full of innovation, depth, and challenge, and yet does not connect with the people around—inside or outside the church—then clearly we are failing, and we all know that that means we need to work harder at understanding where we are. Understanding this improvisationally rather than programmatically, however, shapes how such investigation might take place. Improvised performances take off when they follow the energy; when the performers interact with one another and the audience in responding to response and pushing it just a little further and a little further again. That is, rather than noticing where there is a lack, and trying to fill it, it is about noticing what is generating energy, and taking another step. It is all too easy, when we are sticking to our scripts, to notice what is not happening, and according to the script ought to be, and to try and make it happen. An improvisational ministry, on the other hand, pays attention to what is happening, and takes the next step on that path, to see where it might lead. This involves a preparedness to pay close attention to what is, to see as clearly as we can, and sometimes even to let go of what we feel called or committed to.

Finally, in thinking about preparation, I want to go back to prayer and living in Scripture, already mentioned above. An improvisational ministry is one that depends ultimately on responding to the one Actor, the Risen One, whose story the whole thing is. The question, as we seek to dwell in the given script, and to live it out in our service and ministry, is less "What would Jesus do?" and more "What is Jesus doing—and how can I join in?" Such a question demands of us an attentive, careful, and sometimes slow indwelling not only of Scripture, but also of our world, in the expectation and faith that God is at work—or perhaps at play—and we get to join in.

For surely this is what underlies any form of ministry, and therefore must be acknowledged in reflecting on ministry as improvisation. As we act with, interact with, and react to those around us, and the scenes in which we find ourselves, the givenness of our situation, we are always aware that the Actor we call God is the author, the fellow participant, and the inspiration of what we are about. In improvising, we are not free to do anything at all. We have a script, but even more, we live in the presence of Another who is the ultimate in taking what is offered and weaving it into the great scene. I referred above to resurrection as the epitome of improvising in the face of disaster; that is, taking what is complete failure, a ministry that ended in absolute rejection and execution, and bringing something new into the scene that transforms it completely; where there was no future, now there is an unfailing future.

It is in that context that we dare to offer any kind of ministry, and in particular an improvisational one, in the trust, hope, and faith that the One to whom ultimately we are responding will take whatever we offer and use it, work with it, renew and uphold it so that the purposes begun in creation and made certain in resurrection will be fulfilled.

For that early-morning phone call and the reassurance he gave me, and for many other moments of insight, encouragement, and friendship, I remain deeply grateful to Paul. But above all, for the reassurance that "making it up as I go along" is not to fail, but is to be a human person, living in the presence of a present God.

7

MINISTRY AND WINE

Rob Ellis

PAUL GOODLIFF IS A PASTOR and theologian—or better, a pastor-theologian. His theological research and writing reflects this concern for ministry and his theologizing has been *for* ministry, the church, and the proclamation of gospel. Just as theology is the theory that underpins and shapes practice, every minister's pastoral practice(s) is itself practical, *enacted* theology.[1] Goodliff's work as pastor and theologian demonstrates this duality. His texts on pastoral care and sacramentally understood ministry each broke new ground and both show that ministry must be understood as enacted theology. Theology is a practical discipline: it shapes and is shaped by practice, and is lived in practices. Goodliff is a practical theologian.

Connecting wine with practical theology may seem an unusual move. I have had the pleasure of dining with Paul and Gill Goodliff on several occasions. Paul is an excellent cook, and serves very good wine with his meals too. He is a particular connoisseur of port—the fortified wine produced in Portugal's Douro Valley, and often considered to be the appropriate way to conclude a fine meal. Paul has followed the port wine tours and speaks knowledgeably about the vintages and houses. Coming as it does from a very specific region, port offers a very particular example of the connection between wine and a place.

---

1. Gerkin, *Introduction to Pastoral Care*, 121.

What then of wine and practical theology? Beginning from an understanding of ministry as enacted theology, and theology as shaping and informing ministry, I want to reflect upon the ways in which a consideration of certain aspects of wine might shed light on our practical theologizing. Wine, we might say, illuminates the task and the practice of practical theology—a theology for ministry and enacted in it.

BACKGROUND

Wine and Scripture

There are many biblical texts relating to wine. Many of these texts may have been problematic for Christians from a tradition which has been, for some generations, associated with abstinence because Scripture appears to present a very positive view of wine. We will not simply pile up the texts (there are enough to make a pile) but touch on some of their main themes.[2]

With the Old Testament we might first think of wine as part of God's good creation. Old Testament writers often include the experience of wine within their theological *joie de vivre* as well as their eschatological hopes. In prelapsarian Eden God sets a cultivated garden (no wonder we often seem to have presentiments of paradise in our own gardens). Gisela Kreglinger observes that the Hebrew wordplay between *'adam* (man, humanity) and *'adamâ* (land, earth) accentuates the close relationship between humanity and the earth.[3] It is true that there is no mention of a vine in this garden, but its human stewards are instructed to eat its fruit. Later, Isaac's blessing of Jacob includes "plenty of grain and wine" (Gen 27:28), and prophetic visions of harmony and peace also focus on similar characteristics (e.g., Mic 4:4).[4] Amos is among those who testifies to the significance of wine—symbolic and literal—in God's good future: "They will rebuild the ruined cities and live in them. They will plant vineyards and drink their wine; they will make gardens and eat their fruit" (Amos 9:14). There are blips—Noah's drunkenness being one of the most egregious—but Judges 9:13 speaks of wine cheering "gods and mortals,"

---

2. Krelinger gives a more comprehensive survey in *Spirituality of Wine*, 11–36.

3. Kreglinger, *Spirituality of Wine*, 18.

4. See also 1 Kings 4:25.

and Psalm 104:15 of wine gladdening human hearts. Wine is also used medicinally and in religious ceremony and celebrations.

Layered onto all this is a metaphorical use which explores (Isaiah 5) the relationship of God and God's people, and it is with all these layers of relationally informed, eucharistically aware celebration of life that we encounter Jesus at the wedding in Cana in John's Gospel (John 2:1–11). Here wine is the vehicle for and sign of Jesus's transformation of human life, and, as so often in John, the Lord's Supper is prefigured. Underlying so much of the language of wine and wine-making in our reading of Scripture, preaching and eucharistic practice, is the notion of Christ the True Vine. In John's Gospel one traces a line through the wedding at Cana, the feeding of the five thousand, the True Vine, to the glorification of the cross and a meal by a lakeside. In John 15 we hear that there can be no fruitfulness without our being deeply united with and drawing nourishment from the True Vine. Without this there is only failure, and even with it there will be moments of painful growth.

Wine and the Church

The early church grew in a culture where wine-drinking was normal in its Jewish and Graeco-Roman settings. But some ascetics soon began to see dangers in the abuse of wine. The objections to wine offered seem more personal and precious than the much later temperance movement's concern (at its best) with social conditions and poverty, but theologians such as Cyprian (200–259 CE) and Clement of Alexandria (150–215 CE) argued strongly that wine was a gift of God, essential in the Eucharist and a blessing in life generally. It is to the developing monastic communities that so much of our modern viticulture can be traced: those devoted to the spiritual disciplines of prayer also engaging in the nurturing of vine and the processes of wine-making as part of their daily labour. Martin of Tours (316–397 CE) was not only a major figure in the growth of monasticism, but has also been described as the father of wine-making.[5] Kreglinger speaks of later monastic practice in viticulture as "a deeply spiritual practice that was often accompanied with recitations of the Psalms."[6] A similar view is expressed by Hugh Johnson, who describes Cistercian

---

5. See Ladonne, "Taste of the Divine"; and Johnson, *Story of Wine*, 97.

6. Kreglinger, *Spirituality of Wine*, 50.

wine-making as "the laboratory of their pursuit of perfection,"[7] also making the connection between the work of prayer and the work of viticulture.

We might speculate whether wine-making in particular among horticultural labour might have been seen as a spiritual practice had it not been for the rich seams of scriptural texts to which we have already referred, and its central place in the Eucharist. Another factor might also be the peculiar variety of characteristics which wine produces, and which often seem *local*: to produce a fine drink in one place does not guarantee its straightforward replication in another. Trial and error, what we might call a kind of reflective practice, are required in the ongoing quest for a wine which is just right.

The imagery drawn from wine-making which made it so useful to biblical writers is another factor. The wine press, with its bursts of red liquid, makes a ready image for judgement; the pruning process speaks to discipline and growth through pain and self-control; the use of wine as a sign of blessing and luxury, of the celebration of harmony and peaceful coexistence; and as a symbol for the redemptive work of Christ—all this connects with the "pursuit of perfection" of which Hugh Johnson speaks, and has been inspiring Western culture and its art for centuries.

Wine and Baptists

All this may make calls for abstinence appear to be an odd historical quirk. It's worth recalling that alcohol was served at early Baptist meetings, though one must also recognize that this was at least partly because water quality was much less trustworthy then.[8] When a group met in the King's Head public house in the city of London in 1752 to begin to dream Regent's Park College into existence,[9] we may assume that they supped an ale or two as they talked.

Yet many British Baptists, on consulting their church's trust deeds in the late twentieth century, will have found alcohol to be banned on the premises—particularly when these churches were founded or had their

---

7. Johnson, *Story of Wine*, 130.

8. That also goes some way to account why a group of Puritans emigrating from England to Boston in 1630 packed ten thousand gallons of wine and three times as much beer as water; Kreglinger, *Spirituality of Wine*, 58.

9. Clarke and Fiddes, *Dissenting Spirit*, 16.

buildings erected in the second half of the nineteenth century. While not having the hard line associated with Methodism or the Salvation Army, Baptists have had a reputation for abstinence. The changes from meeting in a public house in the middle of the eighteenth century, to abstaining trust deeds of the twentieth, to common current practice require some brief reflection.

The temperance movement traces its formal origins to the early years of the nineteenth century in the US[10] and from 1828 in Britain.[11] Churches were key players in the movement from the beginning, arguing that alcohol induced poor behaviour, diverted resources needed to support families, and hastened poverty and social degradation. It made it difficult for an individual to meet the requirements of religious observance. As well as a personal vice, it was a social evil. Temperance's growth from fringe interest to mainstream orthodoxy is explained by this mix of a concern to address questions of both piety and social cohesion.[12] The drive towards abstinence took root early on in Baptist communities on both sides of the Atlantic, with Baptists in the Southern states of the US campaigning before the 1830s. A survey of British Baptist ministers in 1886 showed that more than half were committed teetotallers (though as many as five of six Congregational ministers had signed the pledge by this time).[13]

But things have changed significantly in a generation or two, with the temperance movement losing momentum after the failure of prohibition in the US in 1933 and as social conditions more generally improved, mitigating some of the circumstances in which alcohol abuse was most heinous. It took several decades for a change in attitudes to be acknowledged. A personal anecdote might illustrate the point. When I was elected to the Council of the Baptist Union of Great Britain in 1990, I attended my first meetings at a Christian conference centre. After the evening sessions Council members sat around talking in the bar area. When a senior member of staff was asked why the bar wasn't open, he replied a little stiffly, "Because no one wants it open." I suspect this reflected his own views rather than an already changing consensus. Within a decade,

10. Britannica, "Temperance."

11. Harrison, *Drink and the Victorians*, 21.

12. See Harrison, *Drink and the Victorians*, 167–81; Harrison also notes here some of the theological tensions which arose when churches campaigned on temperance issues.

13. See Roach, "Baptists and Alcohol"; and Simkin, "Temperance Society."

many Council members were ordering beer, wine, and spirits at the bar after sessions—Council had a remarkable number of whisky aficionados who broke cover as attitudes became more open. The reality was, almost certainly, that most Council members had been enjoying a leisurely pint, and a glass of wine with some of their meals, for many years before the embargo on the Council bar was broken.[14]

This background serves as a wider context to the focus of this essay: to reflect to upon the ways in which a consideration of certain aspects of wine shed light on the practice of practical theology.

TASTE AND SEE: ATTENTIVENESS AND PARTICULARITY

From the Psalter to the vineyards of Bordeaux

"O taste and see that the Lord is good" (Ps 34:8). Psalm 34 is striking in its appeal to the senses. The psalmist looks, hears, and uses images drawn from touch. Though there is here no mention of the fragrance of an offering, taste and smell are intimately connected. "Little wonder that such a poet with a keen sensual touch would ask the hearer to 'taste and see' that the 'LORD is good,'"[15] though the psalmist's appeal to our sense of taste as a means of speaking about the experience of God's goodness and grace is unusual. Tasting is an intimate experience—that which we taste we have already taken into ourselves. Taste engages, enlivens, or repels us.

Some years ago our family holidayed in southwestern France and one afternoon we enrolled in a vineyard tour near Saint-Émilion. My wife and I walked around the sun-bathed vineyards with interest, listening to the owner speak about the processes of husbandry and harvesting which preceded the crushing of grapes and the beginning of fermentation. Our teenage son, who was with us, lolled with boredom and wished he was back in the campsite pool. He thought wine was "disgusting." At the end of the tour we were all ushered into the "cave" for a tasting, and formed an orderly queue to sample the wine made from the vines and in the vats that we had just been looking at. By some accident our son had gotten himself to the front of this queue and we found him approaching

14. It should also be noted, in fairness to the 1990 staff member, that Council passed a resolution urging Baptists to adopt total abstinence in the 1920s, and has never revoked the motion! See Edgington, "Hope UK."

15. Richards, "Psalm 34," 177.

us, animated, waving an empty glass. "Dad, you have *got* to buy some of this stuff—it is amazing!" And so another convert was made, a Saint-Émillion Grand Cru doing what parents alone could not. "O taste and see!" (We did buy some, by the way. It *was* amazing.)

Casual wine-drinkers will often read the label on the reverse of a bottle of wine with some amusement. One of our household regulars says, "Seriously intense Carignan gives a boost of inky dark fruit to soft, spicy Grenache in this stonking, velvety, southern French red. Big, rich and smooth with mouth-staining red and black fruit. Aroma of bright cherry, raspberry, blackcurrant and sweet spices." Most drinkers will get the smoothness and the berryish flavours, but may struggle to be quite so specific in the naming of parts. Wine-tasting has developed its own mystique and this can often be rather alienating to the ordinary drinker. But learning to notice some of the subtle differences in flavours and bouquet can add appreciation and enjoyment to what one instinctively feels is "amazing" (or not).

Kreglinger helps her readers appreciate the differences in sweetness and acidity, and the balance between them, in fine dessert wines; and speaking of red wines she talks of the layers of flavour in a typical Burgundy—with mushroom, mineral, tobacco, and leather "notes" among the ones to train one's palate to detect.[16] She helpfully shows how taste and smell go hand in hand—indeed, what we usually consider to be our sense of taste is very strongly connected to, and in some ways dependent upon, our sense of smell. "What we recognize in our brain as a flavour is made up of taste (gustation), smell (olfaction), texture (consistency, liquidity, structure), and temperature. We taste with our mouth, but we smell with our nose and our mouth." She tells us that our tongues have several thousand taste buds which constantly renew themselves, with each taste bud holding about a hundred receptor cells which send messages to the brain. Our olfactory cells are not just found in our noses but also at the back of our throats—again, a thousand or more—and these receptors of taste and smell are "deeply integrated."[17]

This demonstrates the very sophisticated equipment we have for tasting and smelling. When we *eat to live*, most of the wonder of flavour passes us by. Industrial farming, mass production of food, and processed food which delivers on the salt and sugar that manufacturers think we

16. Kreglinger, *Spirituality of Wine*, 114–15.
17. Kreglinger, *Spirituality of Wine*, 101.

want may also have something to do with this. When we *live to eat* (once we have got over the rather sybaritic sound of the phrase to our puritanically trained ears), we might have more time to savour, explore, delight. It is precisely this lingering to savour, explore, and delight which wine invites. And doing it requires that we pay attention and learn to notice the details of our food and drink.

An Example from Ethics: Ryle, Austen, Wine-Tasting, and Noticing Character

In an essay on the novels of Jane Austen, Gilbert Ryle writes about Austen's three-dimensional characters and the writer's interest in them as moral agents. There is no facile moralizing in the novels (or very little, at any rate). Rather, Austen offers us characters who are believable but also help her readers to explore moral questions by locating them within extremes.

> *Sense and Sensibility* really is about the relations between Sense and Sensibility or, as we might put it, between Head and Heart, Thoughts and Feelings, Judgement and Emotion, or Sensibleness and Sensitiveness. *Pride and Prejudice* really is about pride and about the misjudgments that stem from baseless pride, excessive pride, deficient pride, pride in trivial objects and so on. *Persuasion* really is or rather really does set out to be about persuadability, unpersuadability and over-persuadability.[18]

As the brief analyses of the novels he then offers demonstrate, each of the characters in, say, *Sense and Sensibility* falls somewhere on a continuum on the themes he has elaborated: ". . . it is not only Elinore, Marion and Mrs Dashwood who exemplify equilibrium or else inequilibrium between judiciousness and feeling. Nearly all the characters in the novel do so, in their different ways and their different degrees."[19] There are few out-and-out villains; few completely virtuous. Austen's characters are real, and it is only by comparing them one to another that we see the fine grain in each character.

Ryle says that "Jane Austen brings out the precise kinds of the sensibility exhibited by Elinor and Marianne by her wine-taster's technique of matching them not only against one another but also against nearly

---

18. Ryle, "Jane Austen and the Moralists," 287.
19. Ryle, "Jane Austen and the Moralists," 287.

all the other characters in their little world."[20] Austen brings out the fine differences between her characters with this *wine-tasting technique*—of noting detail, of paying attention, of seeing differences. He goes on:

> The contrast between Lucy Steele and both Elinor and Marianne is the contrast between sham and real sensibility or emotion; the contrast between Willoughby and, say, Edward is the contrast between the genuine but shallow feelings of the one and the genuine and deep feelings of the other. Lady Middleton's feelings are few and are concentrated entirely on her own children. Her husband's feelings are spread abroad quite undiscriminatingly. He just wants everyone to be jolly.[21]

Thus, Ryle suggests, this careful attention to detail—a wine-taster's attention—means that she can refuse to demonize or to suggest lazy binaries. Paying attention to detail, what Ryle thinks of as a wine-taster's skillful practice, enables what he elsewhere calls "thick description," and will also enable a practical theologian to notice the particular. And it is with the particular that a practical theologian must always begin. The practical theologian would do well to cultivate such a wine-tasting technique.

Wine-Tasting, Practical Theology, and Attentiveness to the Particular

An initial step to learning more about wine and appreciating its distinctiveness, without embarrassment or exposure to too much highfalutin jargon, is to be begin with the bottle in front of you. It should be a decent bottle, of course. Not the cheapest from the supermarket and probably a wine originating in one vineyard rather than some kind of regional or industrial blend: all of that ought to be clear from the labelling. Read the label on the back—it will probably have something along the lines of the example I quoted above. Pour some wine into a large glass but only fill it at most one-third full. Swish it gently around in the glass and then put your nose into the glass and note the aroma. What other smells does this current sensation bring to mind? Grass? Oak? Earth or mineral of some kind? Fruit—citrus (common with white wines)? Berries (common with reds)—and if so, can you say which ones? Can you identify any of the things mentioned on the label? Chances are, you will be able to note one

20. Ryle, "Jane Austen and the Moralists," 288.
21. Ryle, "Jane Austen and the Moralists," 288.

or two of the things listed. Then take a sip and swish again, but this time around your mouth, because your tongue will be alive to different flavour sensations in different places: if you just swig it down you will miss the range of the wine's taste.[22] And then notice the finish: does it leave a good sensation in the mouth after you have swallowed? It will take some practice at tasting, some refinement of skill, to be able to discern multiple and similar flavours—no one becomes an expert overnight, but it's fun trying.

Wine-tasting is an exercise in attentiveness. Instead of gulping it down, actually *taste* it: and to do that you have to let it linger, and you have to *notice*. One of the distinctive things about wine which distinguishes it from many other drinks and food stuffs is the complexity of its flavours, with sweetness, acidity, and bitterness present in different ways, and also developing over time in the glass as the air does further work.[23] In order to boost sales and market presence some New World wine-makers have opted to simplify some of this complexity of flavour, making wine with a bigger and more "obvious" flavour hit and this can be a good way of introducing people to wine though "as one grows in wine appreciation, one looks for more complexity."[24]

This attentiveness to particularity is an essential part of the discipline of practical theology too. In attending to the "situation," the greater level of detail that can be assembled, generally, the better. Practice will teach practitioners to screen out irrelevant details, but also which elements can and should be described and brought into focus. Gilbert Ryle first coined the term "thick description,"[25] though it is more often associated now with anthropologist Clifford Geertz, who used it in talking about required practice in ethnography.[26] Ryle used the expression to indicate that two apparently similar actions or events can and should have very different meanings—his celebrated example is of two boys who contract their eyelids, one of whom has an involuntary twitch, while the other is winking. It isn't simply that one boy means something whereas the other may not even know that he has done anything; rather, to understand the significance of the wink, the person to whom he is directing that wink

---

22. If you are just after the *effect* of the wine, after all, you are probably better off drinking shots!

23. The very best wine is often better decanted to allow it to breathe.

24. Kreglinger refers to these wines as "one-dimensional" and as "fruit bombs"; *Spirituality of Wine*, 116.

25. Ryle, "Thinking of Thoughts," 497–504.

26. Geertz, *Interpretation of Cultures.*

has to understand the codes and messages—and at a basic level has to understand what a wink is at all. The point Ryle labours is that the winking boy is not doing two things (or more, actually): not contracting his eyelid *and* sending a message. He is only doing one thing, but this thing means something, perhaps more than one thing. It is layered. The person who understands both the use of winks and what this particular wink might mean in this situation is able to offer a much "thicker" description of what is going on.[27]

Geertz builds on this, proposing that culture should be "read" like a text. Its meaning(s) will not always be apparent on the surface, but the meaning(s) will be shared and held in common by those who share a culture. For Geertz and those who have come after him, a thick description of a culture would involve an analysis of its signs and symbols, its shared assumptions and behaviours, and inevitably requires interpretation. It will involve listening to the actors in any given situation as well as trying to understand the systems—social, political, economic, cultural, religious—in which they are acting and acted upon. After referring to Ryle's account of winking, which he regarded as typical "of the little stories Oxford philosophers like to make up for themselves,"[28] he presents an extract from his own field diary, which he suggests mirrors Ryle's account in indicating "the sort of piled-up structures of inference and implication through which an ethnographer is continually trying to pick his way."[29] After the long diary extract, he goes on:

> In finished anthropological writings . . . this fact—that what we call our data are really our own constructions of other people's constructions of what they and their compatriots are up to—is obscured because most of what we need to comprehend a particular event, ritual, custom, idea, or whatever is insinuated as background information before the thing itself is directly examined . . . Analysis, then is sorting out the structures of signification . . . ethnography is [this kind of] thick description.[30]

For the practical theologian, attending to a situation similarly requires attention to detail, an analysis of significance, a listening to the actors, and an awareness of the contexts in which they operate. Such

27. Ryle, "Thinking of Thoughts," 498.
28. Geertz, *Interpretation of Cultures*, 7.
29. Geertz, *Interpretation of Cultures*, 7.
30. Geertz, *Interpretation of Cultures*, 9–10.

descriptions do not come naturally or easily to everyone at first, and they are a discipline to be learned by attempting them. As Geertz also remarked, no interpretation is ever final—there will always be more to be said, and more to be learned: "Cultural analysis is intrinsically incomplete. And, worse than that, the more deeply it goes the less complete it is."[31] Given that some theologians expect a definitive quality in their science, this may be challenging. But practical theology, like ethnography, is also generally considered untidy and incomplete. It "provides shafts of light into situations and issues rather than final answers or durable solutions."[32]

As the comparison with ethnography hints, practical theology extends the theologian's toolbox beyond the kind of literary, historical, and philosophical approaches common in theology for centuries, to include tools from the social sciences. In offering a thick description of a situation (a restive church meeting, a moral crisis, a financial challenge, a missional opportunity) the practical theologian will draw upon traditional theological skills—though these are likely to be foregrounded at a later stage in the cycle of reflection—but also need to borrow from this new set of instruments. Those teaching the skills of thick description can develop templates of questions to guide those new to the task, and sometimes models originally designed for other uses can be helpful. In this regard, Charles Gerkin's diagrammatic model to explicate the role of the local pastor in pastoral care can be adapted to help with the required description of a situation.

Interpreting the Particular

Gerkin develops a model of pastoral care that also gives a prime position to the practice of interpretation.

31. Geertz, *Interpretation of Cultures*, 29.
32. Pattison and Woodward, "Introduction," 14.

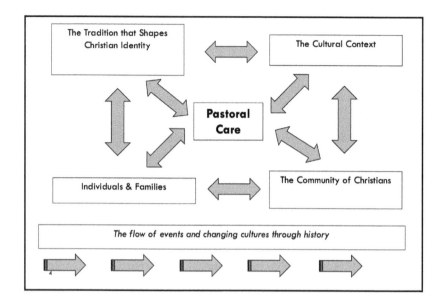

He construes the pastor as an "interpretive leader"[33] and offers a diagrammatic representation of the multiple interpretations with which the pastor must work.[34] Gerkin's pastor is involved in interpreting each of these to one another, and pastoral care takes place within the nexus represented in the diagram—indeed it is only properly possible within this nexus. But Gerkin's model may also serve a broader purpose in conceptualising the work of practical theology. When a "situation" (in Gerkin's treatment, usually a presenting pastoral situation of some kind in a congregation) requires our attention, his model serves to assist the practitioner in teasing out a range of questions which might need to be asked in order to arrive at the thick description of the situation which will facilitate further theological reflection. In particular, we note the "cultural context," which provides the backdrop within which the situation arises, and both the "community of Christians" and the "individuals and families" within that community—which sometimes are in alignment and sometimes more or less in tension. To describe anything is to interpret it in some way, but the questions which probe the details of any given situation will help uncover what Geertz described as "our own constructions

33. Gerkin, *Introduction to Pastoral Care*, 117–36.
34. Gerkin, *Introduction to Pastoral Care*, 35.

of other people's constructions of what they and their compatriots are up to."

Goodliff engages in precisely this kind of interpretive thick description in his own writing. His own text on pastoral care very clearly sets the questions of pastoral care in the cultural context of postmodernity; his study of shame is a deep dive into one of that culture's characteristics; his published doctoral work in which he uncovers and explores an emerging sacramental understanding of ministry among contemporary Baptist ministers is a very fine example of listening to "our own constructions of other people's constructions of what they and their compatriots are up to" and offering an understanding of some of the ways in which some pastors think about what they are doing and how various contexts have shaped such understandings. Each in their way is offering a thick description, albeit painted with large brushstrokes, so to speak.[35] The attention to detail required in this can be helpfully compared to, and can learn from, the practice of wine-tasting.

TERROIR AND LOCAL THEOLOGY

Wine and Place

In ways that are difficult to analyse and explain, wine and its taste are linked to place. Wine can teach about particular places, according to Kreglinger,[36] and she claims that "many Burgundian vintners work hard to let a particular parcel of land sing its earthy and haunting song through the wines it produces."[37] This is a memorable metaphor. But, while scholars and scientists do not fully understand the mutuality of land, vine, climate, and vintner in wine production, there is widespread agreement that wine has a particular and definitive relationship to the land in which it is cultivated.[38] The details appear to matter—the soil

35. Goodliff, *Care in a Confused; With Unveiled Face; Ministry, Sacrament and Representation*.

36. Kreglinger, *Spirituality of Wine*, 103.

37. Kreglinger, *Soul of Wine*, 30.

38. See Maltmann, "Vineyard Geology," 6, an article to which a Kreglinger endnote drew my attention. Maltmann concludes that a direct connection between very specific geological factors and the specific "typicity" of wine is difficult to establish, and indeed improbable—but vintners' claim is usually a little more subtle than this, speaking of the combination of certain factors (including soil type) in shaping the character of a wine.

and the rock beneath it, the direction of the slope, the rainfall, the hours of sunshine—even more than for other crops. Despite some caution over the most extravagant claims, Kreglinger asserts that wine "can create . . . bonds as it reflects and connects us with a particular place and time (vintage). Wine can take you to places you've never thought you would know. A Chianti Classico will take you to Tuscany . . . a Riesling to the Moselle region in Germany . . ." and so on.[39]

In the world of wine-making the notion of place is referred to with the term *terroir*, derived from the French *terre*, "land." Originating in France, the term is now used universally. *Terroir*

> covers all the natural and climatic elements linked to a particular vineyard area. The *terroir* is the primary influence on the character of the wine, though the grape variety and the methods used by the wine producer remain important factors . . . Contrary to commonly held beliefs, [*terroir*] does not simply refer to the soil and what lies beneath the vines (granite, limestone, etc.). It also includes other local factors, such as the slope (hillsides or plain), altitude, exposure, environment (proximity to a forest, lake, etc.), and of course the climate. The terroir is the combination of all these factors and it gives each wine-producing site its unique identity.[40]

While vines will grow almost anywhere, vines prefer drier soil and the best wine-producing *terroirs* are often found in what might otherwise be considered to be poor soil on well-drained hillsides (ideally facing the sun for long periods). Gravelly, sandy, or stony soil on a hill will usually produce better wine grapes than lush soil on the plains: an interesting variation on the Parable of the Sower.

Place and the "Terroirs" of Church and Theology

Despite controversy about the exact relationship between place and the wine it produces, there does seem to be something in that notion of the land singing its song through the wine if we think in terms of the concept of *terroir* with its much broader range of signification. Of particular note is the indication that the *terroir* is more significant even than the grape. A leading sommelier is unequivocal on this: "The fullness of its expression

39. Kreglinger, *Soul of Wine*, 38.
40. *Larousse Wine*, 26.

comes more from its *terroir* than from the grape variety or the year in which it is grown."[41] This will come as a surprise and seem counterintuitive to many wine-drinkers.

In terms of the notion of thick description that we have been considering, *terroir* acts as a kind of shorthand, a pointer to factors that need to be considered in describing a wine. Any description of a wine which fails to include the factors covered by *terroir* will be incomplete. Furthermore, when we serve a wine and say "This is a sauvignon blanc" or "This is a chianti," we discover that we have not said the most important thing about it. Its local provenance turns out to be its key element. Perhaps something similar must be said about our theologies, perhaps they must inevitably be contextual?

Martyn Percy uses *terroir* in a similar way. The particularities of *terroir* explain, he notes, why "one Burgundy tastes quite different from another, even though they might be from the same village."[42] By analogy, he suggests that the concept also sheds light on neighbouring churches.

> On one level, church is church, just as wine is wine. Yet to the refined palate, the difference is detectable and telling. The ecclesial history and ethos of one rural church might be composed through all manner of stories, buildings, forms of organisation, ecclesial and theological accents; and in adjacent church, yet in a similar context, turn out to be entirely different. And arguably, it is only through deep and patient immersion and reflection — the refining of the palate, in effect — that good mission can be undertaken.[43]

I want to suggest that this kind of thick description ("stories, buildings, forms of organisation, ecclesial and theological accents," etc.) is required for every church and all aspects of its ministry and mission. Any theological reflection on a given situation or issue must take into account the community's *terroir*. As Percy argues, those who seek quick or "off the peg" solutions to problems in church have failed to understand the *terroir* that forms it.[44] We recall that the *terroir* is even more significant than the differences between varieties of grape. And similarly, I suggest, a

41. Oliver Poussier in *Larousse Wine*, 29.

42. Percy, *Shaping the Church*, 102.

43. Percy, *Shaping the Church*, 103.

44. Percy, *Shaping the Church*, 114.

congregation's *terroir* is more important in critical ways than its espoused theological positions or (even?) its denominational label.

Percy speculates that there may be a denominational *terroir*—in his case for the Anglican Church. This too makes some sense. Churches, associations, networks exist, live, thrive, fail, in a variety of contexts, as that Gerkin diagram suggests. Part of the "Tradition that Shapes Christian Identity" will be the denominational or ecclesial histories and structures that shape us, and part of "The Community of Christians" will not only be the congregation as we encounter it now, but must take account of the church's story through time (Gerkin's arrows across the bottom of his diagram can go a long way back). Thus Percy reminds us that "there is one church, one faith, and one Lord, to be sure: but many dialects, perspectives and particularities that identify one part of the body from another."[45]

This notion of *terroir*, then, borrowed from the world of wine, steers us to a key idea in practical theology: the importance of the local, and of noticing—of paying attention to, and carefully describing and analysing—the particularities of any particular place which we encounter.

"Terroir" and Local Theology

There have been various attempts at defining and, indeed, doing "local theology." American Catholic theologian Robert Schreiter's work is significant here, as well as that of the English Anglican John Reader[46] and the Austrian Catholic Clemens Sedmak. We might add Anglican Bishop Laurie Green here, and also the Latin American liberation theologians so often mentioned with him. I have, in a rather laboured way, attempted to *situate* each of these writers, if only minimally. At its worst, "local theology" is understood in the West as something that happens elsewhere—in Ghana or Japan—as opposed to the (it must be supposed) "universal theology" written and taught here. But our theology is also local; its questions and answers are the questions and answers of those living in a particular place, time, and culture. As those such as (American

45. Percy, *Ecclesial Canopy*, 149. He goes on also to point out how the concept can help us think about the relationship between church and culture—making some high-level comparisons between the churches of the USA and China and their respective *terroirs* (156–58).

46. Schreiter, *Constructing Local Theologies*; Reader, *Local Theology*; Sedmak, *Doing Local Theology*.

Catholic!) Stephen Bevans point out, all theology is contextual even though there are "constants."[47] Practical theology recognizes, celebrates, works on and with the localness of theology. Priests and ministers know this instinctively even when not consciously acknowledging it, or even when trying to occlude it. It is impossible to be a good preacher to a local congregation without being a somewhat competent local theologian.

There is much here that resembles the work of the wine-maker. Kreglinger describes the work of the vintner in terms of caring for the earth (the vintner becomes part of the *terroir*) but also as discerning what will grow best and flourish in the given place, and indeed reflect that place. She hears a wine-maker liken their work to that of a midwife, with the yeast the mother of the wine.[48] We place this alongside one of her other insights: that our lives before God are lived in certain respects like the crushing of grapes, and the Holy Spirit hovers over our lives to transform them as the yeast hovers over crushed grapes waiting and working to transform them into wine.[49] Here is the minister-midwife-vintner as pastor and local theologian.

THE LANGUAGES OF OENOLOGY AND THEOLOGY: ALIENATING OR INVITING?

Language and Accessibility

One of the dispiriting things for this writer looking back on thirty years' membership of the Baptist Union Council is noting how difficult Baptists have found it—in this context at least—to engage in theological (and theologically informed) discussions. Reports were dismissed as too "technical" or "academic" and there was a constant temptation to respond in pragmatic ways, or in ways reflecting the latest trends from the latest church leadership conferences. If that body found such discussions difficult, local congregations might be forgiven for finding them even more challenging. It has to be acknowledged that sometimes we *do* become too "technical" and at least give the impression of being too abstracted from the here and now. The practical theologian must be a theologian, but she must also be a vernacular theologian, helping others find and deploy the

47. Bevans, *Introduction to Theology*; Bevans and Schroeder, *Constants in Context*.

48. Kreglinger, *Spirituality of Wine*, 131.

49. Kreglinger, *Soul of Wine*, 77–79.

vocabulary which will enable them to think about and act upon their local concerns.

The world of wine has similar problems. Its language can seem obscure and elitist. The casual wine-drinker can be as flummoxed and disempowered by the tasting notes with their tipple over Sunday lunch, as the not-so-casual churchgoer feels when peppered with Hebrew vocab, arcane history, and obscure doctrines on a Sunday morning. Preachers, who should be local theologians *par excellence*, can be among the worst culprits.

Kreglinger recalls an episode where she took a group of wine novices to a tasting, hoping to encourage them to find their own taste and their own voice. Instead, a young expert dazzled them, showing off and going beyond the novices' capacity to truly grasp what was being described.

> And I began to wonder what this way of presenting wine does to us. Yes, it can be incredibly enlightening, but I felt there was much that was getting lost. The guests couldn't hold all the information and process the sensations of the smell and taste of wine at the same time. The verbal onslaught was too powerful and blocked something within them. They lost trust in their own ability to encounter the wine, and they became obedient and compliant consumers in the presence of an expert.[50]

Does this sound a little familiar to those of us in churches?

Kreglinger's other observation about the use of oenological language is more disconcerting still, suggesting that impenetrable wine language is deliberately promoted by marketing experts to disempower and manipulate aspirational but insecure shoppers.[51] To suggest that something like this is being deliberately pursued in our churches would be very disturbing, a vision like something out of Philip Pullman's novels. There is, however, perhaps a grain of truth in this. The use of theological knowledge to distance, control, manipulate, and subdue—there have been times in Christian history where something like this appears to have been happening, and I fear there have been some congregations where the pastor and others have ruled in such ways.

The wine-tasting instincts that Kreglinger displays have much to show us about helping ordinary Christians find their voices, learning to describe their own experience and accessing the treasures of theological

50. Kreglinger, *Soul of Wine*, 114.
51. Kreglinger, *Soul of Wine*, 108.

discourse that might help them to do so, and to address the concerns of their time and place as they do it—rather than to keep them at arm's length and to make sure that only the professionals or zealots control the language of theology.

The challenge for the practical theologian is not dissimilar to that facing the wine-buff who wants to nurture the appreciation of others for their passion. Language does not just describe experience, but also in some measure makes it possible. Without the vocabulary to name something in our experience, it may evade our notice or grasp, or remain fundamentally mysterious beyond all analysis or reflection. This is why the wine-taster deploys the language of "fruitiness," "minerality," and so on to try to lead us into a recognition of the complexity of flavours. But it has to be done in a way that is accessible—one might even say digestible. There are parallels here with our theological helpmeet the hermeneutical circle, and in another academic sphere with what historian J. H. Hexter called the use of "psychedelic" language.[52] Writing in the 1970s, when the term may have had a particular resonance, Hexter spoke of the historian using "psychedelic" language aiming "to assist the reader to translate his experience from a familiar accepted context into a context strange and perhaps initially repugnant."[53] Hexter thought of this as an indispensable tool for the historian in writing about the past, helping "readers . . . learn things about what happened in the past that they could not learn otherwise."[54]

Language, Intoxication, Ecstasy:
Wine and the Work of Practical Theology

The concerns of the temperance movement were far broader than sobriety, but they did include worries about drunkenness and its effects. Wine, like all alcohol, lowers inhibitions. Imbibing a few drinks often results in a lack of volume control and self-awareness. Some go to sleep; others become agitated and aggressive. Kreglinger does not ignore these issues but sees the positive in "gentle intoxication," a state in which we lower our guards sufficiently to become knowable and talk more freely, increase our sense of play and joy in God's goodness. This lowering of our guards is

52. Hexter, *History Primer*, 139.

53. Hexter, *History Primer*, 137–38.

54. Hexter, *History Primer*, 141.

understood not as an unhealthy discarding of proper inhibitions, but as enabling us to "put aside our defences and masks, and to become more vulnerable."[55]

She claims that while severe intoxication can dull our senses and inhibit out motor skills etc., its gentle version can do the very opposite. Her theological basis for advocating "gentle intoxication" should not be overlooked or discounted—the wedding feast at Cana: Jesus provides the best wine when the guests are already tipsy.[56] In pointing us towards the sense of joyous exaltation, or creativity and inspiration, that can come from drinking wine—usually, it must be said, with others in a communal experience of some kind—she is pointing us towards a kind of ecstatic experience through wine.

Wine-drinkers will know—even very casual ones—that there is something luxurious about drinking a good wine. It feels like a treat to most of us, a way of marking a special occasion even if we also drink it at more ordinary moments. The feel of the wine in one's mouth has a lavishness to it that makes it distinctive among other food or drink. It makes the drinker feel special, and it leads to that gentle relaxation that we have discussed. There *is* something of the *ecstatic* about wine. Trying to describe this to a person who has no interest in or taste for wine is a little like trying to describe spiritual comfort to the avowed atheist. Wine is for the feast and it gladdens us and make us happy; it feels luxurious and special. Legend has it that Dom Pérignon (1638–1715), who first discovered the process of secondary fermentation which gives champagne and other sparkling wine its distinctive character, called his monks in excitement, saying, "Come quickly, I'm drinking stars!"[57] Good wine does indeed inculcate some kind of wonder.

If one thinks of ecstasy in theological circles, it is often en route to a discussion of the gifts of the Spirit. We have noted the image of the Spirit hovering over our broken lives like the yeast hovering and waiting to transform the crushed grapes into wine. And at this point I want to suggest that there is something of the ecstatic about the work of practical theology too. I have compared the work of the pastor/practical theologian to some of the ways in which Kreglinger describes the work of the

---

55. Kreglinger, *Spirituality of Wine*, 95.
56. John 2:1–11; Kreglinger, *Spirituality of Wine*, 98, 180–99.
57. Kreglinger, *Spirituality of Wine*, 50.

wine-maker.[58] If the vintner's goal is to "craft a drink that can bring joy and delight, wonder and amazement, to those who have eyes to see, noses to smell, and tastebuds attuned to taste with all their blessed might,"[59] a parallel goal must also energize the practical theologian. Their task (as the midwife of transformation) is also to produce joy and wonder, delight and amazement. While faith is and must be challenging, and Christian discipleship never cheap or lazy, it should also offer hope, gladness, and fascination. It might produce in us a willingness to drop our masks and become vulnerable to God and to one another as the Holy Spirit hovers over our brokenness, so that we too might be transformed into something luscious and wonderful. The use of "psychedelic" language by which we lead one another into new understandings of experience and possibility, of God and community, may be a part of this process of ecstatic theologizing. Our language as practical theologians of various stripes should never close down or intimidate but should open up possibility, joy, and hope. This is the way to speak and do theology: ecstatically.

CONCLUDING REMARKS

Wine gladdens our hearts and lubricates our fellowship. We might paraphrase Kreglinger in such terms, but the statement works as a commentary on the Eucharist too. We give thanks and we enter into communion with the risen Christ as we share wine together at the Table. Wine has a special place in Christian worship, spirituality, and theology, though one that has sometimes been overlooked. It is perhaps the rich biblical and eucharistic associations which underwrite the metaphorical usefulness of wine when thinking about our enacted theologies. Wine teaches us to pay attention to detail, to learn to develop thick descriptions of our encounters, and to reflect deeply on our locations and what it is about them that makes them distinctive, framing our questions and answers. At every step we must *notice*. The language of wine can be as opaque as that of theology. But the competent theologian uses language to empower

---

58. Kreglinger does devote a chapter to "the vintner as a practicing theologian," but her concerns there are rather different from mine. She sees the making of wine as literally a theological exercise—and I have no argument with this. I am suggesting that wine-making can also illuminate the practical theologizing of others in quite different contexts. It may be that these two claims, hers and mine, have some kind of mutuality. See Kreglinger, *Spirituality of Wine*, 121–42.

59. Kreglinger, *Spirituality of Wine*, 117.

and to nourish. And, as with the gentle freeing action of a good glass of wine with others, our theological language should lead us ecstatically into community and offer hope and joy. I raise just this glass to our good friend Paul Goodliff!

8

Ministry as Gardening

Pat Took

The day before yesterday, as I was walking the round of the cloister of the monastery, the brethren were sitting around forming as it were a most loving crown. In the midst . . . of the delights of paradise with the leaves, flowers and fruits of each single tree, I marvelled. In that multitude of brethren I found no one whom I did not love, and no one by whom, I felt sure, I was not loved. I was filled with such joy that it surpassed all the delights of this world.[1]

THIS HEART-WARMING EXPERIENCE, RECORDED in the twelfth century by Aelred, Abbot of Rievaulx, is one which many men and women who exercise pastoral charge will recognize. It attests the deep love that can flourish in the community of Christ and that can bind together people of varied, even incompatible temperaments and diverse opinions. In this book celebrating the ministry of Paul Goodliff, we acknowledge his diligent labour to enable such life-giving community to flourish, and to come alongside those ministers and congregations for whom this vision of life together lies the far side of improbable. I have appreciated Paul's dedication, his friendship, and his patience, and especially the quality of seriousness which has been his hallmark—the seriousness appropriate to those called to the service of the gospel and the care of God's family.

---

1. Aelred, *Spiritual Friendship*, 122.

THE METAPHOR OF THE GARDENER

The metaphor of the gardener is an intriguing suggestion by the editors of this volume. Alongside chapters which explore traditional tasks—prayer, education, counselling, and preaching—they offer metaphors drawn from the creative arts—music, poetry, literature, wine, and art—metaphors refreshingly at variance with bureaucratic or managerial notions of ministry. They suggest the possibility that through creative and suggestive metaphors we can encourage a fresh appreciation of the art and craft of ministry, a glimpse of its heart. Gardening appears to tap into this stream of imaginative and creative images. Aelred used it to convey that which is Edenic, paradisal, about the tie that binds our hearts in Christian love. Hopefully we can use it to find fruitful parallels between the role of gardener and that of minister.[2]

THE GARDEN: "A LOVESOME THING"?

A garden is a lovesome thing, God wot!
Rose plot,
Fring'd pool,
Fern'd grot —
The veriest school
Of peace, and yet the fool
Contends that God is not —
Not God! In gardens! when the eve is cool?[3]

The garden has a special place in both imagination and experience. Gardeners or not, we treasure the notion of paradise—the paradise where we began, the paradise we have lost, the paradise we sometimes glimpse like Aelred in his cloister, the paradise we yearn for and hope will be our ultimate home. Whether an enclosed park of royal recreation, or simply the lawn, lilacs, and roses with which we embellish our homes, the garden is generally thought of as a place of delight and restoration, of beauty, solitude, quiet, fragrance, birdsong—all very desirable in the clamour of the modern world. We feel exalted there, open to good and wholesome influences. In the children's book *The Secret Garden* three unhappy and

2. Soskice explores the creative aspect of metaphor in *Metaphor and Religious Language*.

3. Brown, "My Garden."

lonely characters find new life and hope through the discovery and cultivation of a garden where happiness once lost is restored. The resurrection motif runs clearly through the story, and culminates in the moment
when the Parsifal character—the peasant boy Dickon—leads the singing
of the doxology at the heart of the garden.[4] But are you not actually nearer
to God on the Central Line, at Bank station in pre-COVID rush hour,
pressed up against an armpit and smelling garlic? *The Secret Garden* is a
book of Victorian sentiment, not a metaphor for ministry. In exploring
this metaphor we will have to stand guard against sentimentality.

In Scripture the garden is the setting of our original bliss, our first
home, our proper purpose, and the place where sorrowing Mary meets
the resurrection and the life. And yet, beyond these framing images,
the little there is in Scripture that speaks of gardens is ambivalent. We
encounter gardens as the setting of moral dilemmas. It is there that Eve
and Adam fall prey to the serpent's beguiling and hide from their divine
companion, there that Jesus fights his greatest battle, and there that Judas
betrays his Master with a kiss. Bathsheba must have been bathing in a
garden to be spied on by David, and Naboth was murdered for a vegetable garden. When the Hebrews got tired of wandering in the wilder-
ness, it was for the gardens of Egypt that they hankered, where garlic and
cucumbers were to be found in abundance. A place, then, of temptation?
A place of luxury, as in Esther 1? A setting for disobedience and idolatry,
as in Isaiah 65? A place of disappointment and ultimate futility, as in
Ecclesiastes 2? And then there is the Song of Songs, with its erotic theme
of the sealed garden. Is it of all writings the holy of holies, the celebration of love between God and Israel, God and the church, Christ and the
mystical soul, or is it what it appears to be—a thoroughgoing affirmation
of sexuality, and especially the sexuality of women? "The improper use of
the Song of Songs was much frowned upon" by the rabbis. For the church
too it held many dangers. Ambivalence abounds.[5]

In such an uncertain setting the role of the gardener is also uncertain.
The task of gardening given to Adam by God seems to be fundamental
to our humanity. And as a metaphor for ministry those with postmodern
sensibilities will value its corrective to twentieth-century emphases on
institutional analyses, leadership programmes, and capitalistic growth
strategies. For those looking for characteristics, skills, and gifts for

4. Burnett, *Secret Garden.*
5. See Goldstein, "Introduction."

ministry it suggests patience, perseverance, gentleness, enthusiasm for life, imagination, creativity. This minister stands in the monastic tradition of prayer and contemplation and understands the church as organic rather than commercial. She appreciates how the church year reflects the changing seasons. And if we are approaching ministry from a participative-representational point of view as a role which demonstrates the call of God to all Christians[6]—indeed, to all humans—it demonstrates our current concern with the surviving and thriving of all created things. Here are some connections between the minister and the gardener.

And yet there are places where it does not fit. These misfits highlight the danger that this metaphor, and any metaphor, might take us beyond an illumination of ministry into approaches that undermine our fundamental principles. To examine the places where the image is illuminating, while looking out for the misfits, I ask: what garden are we talking about? Is the garden the minister tending the garden of her own soul or is it the garden of the world? Or is it the garden of the church? In which of these settings might the metaphor function helpfully and what are its limits? What role does the minister play in each setting? What is the nature of her responsibility, the limit of his power?

THE GARDEN OF THE SOUL

> A beginner must look on himself as one setting out to make a garden for his Lord's pleasure, on most unfruitful soil which abounds in weeds. His Majesty roots up the weeds and will put in good plants instead. Let us reckon that this is already done when a soul decides to practice prayer and has begun to do so. We have then, as good gardeners, with God's help to make these plants grow, and to water them carefully so that they do not die, but produce flowers which give out a good smell, to delight this Lord of ours.[7]

The image of the garden of the soul runs through Catholic lay piety, from the thirteenth-century *Little Flowers of St. Francis* to the nineteenth-century cult of St.Thérèse of Lisieux, the Little Flower of Jesus.[8] As holy gardeners we all have a sacred responsibility to tend our souls, living before God in obedience and producing the fruits of righteousness. Our

6. Goodliff, *Shaped for Service*, 106.

7. Teresa of Avila, *Life of Saint Teresa*, 78.

8. See Challoner, *Garden of the Soul*.

call is to "work out our own salvation with fear and trembling" (Phil 2:12). The responsibility is on our own shoulders. And yet "it is God who works in us, to will and to act according to his good purpose" (Phil 2:12, 13). Saint Teresa holds together a robust expectation that we will put our own shoulders to the wheel with a sense of total dependence upon God: "Let his Majesty guide us where he will. We are not our own now, but His. He shows us a great favour when He grants us a desire to dig in His garden, and to be so near its Lord. For He is certainly near us."[9] Our final destiny is in God's hands; all my efforts, my perseverance, my struggles are prompted and fuelled by God's love. Here, as in the other gardens we are considering, the work is collaborative. "In everything God works for good together with those who love him and are called according to his purposes" (Rom 8:28, GNB). If my life should be fruitful or restful or attractive, if the marrows grow and the roses bloom, then God be praised.

Every member of the church is similarly called in the power of the Spirit, who is the Lord and giver of life, to cultivate his own life, her own soul, to the glory of God. The call of Christ is to be, to become, fully and without deviation, the person God has created and named. The minister as a representative Christian stands at the heart of this priestly community, demonstrating this effort to be fully human, labouring with everyone for the purposes of God, the purposes of the kingdom, the purposes of life. It is essential in this scenario that the minister is himself/herself being nurtured, weeded, and pruned by God's Spirit, by their own labour and by the support of their brothers and sisters. We cannot settle simply for how we are, any more than a gardener on inheriting a quarter of an acre of Essex clay can just leave it to the brambles and horseradish. A transformation is needed. But it is a transformation that is led by the Spirit. It is the function of the whole community empowered by the Spirit to encourage each to reach this goal (Eph 4:13–16), but the final shape, the true design, the fruit and the flower, comes from God.

The devotional dimension of ministerial life has been a recurring refrain in the work of Paul Goodliff, with his concern for ministerial formation. The example and inspiration of other pilgrims, the discipline of those to whom we are accountable, and the programmes they devise are intended to shape and underpin ministry. This must be good. And yet I have some reservations. Who decides what form a minister should take? A minister may be a halting preacher, a shy and inept pastor, a poor

9. Teresa of Avila, *Life of St Teresa*, 81.

administrator, and still draw people to Christ by the sincerity of her love. Of course, good preaching, tight administration, and adequate people skills are great asset. And, having, like Paul, had to deal with ministerial catastrophes, with all the grief and shame which they entail, I share his concern that those we offer to congregations as fit ministers should be men and women of integrity, men and women who are serious, who are genuine pilgrims, who are repentant sinners. But one of the delights of serving the London Baptist Association at the beginning of this century was that the city was changing at unprecedented speed, and with it the Christian community. Many of those proclaiming and living the gospel among us, many of those leading significant congregations, did not conform to the pattern of the English, middle-class graduate man that remains the image frequently conjured by the word "minister." They were outsiders; they had not attended any of our colleges, and their formation had been through the company of their brothers and sisters and under the hand of the Holy Spirit. I celebrate all that they have brought to our Association and our city. And I was grateful to Paul, and to John Colwell, Paul Martin, and others for their help in forging new paths into accreditation for those who did not fit the traditional template. Of course diversity is hard to police; risks may be taken and we may come unstuck. But it was, it is, well past time to break the ministerial mould. Certainly not time to create a new one.

And there is always the lurking danger, the insidious seduction of clericalism; the danger that any in our congregations should be expected to be, or expect themselves to be, a caste of the super-spiritual.[10] When we speak of ministerial formation we need to be careful to avoid any insider/outsider thinking, any tendency to create private worlds of piety or litmus tests of devotion, or to form clubs, even holy ones. Any ministerial formation which promotes a division at the heart of the church is surely inimical to the gospel. And any attempt to change all our Marthas into Marys shuts down on the creative wealth of God and impoverishes his church. Luther warns, "If you are a lily and a rose of Christ . . . know that you will live among thorns. Only see to it that you will not become a thorn as a result of impatience, rash judgement, or secret pride."[11]

Outside the enclosure of Rievaulx Abbey, where Abbot Aelred held his benevolent rule, a magnificent vegetable garden gives evidence of

10. See Matt 23:1–12.
11. Luther, "Christ Dwells Only with Sinners," 230–31.

consummate skill and expertise. It is planted in a soil rich enough to be the outcome of a millennium of cultivation. I do not know if this garden dates from Aelred's day, but that house would have needed something similar. I doubt whether the aristocratic Abbot himself turned the soil, or knew the remedy for black fly. But someone in the convent would have had that knowledge, and the well-being of the community—perhaps its very survival—depended on that brother serving God in the exercise of this non-clerical skill. I have no doubt that the good abbot knew and acknowledged this expert.

In the garden of the soul, personal piety, personal responsibility, persistent labour and patience are required of every Christian. Here ministers take their place—perhaps, hopefully, an exemplary one—among all the faithful.

THE GARDEN OF CREATION

> O if we but knew what we do
> When we delve or hew —
> Hack and rack the growing green!
> Since country is so tender...
> Where we, even when we mean
> To mend her we end her,
> . . .[12]

When considering the cultivation of personal piety, the image of the minister as gardener simply underlines the necessity for all Christians of that lifelong pilgrimage by which God achieves our formation. When set in the garden of the world, the image is more distinctive. Those occasional references in the Bible to a garden posit God as the gardener, and ourselves as his collaborators. In the work of creation it is the Spirit that broods over the chaos, gradually producing order, rhythm, predictability, beauty, and usefulness. Then we are told "the Lord God had planted a garden in the east, in Eden; and there he put the man he had formed . . . to work it and take care of it" (Gen 2:8). The activities of the gardener—planning, preparing, planting, watering, weeding, pruning—are first of all activities of God himself. This is clear in the teaching of Jesus. Whether we think of the parable of the patient farmer, the sower, the mustard seed, the tree and its fruit, the barren fig tree, the workers in the vineyard, the birds and

---

12. Hopkins, "Binsey Poplars," in *Poems*, 86.

the lilies, or the grain of wheat, always it is God alone who is the Lord and giver of life. Creation is his masterpiece, his demesne, his kingdom. But our role is significant and cannot be abdicated. God offers us a universe that is predictable, that if tended with care will produce a good harvest. But we are under his command to tend this crop, both the literal crop and the crop of righteous deeds which reveal us as living "according to our kind" (in God's image). Many of these parables, like the story of the wheat and tares and the mixed fish, are parables of judgement, in which the question is posed: have you—you as an individual, you as the people of God—brought forth that fruit of generous, humane living that declares you to be children of God? Have you taken the life that was given you and lived it energetically and faithfully in the service of God and neighbour? If not, then the axe is already laid to the root. Useless trees, useless vines, will be chopped down and thrown into the fire. God will wield the axe. The promise and threat of eschatological judgement gives urgency to all that Jesus taught.

For us in twenty-first century this note of judgement has a fresh immediacy. The call of the kingdom has taken on a new urgency, a new revelation. Traditionally the Christian hope for creation lay in an automatic redemption, a global rebirth, which would follow the global acceptance of the gospel. Our call was to evangelise the world, and then the eschaton would look after the rest of the created order. Creation as we know it would pass away before the new act of God:[13]

> Though hills and high mountains should tremble
> Though all that is seen melt away,
> Thy voice shall in triumph assemble
> Thy loved ones at dawning of day.[14]

This expectation, in which humanity played no role in the salvation of creation—had no responsibility for it—has in recent years given way to a new realisation that the well-being, the salvation and survival of the created order is a matter for our concern, our labour, and our sacrifice. Righteous living is increasingly understood as exercising a proper stewardship, a godly care of all that God has made. "What is man, that you are mindful of him? . . . You made him ruler over the works of your hands; you put everything under his feet" (Ps 8:6–8). This has become a big ask,

13. See Matt 24:14 and 35.

14. H. Elvet Lewis, "The Light of the Morning Is Breaking," no. 193 in *Baptist Hymn Book*.

a huge challenge. We may be about to fail—we may already have failed. We teeter on the line between paradise and the waste land.

If it is too late, where is redemption to be found? The image of the garden as the site of human fall and human redemption gains fresh significance. Just as the garden was the scene of God's call to men and women in their innocence, so too it was the site of their betrayal, of alienation and fear, of shame and hiding and banishment. It was fitting then that the redeeming action of God in Jesus—his greatest battle, his betrayal, and his resurrection—should take place in a garden. As we are redeemed so the garden once again becomes the scene of our companionship with our creator God. But what if we destroy the garden? God is the giver of life and fruitfulness, but he recruits us into his enterprise. Perhaps our creative (or destructive) efforts might impinge upon God? Change God's purposes? Add to God's imagination? Compliment God's grief or delight? Perhaps he makes space for that? Perhaps the garden of Eden is a foretaste of how the whole of creation is intended to be as the result of a proper collaboration between God and humanity, a collaboration in which humanity is given dominion over—responsibility for—all created things? The first call of God to Adam is today acutely reaffirmed.[15]

In this situation ministers are called to take responsibility for their own righteous living alongside their brothers and sisters but also to offer a prophetic challenge. This issue, of immediate and contemporary relevance, means more carefulness in us as individuals, but also new habits for our congregations. It does occasionally happen that congregations, churches, choose not to store up treasure on earth—not to pull down and build bigger barns—but to act as stewards of the good things God has given them, producing the fruit of generous, non-wasteful living. But the danger of a disconnect between the words of the Gospels and congregational ambition continues to haunt us.

In what sense can the minister contribute to this cosmic drama? Ministers are not responsible for life; they must be relieved of the burden that the flourishing or not of a congregation is the measure of their own devotion or competence. Many a devoted minster serves with no apparent fruit. It is in God's hands what grows and what vanishes. Humanity inherits the curse of Adam—ground that produces thistles, and can only be made productive by the sweat of our brow. We share not only growth and fruitfulness but also frustration and decay. But ministers are the

15. See Gen 2:8 and 15.

guardians and messengers of the salvation story, the harbingers of salvation, the prophets of God's call. They have the responsibility of proclaiming God's Word, God's judgment, for the salvation of the world. This is increasingly a call to men and women to have dominion, to take responsibility, to do what they can through repentance, love, and self-denial to usher in that kingdom, where "they will not hurt or destroy in all God's Holy mountain, because the earth will be filled with the knowledge of the Lord as the waters cover the seas" (Isa 11:9).

It has to be admitted that the church has been slow to discover this vocation. As Jeremy Flack, Green Advocate for the URC, writes, "too often the 'prophets' who see the truth and the challenge for change are outside the church."[16] Much private support for green causes has been generated within the church, but it is good to see an increasing engagement in the wider task of addressing the powers. After COP26 the Joint Public Issues Team, speaking for Baptists, Methodists, and the URC, declared, "Our Churches acknowledge that while we live in an age of individuality and immediacy, this is a journey not of individuals but of a community, the people of God and the people of the earth."[17] Standing within the nonconformist tradition, the task of calling the powerful to account before the Word of God is not new to us. Whether or not our voices are heard, we are called to speak for God and to collaborate with all who have a love for humanity and for life in campaigning for a new approach to the future that will place the survival of all above the comfort of some.

And here the church and its ministry has a distinctive and essential role. During the weeks and months surrounding COP26 we saw many images of disaster, and heard many prophecies of doom. The knowledge of what is happening and what has happened is crucial if we are to make creative decisions and live well and righteously. But the church has a further message for a struggling world, a message of hope. We are indeed responsible, and if life on earth fails it will be humanity that has precipitated that disaster. But we are not alone. Without in any way stepping

---

16. Jeremy Flack, "Green Advocate: Environment," https://www.urc-eastern.org.uk/mission-and-ministry/environment-green-advocate.

17. "Response to COP26," statement from the Baptist Union of Great Britain, the Methodist Church, and the United Reformed Church on the conclusion of the Glasgow COP26 summit, November 14, 2021, https://www.jointpublicissues.org.uk/response-to-cop26.

back from our newly discovered—or rediscovered—vocation to protect life, we can still proclaim the hope expressed by Hopkins: even though

> the soil is bare now,
> . . . for all this, nature is never spent;
> There lives the dearest freshness deep down things;
> And though the last lights off the black West went
> Oh, morning, at the brown brink eastward, springs-
> Because the Holy Ghost over the bent
> World broods with warm breast and with ah! Bright wings.[18]

The creative imagination and lifeforce of God is never exhausted. Without this gospel dimension, this dimension of forgiveness and hope and promise, the most natural, and perhaps the most rational, thing for humanity to do is to despair. In this proclamation, which is also an energiser, a summons to action, the preaching ministry has a significant role. But it has to be confessed that the gardening metaphor falls short here, lacking the urgency required by the task in hand.

THE GARDEN OF THE CHURCH

> Such was that happy Gardenstate
> While man there walked without a mate:
> After a place so pure and sweet,
> What other help could yet be meet!
> But 'twas beyond a mortal's share
> To wander solitary there:
> Two paradises 'twere in one,
> To live in Paradise alone.[19]

What, then, of the paradise that is the local church? At first our metaphor seems an attractive opening. In their essay collection *Metaphors We Lead By*, Mats Alvesson and Andre Spicer offer the image of the gardener alongside leadership metaphors of saints, buddies, commanders, cyborgs, and bullies. As a post-heroic metaphor, it carries sympathetic overtones. "Leadership (as gardener) appears as a beautiful thing: it fosters creativity, morality, authenticity, spiritual growth [and offers] a happy image of care."[20] And yet the authors of this book are sceptical

---

18. Hopkins, "God's Grandeur," in *Poems of Gerald Manley Hopkins*, 47.

19. Marvell, "Thoughts in a Garden," 118.

20. Alvesson and Spicer, *Metaphors We Lead By*, 76.

about the contemporary fascination with leadership—"the mystical arts of leadership." Something of the same reserve has been characteristic of Baptist thought. In the pamphlet *Something to Declare*, a study of the Baptist Union of Great Britain's Declaration of Principle, produced in 1996 for the Denominational Consultation, four principals of Baptist colleges maintained that Baptists have a distinctive history and theology, a particular contribution to the church worldwide.[21] And yet that authoritative study contained no reference to ministry. This silence is revealing. It suggests that a genuinely Baptist voice will be non-clerical, offering a communitarian understanding of the church and a congregational understanding of priesthood. Miroslav Volf, in his Trinitarian reflections on ecclesiology, *After Our Likeness*, offers a Free Church model which is charismatic and participative, expressing the practical outworking of the biblical concept of the priestly company.[22] This charismatic understanding is explored by Nigel Wright in *The Radical Kingdom*, an essay which reflects the deep root of congregationalism that runs through Baptist life, and that is the distinctive vision we bring to the wider church.[23] Ministry is a gift to the church, but it is not the church. The corrective to Baptist iconoclasm is not a new priestly caste but a thoroughgoing embracing of the high calling of all the baptized; not the setting aside of the few, but the commissioning of the all to live out this salvific vocation.[24]

Playing God

The metaphor of the gardener cannot express this congregational and communitarian understanding of the church. There are some serious misfits. Jesus included many allusions to cultivation in his teaching, but significantly it is God who stands as the gardener/farmer. Paul too, in emphasising growth and maturity in the church, always finds the dynamic

21. "we locate authority in community and not in hierarchy"; Kidd, ed., *Something to Declare*, 28.

22. "Universal distribution of the charismata implies common responsibility for the life of the church"; Volf, *After Our Likeness*, 230.

23. Wright, *Radical Kingdom*, 122. This Congregationalist theology is reaffirmed by Stephen Holmes: "Christ's active lordship, as understood by Baptists and others in the Free Church/Believers' Church tradition, decisively relativises the authority of ordained clergy"; Holmes, "Radical Ecclesiology," 122.

24. "The specialised purveyor of access to the divine is out of work since Pentecost"; Yoder, *Body Politics*, 56.

and life in God: "I planted the seed, Apollos watered it, but God made it grow. So neither he who plants nor he who waters is anything, but only God, who makes things grow . . . For we are God's fellow workers" (1 Cor 3:6–9). Inevitably, the gardener takes upon himself/herself the task of shaping the vision, of choosing what to plant and what to uproot, what to consider choice plants and what to discard as weeds: "Enabling growth in an organizational context can rarely be separated from weeding, pruning, nurturing, staking and cutting that enable the manager to choose one form of growth above another."[25] And yet surely it is God's prerogative "what to avow or amend there"?[26] It was our original sin to want to play God—it lost us paradise. This metaphor threatens to aggregate dangerous amounts of power to the minister, trespassing on the prerogative of God.

Inappropriate Responsibility

Plants and gardeners are different species. Communication between them is excluded. You cannot hold a conversation with a plant—it will not disagree with you. If you chat to the trees, or begin a debate with a vegetable marrow, you will get little response. Church meeting should afford plenty of response and no little disagreement. It is not a vegetable marrow. Plants are entirely dependent upon the gardener for food and water, and so for survival, while the gardener gets on and pursues his vision. Not so the congregation. If the minister assumes inappropriate responsibility for the vision of the church and the health of the members, she radically curtails the freedom, maturity, and independence of the members. An individualistic and autocratic approach to ministry is a sad falling away from the image of the church as the body of Christ, the company of pilgrims. It weakens and impoverishes the whole. A neighbouring minister once offered me all his old people as a job lot, on the basis that they were slowing down progress. The result of this outrageous piece of human weeding was our enrichment, but it reflected a sad betrayal of the pastoral call. The whole church is involved in the proclamation of the gospel and the service of the kingdom; every voice, including particularly those most easily discounted, must be heard. At the heart of our churchmanship is an insistence that before the cross of Christ all believers stand on level ground and each brings a distinctive

---

25. Alvesson and Spicer, *Metaphors We Lead By*, 83.
26. Hopkins, "The Lantern Out of Doors," in *Poems of Gerald Manley Hopkins*, 53.

contribution. This is the heart of what makes the church both revolutionary and redemptive in a world besotted with power, celebrity, and egoism. No metaphor that involves the level of control and supervision exercised by a gardener will do. Pressed too far, our metaphor would lead us into a form of churchmanship we would disavow.

For all its attractiveness, the image of the gardener creates difficulties for ministry, whether in the private life of the soul, where no special vocation can be discerned, in the garden of the world, where something more immediate and urgent is required, or in the garden of the church, where, as ever, there are difficulties over power and control. Nevertheless, some interesting consonances remain to be explored.

Actuality

Both minister and gardener deal with the real, the actual. There are some professions that work with ideas and ideals, where the life of the mind is untrammelled by the mundane aggravations of life and breath, of fabric committees and drains. The minister may indeed cherish dreams and visions of what the kingdom of God will be like in its fulfilment, of how human beings might be when they are wholly redeemed, of how community might be when filled with such redeemed humans. But today and tomorrow there is the mess and the trouble, the sadness and the hope of this and that life to be dealt with, the difficulties that defy resolution, the challenges of an ideal that has to be enfleshed, incarnate, when the fleshed and the carnate pursue their own agenda. So too the gardener deals not just with catalogues and books, gardening programmes with solutions to every problem, but with this actual soil, claggy or dry, fertile or sandy, and with these growing things which do not unfold as expected or required. This experience of the real must serve to put brakes on our overweening pride and ambition. In *Life Together*, Bonhoeffer suggests that "God hates visionary dreaming; it makes the dreamer proud and pretentious."[27] There is a kind of dreaming that does not go well with ministry. It finds the reality of human life a source of disappointment. Gardener and minister must both be rooted in the real.

---

27. Bonhoeffer, *Life Together*, 16.

Tact

The metaphor is also, particularly in the contemporary setting, a pertinent reminder of our call to collaborate with God in everything for good and for life. In this partnership God is predictable enough to enable us to work, to plan, to create ("while the earth remains . . ."). On the other hand, he is never entirely predictable, never under our control, at our beck and call. His is always the dynamic; our task is to pay attention and offer our work in response. An awareness of the proper balance in this divine collaboration reflects the need in the minister, and the gardener, for a form of tact, a degree of self-effacement, of making space for that which we have not initiated and for the development of the other in the integrity of their otherness. Not everyone has this instinct. Discernment in working with those seeking ministerial accreditation requires that somewhere in the list of skills we seek, both for minister and for gardener, must be a gap, a self-negation, a willingness to become invisible.

Context

Living by the sea in North Yorkshire, I know that there are some plants—fuchsias, for example—that thrive here, but others which flourish in Essex, where I grew up, that wilt under the cold blasts of North Sea tempests. My neighbour repeatedly attempted rhododendrons, but the soil is far too alkali, while the broom I planted withered sorrowfully in the cold. An understanding of context is also crucial for ministry, crucial to defend the minister from exhaustion and disappointment, crucial to enable the congregation to be truly God's planting for that place. In small villages small congregations of dedicated disciples offer God's presence to their neighbours in lives of integrity and welcome. These exist scattered across the nation as salt and light. Meanwhile, large suburban congregations with multifarious, well-resourced programmes draw busy professionals and their children under the sound of the gospel. This diversity is as welcome as the variety of the gardens we create, large or small, urban or village, disciplined and organized or relaxed and free. An emphasis on context has become a positive dimension of ministerial training, but we need to reflect also on which forms of ministry emerge and thrive best in different settings. Good examples and good practice are there to be celebrated; decontextualized visions, which result in disappointed pastors, the accusers of their congregations, need naming as the destructive mirages they are.[28]

Adaptability

Given the cussedness of the real, both gardener and minister have to develop an adaptability that learns the lessons of what will or won't work here, in this weather, this climate, these surroundings. Both need to accept reality and not keeping planting the wretched rhododendrons. Try fuchsias instead. They need to draw on their imagination, learn from the experience of their neighbours, listen to the brethren, think, read, pray, and try something new. In this willingness to adapt, to abandon that which clearly does not work, however wedded they have been to it, and step into the new, ministers—and gardeners—trust that God can be found in the changes. A willingness to persist, to adapt and still to persist, expresses that vigorous commitment to the kingdom that lies beyond our sight which is the hallmark of Christian leadership. The same hope fuels the gardener, who has in his mind's eye a picture of balance, harmony, beauty, and fecundity that drives him on even in the face of bugs and rain. She works with this dream and perseveres in pursuit of the image, despite all setbacks.

Dependence

Gardeners hold together this perseverance with a clear sense of dependence. In the end we are not the lords and givers of life. The farmer sleeps and wakes, and God brings forth the blade and the ear. If, by any chance, I am not a lily or a rose, if instead I am a vegetable marrow, then that is what I am. Both my essence and my outcome are out of my hands. Without this necessary sense of dependence, the minister, like the gardener, is en route for disaster. He or she will eventually despair of themselves, or their garden, as their dream of perfection again and again falls under the impact of the ordinary:

> Indeed at first Man was a treasure,
> A box of jewels, shop of rarities,
>   A ring whose posie was My pleasure:
> He was a garden in a paradise:

28. Bonhoeffer, *Life Together*, 17.

Glorie and grace
Did crown his heart and face.

But sinne hath fooled him. Now he is
A lump of flesh, without a foot or wing
To raise him to a glimpse of bliss:
A sick toss'd vessel, dashing on each thing;
Nay, his own shelf:
My God, I mean my self. [29]

Perfectionism is dangerous, for gardeners and for ministers. It is dangerous for congregations, who are liable to find themselves nagged, bullied, and harassed as the minister asserts his or her agenda and drives forward his or her ambition. The poor church will never live up to the dream. As God is real, and the guardian of reality, to depend upon him is to hold steady in a possible place. Meanwhile, creation itself awaits our rescue, paradise awaits our cultivation, both tasks beyond our powers. As children of Adam and Eve we cannot abdicate from our responsibility, but neither can we forget our dependence, our not-God-ness.

Provisionality

No one completes a garden, and few gardeners start one. Almost always we inherit something, even if just a patch of scratchy grass, a concrete path, and a few lupins. We step into the work of previous gardeners, perhaps many years of loving labour, and must decide whether to uproot and start again or to evolve around what exists already, with the danger that we will inherit pests and weeds as well as raspberries. Wisdom dictates that we take time—at least a year—to get to know the garden and discover what will appear with the passing of the seasons. A gardener who rushes in and digs the whole thing up shows little respect for the labour of others, and loses many plants that may then take years to reestablish. The gardener needs patience and respect for the past, along with a sense of the future and persistence over time with the new. Here the parallel with ministry is strong. Both activities are long-term endeavours. A gardener does not expect to see the full beauty of wisteria for several years, and an introverted church will take several years of patient preaching and example to begin to take down its walls. Gardener and minister must dig in for

29. Herbert, "Miserie," in *English Poems*, 358.

the long haul, working on through every weather, durability being the keynote of authenticity.

We inherit a garden, make a contribution to its development, and trust that it will have a future, that growth and development will continue to unfold during our own time of labour and long afterwards. Those who love to garden know how the labour is fuelled by hopes and dreams. In our imaginations we can see the beautiful row of cabbages, the runner beans climbing high, the roses scaling the wall to perfume the bedrooms. And then there are caterpillars. There is the invisible worm in the bud. It does not rain and the wind blows the runner beans over. And there is the heartbreak of the gardener who has to leave a garden, knowing that her work will probably disappear and that the garden so lovingly cultivated will quite possibly fall into ruin. Leaving a congregation after a particularly creative ministry carries a similar sense of loss and fragility. It faces us with the reality of our ephemeral presence in the world, our mortality.

Indeed it seems that God also experiences the frustrations of all who cultivate the soil when his careful and devoted work results in nothing, no fruit, no response. The metaphors of the barren fig tree and the feral vine reflect this experience of wasted effort, wasted love, which is a recurring theme in Scripture.[30] There is always a shortfall, always disappointment as well as delight, always the unforeseen and sometimes disastrous intervention of nature, always the unforeseen consequences of our own ignorance. As Adam and Eve set out from Eden a flaming sword insists that from now on paradise will always be out of reach—a dream and a yearning, an echo of what might have been, but qualitatively different from the real world in which Adam will tend the soil by the sweat of his brow and Eve will endure the pains of childbirth and the problem of men. But while there are certainly plenty of thorns and thistles, not to mention caterpillars in every congregation, there are also, as in the garden, the delights, the unexpected blossoming, the new beginning, the constant demonstration of the goodness, the fecundity, and the extravagance of God's creative energy. The Aelred experience. For gardener and minister the flaming sword suggests the necessity of seeking a provisional, proximate delight in achieving the best that is possible in given circumstances. Taking on board the fragility, the unpredictability of all creation, the unsatisfactory reality of themselves and of one another, they find delight in proximate ends.

30. See Isa 5 and Luke 13:6–9.

Eschatological Hope

Disappointment will inevitably encounter us, whether in the garden, the church, the world, or ourselves. It can lead to the canker of despair, the blight of despondency. But we are called to reality, not to fantasy. The call of the minister is to stand in the truth of who they and their people are, the truth of the way the world is, and to look for the coming of the kingdom. Unlike gardeners, who depend on the cyclical return of the seasons, ministers do not believe in the wheel that turns and returns, always to the same place. Our conviction is that beyond all the struggles and disappointments God is working towards a glorious fulfilment. So for the minister whose congregation shows little evidence of growth or fruitfulness, trust in God's good future still fires an imagination of how this company of pilgrims might develop, what expression of the kingdom they might fulfil in their generation, how their witness might be given its maximum potential for life and for new life.

We share with God a desire to cultivate, to take what raw material lies to hand and shape it into something of beauty and usefulness, something which is under our hand yet has its own life—a garden, a company, an identity. Like God, we work with material that is recalcitrant and unruly. We are ourselves recalcitrant and unruly, needing ourselves a shaping and disciplining hand. This egotistical warp is present in both the gardener and the minister in the possibility of autocratic, individualistic control and a willingness to discard, weed out, prune back without compunction. There have been ministers who have believed that "it is expedient that one should die for the people" (John 11:50), troublemakers ejected and dissident voices silenced. The myth of Eden resonates with human yearning for the time when all is complete, all is golden, all is right, and no voices are dissident. But the way to this perfect state, whether for ourselves or for our congregations, is barred. Neither my heart nor my congregation, nor indeed the world, will find paradise again until the Eschaton. But we trust in the ultimate fulfilment of love in the paradise garden when the crucified and risen Lord welcomes us to his wedding feast and when perfect love and friendship reign throughout eternity. And in the meantime we take up the trowel.

9

Ministry and Travel

Paul Beasley-Murray

First of all, let me thank Paul Goodliff for his friendship over the years. I first met Paul in the late 1980s when he was one of my students at Spurgeon's College. Later we worked together as members of the board of Ministry Today (formerly the Richard Baxter Institute of Ministry), and then as members of the board of the College of Baptist Ministers. Through personal encounters as also through his writings I have gained many insights into ministry. This leads me now to wish Paul well for his retirement. As Paul will discover, retirement marks the beginning of "Freedom Day," when we are not just free to be ourselves, but free to serve the Lord on our own terms! I look forward to many further insights from Paul through his future writings.

In February 2021 Andy Goodliff wrote to me: "Dad has done various bits of travelling around the world . . . Your chapter might explore, what it is for ministry to be shaped by travel—perhaps leading a church to go places, or helping them glimpse the gospel from a new location of thought. Or you might want to take the metaphor in a different direction." Although over the years I have helped churches "go places," I want to reflect on how I have sought to encourage ministers to "go places" in their personal and professional journeys; or in terms of the metaphor, how I have sought to give other ministers "the travel bug."

A "TRAINING VICAR"

Anglicans have a wonderful system of curacy, which involves every ordinand beginning ministry as part of a team.[1] Would that Baptists had the system! The traditional Baptist pattern of solo ministry stands in stark contrast to the shared leadership pattern of the New Testament.

I began as a solo minister, but as the church grew staff were needed. In my time I worked alongside thirteen younger colleagues, all bar one of whom either were or became accredited Baptist ministers; the one exception now leads a thriving Anglican church. As I look back, I realize that the more experienced I became as a minister, the better a trainer I became. In my thirties I still had so much to learn myself. However, because of all I had learnt in the school of life (with all its hard knocks), I had much more to offer in my final twenty-one years as a senior minister.[2] By then I really knew what effective supervision involved. Bearing in mind John Adair's definition that "a good leader works as a senior partner with other members to achieve the task, build the team, and meet individual needs,"[3] I saw my role as team leader to keep my colleagues focussed on the mission of the church (our task), to continually work at team building, and to ensure that the individual needs of the team were being met through giving them opportunities for development in ministry. The latter role I defined as follows:

> To help staff develop. This is particularly true of colleagues who have come straight from theological college. Along with their church work, they have also books to read and projects to complete. The task of the team leader is to help them have a good experience of ministry, so that they are ready then to take on a church of their own. However, it is not simply the younger staff who need to be developed. The learning process never stops. Everybody is on a journey, including the team leader![4]

1. Not every curacy is a resounding success. Around a third of curates would not recommend their training incumbent to train other curates: see Marlow, *Thriving in Curacy*, 3, 4.

2. For instance, the difficulties I encountered at Spurgeon's College meant that "I now knew at first-hand what it was to experience pain and suffering, misunderstanding and rejection" and as a result I was much better placed to help others; Beasley-Murray, *This Is My Story*, 123.

3. Adair, *Effective Leadership*, 38. This definition of leadership formed the basis of my book *Dynamic Leadership*.

4. Beasley-Murray, *Living Out the Call*, book 2, *Leading God's People*, 75.

The weekly Monday team meetings were an opportunity to reflect and learn together. The informal conversations which took place every day as we worked from our church offices gave opportunities for more personal reflection. Then every month a formal supervision with a view to furthering growth and development.

To what extent was I successful in encouraging my former associates and assistants to get "the travel bug" in their ministerial journey? As part of my preparation for this essay, I wrote to some of my more recent colleagues, asking three questions: "What did you learn from me? How did you learn from me? Subsequently, have there been occasions in our own ministry when came to see the point of something I had urged upon you, but to which at the time you were resistant?" The resulting responses were overwhelmingly positive and showed what a difference mentoring can make to ministerial development.

Although it was suggested that I simply summarize the responses with a view to then drawing out common themes, I have decided to let the responses speak for themselves.

Mike

My four years with you were undoubtedly the most formative years of my ministry and I have taken much of that into the subsequent twentyt-two years of ministry. You took people on the journey with you, you mentored naturally and consistently. In management-speak, you were a "diplomat"—one who valued, encouraged, enabling and empowering the team. That is not to say you were uncritical if you felt things went badly: you held us to a high standard as you gave of your best and wanted us to do the same, striving for excellence. At times good enough has to do if we cannot give any more, but the zeitgeist too quickly follows the philosophy of Mediocrates! Whilst you would be critical (usually in a positive way) to our face, you always supported us publicly, allowing us to be creative and make mistakes.

You were very generous with your time and never gave the impression that you resented giving it. The Monday team meetings were extremely valuable but perhaps it was the one-to-ones, where you shared yourself and let me into the inner world of a pastor, which above all helped me to develop and grow as a person and a pastor. I would also flag our team away days as being formative.

Your perspective on Spirit-led preparation is one area that I was not so sure about in the early years but have increasingly come to value and commend, particularly in prayer. Whilst the heart felt extempore prayer has a place, the well-prepared prayer can transport the spirit to the very throne of God. The evangelical norm seems to be a not very Spirit led or thought-out prayer that diminishes our relationship with God, falling into bland repetition.

Matt N

The time offered me experience of a style and size of church that I had not had before and that has helped particularly as I have gone on to build a team here. I learnt about the importance of drawing alongside me those who are different so there can be a complementing of gifts and a stronger team. I saw the importance of really immersing myself as a pastor in the midst of the people—being accessible and available (whilst at the same time putting the necessary boundaries in place).

Emma

I learnt the importance of pastoral visiting; how hard ministry is—you impressed upon me strongly the pain of ministry in order to ensure I went in with my eyes open; to minister according to who I am—you frequently pointed out that we were very different people and I should not assess my call to ministry based on how much I resembled you; the essential content of gathered worship, including praise, thanks, confession, and petition.

I learnt by going on pastoral visits with you; through one-to-one conversations and pastoral supervision; through weekly Monday team meetings and the annual leadership team retreat, which impressed upon me the importance of gathering the team together regularly; and through hearing you preach and having you comment on my preaching.

Subsequently I realized how often petitions and, even more, confession were missed from public worship. As an intern I used to kick against your insistence on certain aspects of worship; but as a ministerial student I realized you were right all along! Also, when writing an essay on preaching the messianic oracles in Old Testament prophecy, I realized how much your preaching included historical criticism in a way which helped me to integrate this into my own understanding of Scripture and preaching practice.

Nicholas

I learned the vital importance of good organisation, administration, and attention to the executive function as a senior pastor. Preaching and teaching, pastoral care and oversight, leading and vision are clearly vital for a pastor, but being with Paul for a year greatly heightened my appreciation and understanding of those areas. Having been with a senior pastor for six years previously who was focussed on preaching, teaching, and pastoral care, it was a great example to see these other areas of leadership/ministry being exercised well.

I learned the value of ongoing learning and growth in ministry with Paul being someone who encouraged reading, reflection, and development in ministry. Often Paul would give me books to review. I felt challenged in my role to grow and be the best I could be. Paul set a cracking pace and standard of ministry and was not content to sit on his laurels or fade out into retirement, and this lifted the culture of growth and development at the church. I felt held accountable in a healthy way for how I was preparing and spending my time in ministry. I learned too the benefit of regular and clear communication. At weekly team meetings Paul would provide team members with significant print-outs of news, information, and resources pertinent to what was happening in the church. This carried across the church in various publications, Sunday services, etc. Paul was ready to share news or important updates in the context of one-to-one meetings or with our weekly minsters meeting, which made me feel valued and trusted as a cominister. In summary, Paul helped restore my confidence to lead as a senior pastor by being a well-rounded leader who had high competency across a range of importance leadership and pastoral functions.

I learnt above all from Paul's example. The saying "Ministry is more caught than taught" factored in here. I was at a juncture in my life where I was not sure I wanted to continue in pastoral ministry longer term. Spending a year with Paul and the church rekindled my heart and hope for what was possible in the local church. I saw a well-lead, caring, and empowered church that was really making a difference for Christ.

At the time I was much less inclined than Paul to be so on the front foot with visitors and new people. He was very keen to get them signing a welcome card and made it clear he expected the ministry team to be on the lookout at services. My sense was to give people space, respect that they may not want to be made a fuss of, and give them a couple of weeks of coming before seeking details. I now think that Paul's approach was right and that churches must pay attention to newcomers and follow them up well. It is better to err on the side of being too friendly and engaging than on the other side of neglect and being inhospitable. One other thing comes to mind: Paul took me with him to visit a lady from church who was in hospital for minor surgery. She was chuffed to have two ministers visit and made that known. Afterwards, discovering Paul was not particularly fond of her, for in the past she had been vocal in her criticism of him, I sympathized, but he said, "Let's just say we were paying the rent." At the time I felt this sounded demeaning—not to the lady, but as a reflection on pastoral ministry. I now realize that there are times when you just have to perform and do things in ministry to "pay the rent." However difficult or unenjoyable they may feel, however weary you may be, they need to be—"the rent" needs to be paid!

Martin

I learnt from you that looking after my own spiritual health is key if I am to be an effective minister. I learnt not to feel guilty in taking time out for personal spiritual growth. I learnt too the need for good preparation, particularly in sermon preparation but equally for meetings. I learnt the importance of being approachable, both in terms of being physically available to meet with people but also being present with them. I learnt too the need to develop a thick skin; that criticism in ministry is inevitable even though not always justifiable and that not all of it is meant personally. The ability to recognize what is going on and to challenge was part of this learning also. I learnt to have both courage and confidence in my calling, and in turn to be willing to take risks, have a go at things, and lead others by example. Finally, I learnt I needed to be willing to own mistakes and seek forgiveness.

Your example was most definitely the most important factor in my learning. Seeing your commitment to ministry and to the church, seeing you handle both the highs and lows of ministry, taught me more about the calling of ministry than anything else. One-to-one meetings also helped me to learn: the opportunity to talk openly and honestly together and to talk issues through, even if we held different opinions, helped me to think critically about ministry and to be open to other ideas. In addition, regular team meetings, leadership team meetings, and church meetings helped me to learn how to handle different situations. It was important to observe but also to have the opportunity to reflect together as to how things were handled.

Subsequently, I developed a growing appreciation for the lessons I learnt working with you. I understand more than ever the importance of a team covenant which brings openness and honesty within the team. I understand now more about the weight of ministry and my call. You always demonstrated the high calling you felt for ministry, but at the time this was not an issue for me. I now understand the high calling of having been set apart and gifted to lead Christ's church forward.

Leesa

The most important thing I learnt was how to operate as an outstanding team. You showed me that "textbook teamwork" could be a reality. Sadly, teams often fail and fall apart as people struggle to work together, but you gave me an opportunity to experience what an ideal team is really like. The team covenant was so valuable, but only because you modelled it and enabled everyone else to operate within its guidelines. The importance of being honest with each other is so true and helped to build a team that operated with a real strength. You also showed me that it was possible for a team to work in unity even with different opinions and points of view. You encouraged us to say what we thought, although we knew we had to have done our homework as we would need to back up why we had that opinion! But you illustrated how different opinions and constructive conflict helped each one of us to learn and grow and strengthened us as a team ("iron sharpens iron"). In the years we worked together, there were often many different opinions between us as a team, but we never lost unity.

Your example was the most important way I learned from you. Knowing that your door was always open and that I could always talk things through with you was also very valuable. I appreciated our one-to-one conversations.

Subsequently, when I was having to preach every week, I remembered how you said that as long as I had done the prep and said what I thought was right, then I should not beat myself up if I felt the sermon had not been perfect. "Some sermons fly," you said, "and some do not!" Secondly, over the years I came to appreciate your constant reinforcement of the importance of names. Thirdly, the importance of timing, both of the sermon and of the whole service, became more became more significant to me later in my ministry.

Matt R

I grew a huge amount under your ministry and leadership. I came as a pretty blank canvas and you helped turn that blank canvas into something that resembled what I hope is a half-competent minister! You helped me to develop a wider perspective of pastoral care, of preaching, leading worship, church leadership, church politics, and understanding. One of the things I saw most in you is your heart—your heart for the team, for individuals, for the church, and of course for Jesus. I learnt from that the importance of authenticity.

I really appreciated our one-to-one conversations, when I was summoned and enlightened! I am a practical learner, and so being given the opportunity to learn and then reflect with you and learn on the job was also hugely beneficial. Your example was a big way of learning. However, not only did you set an example, you were always open to me even though I was a junior member of the team, allowing me to question why you thought or acted as you did.

Subsequently, when I come across a situation I have never seen before, it can be helpful to think of lessons that I have seen or observed in your leadership that might be helpful and relevant to the situation I am facing. I guess this works both ways—imitating your example, and also developing my thinking and reasoning from your example and occasionally doing things differently too.

A PASTORAL "PROVOCATEUR"

Writing gradually became an important part of my ministry. Like Eugene Peterson, the long-serving pastor of Christ Our King Presbyterian Church in Bel Air, Maryland (1962–1992), I felt it to be a calling arising

directly out of my pastoral ministry. For me there was a strong relationship between the two. Peterson, with his gift for words, described his
"holy vocation of writing/pastoring" in this way:

> Pastorwriter, writerpastor. The holiness of words, the holiness of
> people—both at the same time, neither sacrificed for the other.
> Not many have attempted this, protecting the integrity of these
> two ways of holiness.[5]

My mantra for much of my writing of blogs and articles has been
Hebrews 10:24: "Let us consider how to provoke one another" (NRSV);
or in the NIV: "Let us consider how we may spur one another on." As I
wrote in a blog:

> The Greek noun (*paroxune*), from which we get our English
> word "paroxysm" and which is present here, is a strong word
> full of emotion. It appears in only one another place in the New
> Testament. There in Acts 15.39 it is used of the "sharp disagree-
> ment" which broke out between Paul and Barnabas when they
> could not agree on taking Mark with them on another mis-
> sionary journey. The cognate verb (*paroxuno*) appears twice in
> the New Testament: in Acts 17:16 it is used to describe Paul's
> exasperation—"his spirit was provoked" (AV)—at the sight of
> so much idolatry in Athens, while in 1 Cor 13:4 it describes how
> love is not easily "provoked" (NRSV "it is not irritable"). In all
> these instances the provocation concerned has a negative sense.
> However, here the word is used positively. It is about stirring up
> our colleagues for their good. So the REB translates: "We ought
> to see how each of us may best arouse others." If we look at these
> words through a ministerial filter, then by extension we have the
> thought of provoking or arousing our brother and sister minis-
> ters to fulfil their calling.[6]

I have always been a great believer in "provoking" ministers and leaders to think. For most of my articles and blogs this has been my primary
motivation. In my first church, for six years I wrote a monthly article
entitled "Pastor's Prescription" for a magazine which at first was called
Family and later became *Today*. In my final article written as I moved
to Spurgeon's, I confessed that in all my articles I had "lied through my

---

5. See Collier's biography, *Burning in My Bones*, 205.

6. Beasley-Murray, "Let Us Be Concerned for Our Brother and Sister Ministers," *Church Matters* (blog), March 9, 2017, https://www.paulbeasleymurray.
com/2017/03/09/let-us-be-concerned-for-our-brother-and-sister-ministers.

teeth," for I had only written about the things that worked, rather than failed—strangely, not one person commented. Another lengthy series was "Last Word" in *Baptist Times*—that title caused misunderstanding, for some thought that I was claiming to have "the last word" on any given subject, whereas in fact it was simply a description of my articles always appearing at the bottom of the last page.

In October 2011, at the suggestion of one of my associates, I decided to try my hand at writing a weekly blog. I have been writing ever since. The blog's title, *Church Matters*, contains a deliberate double entendre. Indeed, *Church Matters* has become the title of my website as a whole.[7] In the words of the blurb:

> Are you looking for resources to transform the life of your Church? If so, this website could be what you are looking for. Paul Beasley-Murray is a dynamic Christian leader, who has transformed the life of churches and Christian institutions and enabled them to face up to the challenges of today. This process of change has not always been easy, but the tough times have only served to deepen his faith and to enable him to empathize all the more with others 'going through the mill'. A creative thinker, he is constantly sparking off new initiatives. With over fifty years of ministry, he has developed wideranging expertise in many areas of pastoral life.

There have been times when I have been tempted to give up writing the blog. It is quite a discipline dreaming up a new topic every week, especially now that I am retired. It has become what Donald Coggan once said of preaching every week—"a joyful tyranny."[8]

Yet, compared with preaching, the response has been overwhelming. Every week—and often every day—I have comments from all over the world. Some come from people I know, while others come from people I have never met. Clearly I am meeting a need—and so, for the time being, I continue.

---

7. https://www.paulbeasleymurray.com.

8. See Coggan, *On Preaching*, 3–4: "Preaching *is* a tyranny. I refer not only to the fact that Sunday comes round with an inexorable regularity and makes demands which must needs be met. I refer also to the fact that we know that we must not offer to the Lord a second-rate offering; only the best we can produce will do. I think of the demands which this makes on a man's [*sic*] freshness and devotion and reading and thinking and praying. A tyranny indeed. But a *joyful* tyranny — who would be without it who has been called and commissioned?"

A PASTORAL THEOLOGIAN

With a PhD in New Testament studies and being a member of the prestigious Studiorum Novi Testamenti Societas, some might say that my credentials are not in theology per se. However, much of my reading and thinking has been in pastoral theology as it relates to the practice of ministry; here I have in mind matters relating to such aspects of church life as leadership, mission, pastoral care, preaching, worship, and spirituality.[9] I have a concern for what has been termed "strategic practical theology," which can help ministers to fulfil their calling to be "inspirational leaders, charismatic preachers, creative liturgists, missionary strategists, compassionate pastors and exemplary pilgrims."[10]

While many pastoral theologians are academics operating from a university or theological college, for most of my ministry I have operated from a church. As a pastoral theologian, I have written many books, which often then became the basis for courses I have taught all over the world. In these books and courses I have mostly reflected on what I have learnt from my practice of ministry, with the intention of helping ministers (as distinct from theological students) to grow and develop in their own practice of ministry—and in this way "infect them with the travel bug."

My reflections on ministry fall into a number of groups:

- First and foremost, reflections on leadership as it affects ministry and mission: *Turning the Tide: An Assessment of Baptist Church Growth in England* (1981); *Pastors under Pressure* (1989); *Dynamic Leadership* (1990); *A Call to Excellence* (1995); *Power for God's Sake?: Power and Abuse in the Local Church* (1998); *Transform Your Church: 50 Very Practical Steps* (2005); *Living Out the Call*: volume 1, *Living to God's Glory*; volume 2, *Leading God's Church*; volume 3, *Reaching God's World*; volume 4, *Serving God's People* (2015).

- Secondly, books on preaching: *The Message of the Resurrection* (2000); *Joy to the World: Preaching at Christmas* (2005); *There Is Hope!: Preaching at Funerals* (2021). Hopefully, eventually *There Is Love!: Preaching at Weddings* will see the light of day!

9. Definitions of pastoral theology vary; see Woodward and Pattison, eds., *Blackwell Reader in Pastoral and Practical Theology*.

10. See Beasley-Murray, *Living Out the Call*, in particular book 1, *Living for God's Glory*, 13–14.

- Thirdly, *Faith and Festivity: A Guide for Worship Leaders* (1991), which reflects my deep concern for structure and direction in worship.

- Fourthly, *Radical Believers: The Baptist Way of Being the Church* (1991, 2005), where I expressed my Baptist convictions.

- Fifthly, *Retirement Matters for Ministers: A Report on a Research Project into How Baptist Ministers Experience Retirement* (2018); *Entering New Territory: Why Are Retired Baptist Ministers Moving to Anglican Churches? What Are the Underlying Theological Issues?* (2019); and *Make the Most of Retirement: A Guide for Ministers* (2020) explores the theme of retirement.

- Finally, three more biographical reflections on ministry: *Fearless for Truth: A Personal Portrait of the Life of George Beasley-Murray* (2002); *This Is My Story: A Story of Life, Faith and Ministry* (2018*); and Fifty Lessons in Ministry: Reflections on Fifty Years in Ministry* (2020).

Other writings, as distinct from books, articles, and blogs, are made up of a large number of booklets of various sizes. The booklets include publications by the Baptist Union of Great Britain such as two baptismal courses, a guide for deacons and elders, a marriage preparation course, and a "help in the first few weeks" for the bereaved.

Intimately linked with the writing has been the teaching. For many years as a pastor, and then as a "retired" minister, I have travelled extensively, speaking at conferences for ministers. Initially my expertise was in church growth, and I taught courses in church growth not just in Europe, but also all over Australia. Then, while at Spurgeon's I developed an expertise in leadership and again travelled all over Europe, Australia, and New Zealand, as also the USA. Returning to the pastorate, I developed an expertise in ministry in general, and taught post-graduate courses in ministry at theological institutions in Australia and New Zealand, and also Lebanon and Sri Lanka. In retirement this teaching has continued. What has been significant is that the teaching has almost exclusively been reflecting on what I have learnt from the practice of ministry. Of course, I have read widely—my books certainly reflect that. However, I use my own experience to encourage my brother and sister ministers to get the travel bug and journey beyond their comfort zones.

PROMOTING CMD

CMD (continuing ministerial development) is the church equivalent of what elsewhere is known as CPD (continuing professional development). CPD started in the late twentieth century; the first Anglican CMD course (then known as "ministerial development review") took place in 2011.

My interest in CMD began when as Principal at Spurgeon's College I realized the limitations of gaining higher degrees. How could ministers be encouraged to continue and grow and develop once a professional doctorate (e.g., Doctor of Ministry) had been gained? At Spurgeon's I toyed with the idea of creating a fellowship of the college, membership of which would be given to ministers who displayed an ongoing commitment to developing their understanding of ministry, but in the end other priorities intervened. However, as I came to the end of my principalship I was concerned to discover that between one-quarter to one-third of students whom we had ordained were unlikely to be in ministry when they retired.[11] As a result in the summer of 1992 I began to explore the possibility of developing an institute for ministry, which I proposed be named after the great seventeenth-century pastor of Kidderminster, Richard Baxter, in part because his book *The Reformed Pastor* remains a classic model of pastoral ministry; in part because he is not viewed as a figure belonging to any one denomination.[12]

In 1994 the Richard Baxter Institute for Ministry was formally launched. In the end my dream of a resource centre could not be realized. Along with our annual conference and some training days, our primary focus was on the production of a journal, *Ministry Today*, which came out three times a year. Over the years there were changes: we changed our name to Ministry Today UK. We also changed the wording of our strapline: instead of "promoting excellence in the practice of ministry," we found that "surviving and thriving in ministry" was less threatening to some ministers. They were great days, and along with Paul Goodliff we had some wonderful characters on the board drawn from all the mainline Protestant denominations. However, in 2018 Ministry Today UK closed—primarily because I felt that now since I was retired I should step down, but no successor was to be found!

In the meantime, some of my energies were diverted into The College of Baptist Ministers (CBM), which had a strong focus on

---

11. See Beasley-Murray, *Call to Excellence*, 1–5.

12. See Baxter, *Reformed Pastor*.

ministerial well-being through continuing ministerial education. The origins of CBM went back to a conversation which Paul Goodliff and I had in September 2010. The College came into being in January 2013 and closed in 2021 after the launch of the Baptist Union's own scheme for CMD in the autumn of 2020. Sadly, the development of the College, in my view, was effectively blocked through resistance to the formation of the College by the Baptist Union leadership. As a former distinguished Baptist leader wrote to me:

> We have a lesson to learn from the Roman Catholic Church which through the centuries has mostly opened the door to reform movements that emerge in their ranks. Baptists have a tendency to show the door to those creating new wine skins!

Nonetheless, I wrote to Tim Fergusson, the Baptist Union's Adviser for Ministerial Development, to wish him well for the new Baptist Union initiative in CMD. I was delighted to learn that by Easter 2021 already one-third of Baptist ministers had enrolled. However, my concern is for those who do not enrol. My 2017 research into the reading habits of Baptist ministers, which involved two surveys, showed that although there are many ministers who are disciplined in their reading and study, there is also a substantial percentage of ministers who are not.[13] For instance, it is concerning that:

> 59 percent (longer survey) do not subscribe to a ministry-related journal or magazine;
>
> 56 percent (shorter survey) have not availed themselves of a reading week in the last three years;
>
> 53 percent (longer survey) only read irregularly (as opportunities arises)—and 2 percent never read;
>
> 44 percent (longer survey) do not access any ministry-related website;
>
> 36 percent (longer survey) have less than 250 books;
>
> 31 percent (shorter survey) bought two or less books in the last six months—and 9 percent did not buy a book at all;
>
> 21 percent (longer survey) read six or fewer hours a week;

---

13. See Beasley-Murray, "Ministers' Reading Habits."

19 percent (longer survey) don't have a regular pattern of reading the Bible;

12 percent (shorter survey) normally use only one commentary for sermon preparation—and 3 percent don't use any commentary;

8 percent (longer survey) have not read a ministry-related book in the last six months;

7 percent (longer survey) have not read a general book in the last six months.

My dream—which I share with the Baptist Union—is that CMD becomes part of Baptist ministerial culture.

AN UNRETIRED RETIRED MINISTER

I retired in March 2014, after forty-three years in stipendiary ministry. I now have opportunities to be more involved in the wider community. I have been president of my Rotary club; I am currently chairman of a Cambridge alumni society in Essex; I belong to a local political party; and I am delighted that I no longer am out most evenings either visiting or in meetings. However, I believe that God has still a call on my life. I may no longer be leading a church, but there is still a Lord to serve. Ministry does not end with retirement.

Unfortunately, this is not the view of the leaders of the Baptist Union. This is seen in the way in which, with the notable exception of the South West Baptist Association, most regional associations and their regional ministers have little concern for the well-being of the retired, let alone any interest in using their experience. As a result of my research into how Baptist ministers experience retirement, I discovered that although 81 percent believe that "ordination is for life, so God continues to have a call on my life," most retired ministers feel abandoned by the denomination which they served. I was shocked by my findings:

54 percent do not feel that they belong to the Baptist family.

75 percent are not content with the support they receive.

79 percent had no contact with a regional minister since retirement. "Even after the death of my wife I had no contact," said one."[14]

The Baptist Union position is that retired ministers are the responsibility of the local church. Yet many churches do not know how to care for retired ministers, while some pastors find retired ministers a threat:

40 percent feel that they have no support from their local church.

43 percent said the minister was not their friend.

19 percent feel "at the edge" or "very much at the edge of the church."[15]

Thankfully, not all is gloom and doom:

74 percent are "happy" to be retired.

62 percent said that "retirement has given me new opportunities to serve God."

53 percent were "glad to pursue new interests outside the church."

38 percent agreed that "retirement is a great adventure."[16]

This is the context in which I wrote *Make the Most of Retirement*, the first guide to retirement for ministers in the UK. There I wrote:

"Retirement offers new opportunities and new challenges. Retirement can be an exciting period of life. Apart from childhood, it is the most dynamic stage of life. Change follows change.

As I reflect on retirement, a poem which sums up my experience so far is *The Terminus*, written by David Adam, a former Vicar of the Holy Island Lindisfarne: [17]

The Terminus is not where we stay,
It is the beginning of a new journey.
It is where we reach out beyond,
where we experience new adventures.
It is where we get off to enter new territory,
to explore new horizons, to extend our whole being.

---

14. Beasley-Murray, *Retirement Matters for Ministers*, 85–89.

15. Beasley-Murray, *Retirement Matters for Ministers*, 99.

16. Beasley-Murray, *Retirement Matters for Ministers*, 96–98.

17. Written by David Adam for a greeting card published by Tim Tiley Ltd, Bristol.

It is a place touching the future.
It opens up new vistas.

> Retirement is about the beginning of a new journey. There
> is nothing static about retirement. Retirement . . . is an oppor-
> tunity to discover new ways of living that fullness of life that
> Jesus promised (John 10:10). True, the opportunity needs to be
> seized. Sitting around in the "terminus," watching daytime TV,
> is a diminishment of life. For me retirement opens the door to
> further growth and selfdevelopment.[18]

Much of which I wrote was from my own experience of retirement—at
that stage less than seven years. However, the book's last main section is
entitled "Preparing for the Final Journey," which I have yet to experience.
I wonder how I, an activist, will rise to the challenge of old age, when I
can no longer *do* but can only *be*. There I drew upon the experience of
others:

> In the words of Paul Tournier: "What is important for the aged
> is not what they are still able to do, nor yet what they have ac-
> cumulated and cannot take with them. It is what they are."[19] Or
> as he wrote on another occasion: "From then on a man's value
> is judged not by what he does, but by what he is, not by the
> position he occupies or by his titles, but by his personal ma-
> turity, by his breadth of mind, by his inner life, by the quality
> of his love for others, and by the intrinsic, and not the market,
> value of what he brings into the world."[20] Tournier was right: so
> many older people, including some of us retired ministers, fail
> to reach that point of understanding and maturity."[21]

Paul Clayton, an American minister in the United Church of Christ,
helpfully developed that point in his book on ministers finding meaning in retirement. In a chapter entitled "Don't Just Do Something, Stand
There," he said: "We are called not only to do God's work in the world, but
also to be God's people in the world . . . That identity is marked by integrity rather than greed, care for others rather than self-absorption, humility
rather than arrogance."[22] When illness strikes and death perhaps loom

---

18. Beasley-Murray, *Make the Most of Retirement*, 18–20.

19. Tournier, *Seasons of Life*, 54.

20. Tournier, *Learning to Grow Old*, 204, 205.

21. Beasley-Murray, *Making the Most of Retirement*, 101.

22. Clayton, *Called for Life*, 88.

and there is nothing perhaps we can do, what counts is our "witness of courage and faith."[23]

As we grow older, there is the comfort of knowing that "even though our outer nature is wasting away, our inner nature is being renewed day by day" (2 Cor 4:16). However, that is also a challenge for the retired to engage actively in this journey of inner renewal by immersing ourselves in the daily disciplines of reading Scripture and of prayer, and in this way stir up "the travel bug" for the ultimate life of eternity.

IN CONCLUSION

One of the first descriptions of the Christian faith was "the Way" (see Acts 9:2; 19:23; 22:4; 24:14). Men and women of the Way are by definition travellers. What is true of Christians in general is also true of the Christian minister. We are travellers engaged on the long walk to God.

I am struck by the account Abraham's journey of faith in Genesis 12:9: "And Abram journeyed on by stages" (NRSV). The term "stages" speaks to me of an ever-changing journey. As I look back on my past fifty years of ministry, my life has been a journey marked by ongoing change and stages. Through my varied ministry I have sought to pass on what I have learnt from my journey to younger generations in the hope that this would enable them to be more effective in the ministry to which Christ has called them. Inevitably their journeys will be different from mine. Hopefully, however, I have encouraged them to get "the travel bug."

23. Clayton, *Called for Life*, 97.

10

Ministry and Education

Sally Nelson

Formation for ministry is a holistic understanding of the processes
engaged in the preparation of men and women for ministry. It is the
shaping of a whole life that is of concern here, not merely the impart-
ing of knowledge or the acquiring of skills.[1]

EVERY TIME WE PRAYERFULLY send students out from theological college
into ministry at the end of the academic year, we trust that we have done
our part in fulfilling the aim that Paul Goodliff describes. A person who
is called to ministry (of any kind, recognized or not) is a gift of God to the
church (Eph 4:11–13), and all who participate in delivering theological
education and formation[2] have a primary responsibility to cherish and
nurture each person so called. A key task for theological educators is thus
to reflect critically and often on the shaping and equipping to which Paul
refers: the process of formation—and indeed of transformation—which
leads, for Baptists, to the corporate recognition of a person's ministry
among us.

1. Goodliff, *Shaped for Service*, xv.

2. "Formation" is the language now commonly used to embrace the sense of ministry as a vocation and calling as much as a set of competencies. I acknowledge the
common distinction between "theological education" (about knowledge) and "formation" (about developing the person for ministry), although I do feel it is unfortunate—
theological education conducted in a faith setting should always be formational. Nigel
Wright's summary is apposite: *How to Be a Church Minister*, 16.

Paul published *Shaped for Service* in 2017, shortly after the *Ignite Report*, which explored a vision for the future of Baptist ministry in the denomination, was published in its final version in 2015.[3] Both publications helpfully refocus attention on the *character* of those called to ministry and away from professionalization in the sense of "skilling" (although essential competencies are, of course, needed). At the time of writing this essay to honour Paul, just a few years later, much has happened in our national life which profoundly affects church, mission, and ministry. Our UK context can now be summarized as post-Christendom, post-religious post-denominational, and COVID-shaped.[4] Churches have less resources and less national significance than at any time since Christianity came to Britain. Certainly in the north of England, where I work, the ministers-in-training at the centre of this discussion struggle for money, initially to pay for the formation period, and then later, when their churches cannot find stipends, they also struggle to achieve serious public recognition of their calling. The forms of church that were the norm in the mid-late twentieth century (a building, a gathered congregation, a pastor, and a stipend) are no longer guaranteed. The Baptist Union of Great Britain has responded to this new landscape by developing different categories of ministry, to give formal recognition to new forms of pastoral service (chaplaincy, youth ministries, pioneering, etc.). In college, then, we are offering education and formation for . . . what, exactly?

Even a superficial survey of published books and journals will show that theological educators do engage deeply in reflection on their practice, demonstrating the high degree of commitment by many of those involved in it. Educating people well for Christian service *should* be challenging (particularly, perhaps, for nonconformists, who have historically faced, and still face, particular questions of principle, funding, and status). I believe we can be both encouraged and challenged as we confront new horizons in theological education for ministry. Encouraged, because Baptists have often been pragmatists whose theology follows practical change—and we are in principle uniquely free to adapt and respond to such changes. Baptists comprise a movement shaped by, and which inhabits, the story of Jesus, interpreted afresh in each gathering of disciples as outlined by our Declaration of Principle[5]—this is a

3. Baptist Union of Britain, *Ignite Report*.

4. See, for example, John et al., "Life-Changing Learning for Christian Discipleship," 300; and Wayman, "Imagining the Future of Theological Education."

5. https://www.baptist.org.uk/Groups/220595/Declaration_of_Principle.aspx.

dynamic way of being the people of God. Challenged, because human tendency is to cling to the parameters of the past and Baptists are not exempt, as *Ignite* recognizes.[6]

Stories move in one direction: forwards—if they do not, they are only memories. In response, the *Ignite Report* made many practical recommendations about ministry and formation, many of which have now been implemented. However, it was not *Ignite*'s remit to analyse what we might call the "spirit" of theological education, which is the focus of this essay. Are there internal pressures that bear exploration? Here are three.

Academic Pressures

The research stage of the *Ignite Report* revealed that some people do not offer themselves for formation because of the perceived academic nature of the process.[7] Anecdotally, "I just don't have money or time for college and all that reading: I already have a busy ministry, a job and a family" is a rationale for holding back that I have heard more than once during "Explore Your Calling" events. Some potential candidates may feel they are not academic enough, and *Ignite* recommends the development of creative alternative pathways for such candidates.

Theological colleges are embedded within the economic and cultural framework of wider society. Most are linked to secular universities and impacted by the academic, structural, and political discourses of those validating hosts, and there is an unavoidable pressure on students to achieve academically. While ministers *must* be able to handle God's Word, the pressures and expense of the current process are considerable, and the routine of essays or exams and marks can lead to anxiety among students. For staff, the burden of administrative meetings and organisation can rob life from the joyful aspects of teaching and mentoring.

6. Baptist Union, *Ignite Report*, 3.

7. Baptist Union, *Ignite Report*, 36–37. This is not the sole reason—a lack of encouragement to consider ministry is another identified issue.

Fragmentation and Loss of Pastoral Confidence

Edward Farley wrote in the 1990s about "fragmentation" in theological education.[8] A reductive approach to education has led to specialisations within theology (biblical studies, pastoral studies, doctrine, etc), and to topics within those specialisations—for example, doctrine is often broken into Trinity, Christology, soteriology, etc.[9] These subdivisions have the potential to reduce theology to categories that are less than the sum of its parts, with two unfortunate consequences. One, students become anxious about mastering competence in all areas; second, it can be hard to reintegrate the areas conceptually, as becomes evident in theological reflection assignments. For example, in some current (unpublished) research I have been exploring pastoral anxiety—a concern among students that they have not covered enough specific areas of pastoral care to be competent (for example, mental health, dementia, youth sexuality, or whatever is current in the student's context).

Embedded Power

One of *Ignite*'s hanging questions is about diversity and inclusion among ministry candidates.[10] A subtle dimension of higher education is explored in Willie James Jennings's challenging book, *After Whiteness*, in which Jennings asks us to consider whether the system of Western higher education—and theological education in particular, because of its appeal to ultimate authorities—is birthed in, and perpetuates, a slave-and-master mentality. Jennings argues that the seminary is irredeemably flawed in its cyclical propensity to deliver more of the same. "White self-sufficient masculinity is the quintessential image of an educated person, an image deeply embedded in the collective psyche of Western education and theological education, flexible enough to capture and persuade any and all persons so formed to yield to it. It floats through our curricular imaginations, our pedagogical practice, and the ecologies

8. Farley, *Theologia*, chs. 1–2.

9. John Colwell's *Rhythm of Doctrine*, which explores doctrine through the church calendar rather than through topics such as the Trinity, creation, and redemption, is an attempt to reintegrate theology within the metanarrative of the story of Jesus. Helen Collins's book *Reordering Theological Reflection* suggests that reflection should start with Scripture rather than with experience, for a similar reason.

10. Baptist Union, *Ignite Report*, 34.

of our academic institutions."[11] Jennings's challenge is important and has profound implications for the whole process of ministry preparation, especially for Baptists, for whom justice is at the heart of practice and culture.

Do such questions mean that one of the biggest challenges to ministry formation is not out there in culture, nor even in the churches? Perhaps instead we should be most afraid of an imprisonment within our own story, in a way that commits the future to being an iteration of the past. The uncomfortable question is whether the very structures of theological education are complicit.

It is without question that we must nurture and bequeath the key features of Baptist life and mission: a radical commitment to the rule of Christ, to personal discipleship, to congregational discernment, and to covenant. However, none of our colleges is now a purely Baptist formational setting, and realistically cannot be so under the multiple pressures of the academy and the economy; so how do we both embrace the context and safeguard the tradition?

This book to honour Paul has a theme of metaphor, and in the spirit of that I will suggest that a metaphor of dialogue as a model for education and formation might help us to birth and support new Baptist stories, by focusing the theological objective of formation on developing personhood. This metaphor seems to address the shaping of lives that Paul identifies.

I will now explore some of the expectations we have of theological education, to set the scene for developing the metaphor itself.

EXPECTATIONS OF FORMATION

What is Baptist ministry, for which we in ministry are all in formation—since none of us ever stops being formed? The terminology around ministry in contemporary discussions often seems polarized between opposites such as "minister" or "leader," "pioneer" or "church-based," "professional" or "vocational."[12] Even the language of "training" or "formation" is used inconsistently (we have ministers-in-training who are in formation for ministry, for example). Our congregationalism does not always help us to

11. Jennings, *After Whiteness*, 32.

12. Anthony Clarke's recent *Forming Ministers or Training Leaders?* offers a dialectic approach that tries to navigate this territory holistically.

define what we mean theologically by "minister" or "ordination," although I like Paul Fiddes's exploration in *Tracks and Traces* of authority existing dynamically between pastor and congregation,[13] while Steve Holmes gives a useful survey of concepts of ministry in *Baptist Theology*.[14] There is, however, a term used by Goodliff in *Shaped for Service* that I have found especially helpful because it focuses on the person, not the task, and includes all the forms of ministry that the Baptist Union recognizes. This term is "exemplary disciples."[15]

To explore this idea of exemplary discipleship, let us think about what it is that Jesus calls his followers to be. Perhaps it might help to imagine the scene of the Beatitudes in Matthew 5, where Jesus calls the disciples to him for instruction. This ethical life standard is for those who are serious about the Way. Far more than just a set of holy habits, it is a calling to become more like Jesus, and one way of thinking about what it means to *be a person* is to be formed in the image of *this person*, Jesus. Ministers are, first and foremost, persons: created and contingent beings, called into existence by God and formed in his image.[16] All persons share this status, but a minister of Christ should be constantly attentive to her personhood and its potentially revelatory significance. The expression "exemplary disciples" does not mean that the minister is more holy, more godly, or more biblically learned than others, but rather that she has vowed before God, and before brothers and sisters in Christ, to return willingly and often to Jesus's feet, in spite of personal failing and sin. This is a constant reengagement with human personhood as created, redeemed, and purposeful (meaning that we have a sense of *telos*). The tasks of ministry (Word and sacrament, mission, justice, and love) follow from this frequent recommitment to the rule of Christ. A key aim of ministry is then not to *care for* or to *do for* or to develop and deliver programmes and projects, but to draw others into growth into the *imago Christi*: growing up in Christ is *the* ultimate pastoral goal.[17] The process of growing into the *imago Christi* (both for ministers and others)

---

13. Fiddes, *Tracks and Traces*, 87.

14. Holmes, *Baptist Theology*, 111–18.

15. Goodliff, *Shaped for Service*, 94.

16. *Imago Dei* has many interpretations. See a summary in McCortez's *Theological Anthropology*. For the purposes of this essay, let us think in terms of growing into the image of Christ.

17. Contemporary writers often use "discipleship" in preference to "pastoral care."

is a theological undertaking that is *caught* as much as it is taught, which is significant for our formation processes.

With these observations in mind, I asked a small sample of students in ministry formation two questions about their expectations:

1. Why did you enrol to study at theological college?

2. What key thing do you hope for from your theological education?

The responses fell into two broad categories that were refreshing in their simplicity: first, a practical desire for the essential skills, knowledge, and competencies of ministry/leadership; and secondly, a more reflexive acknowledgement that there is work to be done in learning to love the Lord better and to grow in spirituality. These hopes are primarily about *shaping the person*, which is encouraging for theological educators swimming in the multiple demands of university, church, and culture.

In a recent issue of *Practical Theology*, Graham Stanton comments on the complexity of ministry:

> . . . Christian leadership is complex in that it is characterised by an underlying unpredictability and uncontrollability . . . It is necessary for the practice of Christian leadership to take account of the challenges of living in an everchanging and unpredictable world . . . Churches and training institutions face the difficulty of training and equipping ministry candidates for future challenges that are both unknown and unknowable.[18]

Stanton notes further that taking a complexity approach encourages us to engage with the *dynamics* of a changing organization's (church's) life. The "future challenges . . . unknown and unknowable" to which Stanton refers may be unwelcome, but they are a given. In my pastoral studies teaching, I ask students to think about the fact that they cannot possibly know what will confront them pastorally from day to day, and that we cannot equip them for every *specific* eventuality. What we *can* do is to give them a deep theological understanding of what it is to be a human being in relationship with other human beings, to explore the dynamics of those relationships, and to set them in the context of our ontological contingency before God. Ministry is highly personal in nature. We bring ourselves to the task and we work within our given gifts and aptitudes, so each minister is unique in her approach.[19] We engage with other unique

18. Stanton, "Theology of Complexity for Christian Leadership," 147.

19. ". . . there is a calling to be a minister as the way in which this particular person

persons and so we minister within a complex web of interpersonal relations. Ministry is thus not reducible to skills or competencies but is infinitely variable and unpredictable.

The context of ministry is also fluid. In twenty-first-century Britain, future rapid cultural change seems guaranteed, focused around the continued outworking of the subjective turn,[20] and experienced in ministry as the swing away from "big religion" to "my spirituality" and the decline of institutional church (though not spirituality). Colleges not only have to address this but to implement an overdue shift in recruitment focus and in pedagogy as a result of postcolonial attitudinal changes; to adopt digital and block teaching as a response to student financial and domestic pressures, coronavirus, and environmental considerations; and to manage the impact of straitened economic circumstances on the churches that have historically fed colleges with students and can no longer afford to do so.

A further dimension of complexity for formation is that the breadth of experience of incoming students and the variety of settlement contexts means that expectations of, and pathways through, formation are now often highly individual. This bespoke nature of formation itself raises questions: How can we prepare and compare quality pathways for diverse situations—say, a pioneering community work and a pastor-scholar pulpit ministry—within the same (often small) cohort? Is an academic outcome (currently a diploma for national accreditation) always the best test of ministerial fitness? These questions are indicated in *Ignite* and have also emerged in different forms over the history of Baptist theological education,[21] and they raise questions for colleges about how they are to deliver robust yet flexible pathways for formation against such a diverse range of requirements.

FORMATION CULTURE

In *Reenvisioning Theological Education* (still good to read even though it was published in 1999), Robert Banks quotes Karl Barth's farewell lecture in Basel in March 1962:[22]

---

is called to be a Christian," says Chris Ellis in "Being a Minister," 57.

20. Taylor, *Ethics of Authenticity*, 26.

21. See, for example, the comprehensive survey of Cross, *"To Communicate Simply.*

22. Banks, *Reenvisioning Theological Education,* 215 16; citing Wolff, *Joel and Amos,*

> . . . the real relation of God to theology and theologians must
> be described by a variation of the famous passage in Amos 5:
> "I hate, I despise your lectures and seminars, your sermons,
> addresses and Bible studies, and I take no delight in your dis-
> cussions, meetings and conventions. For when you display your
> hermeneutic, dogmatic, ethical, and pastoral bits of wisdom
> before one another and before me, I have no pleasure in them: I
> disdain these offerings of your fatted calves. Take away from me
> the hue and cry that you old men raise with your thick books
> and you young men with your dissertations! I will not listen to
> the melody of your reviews that you compose in your theologi-
> cal magazines, monthlies, and quarterlies.

The immediate textual context of this quote is important. Barth's concern,
explored also in *Evangelical Theology*, is to remind us that while theology
is important, it is not so for itself—the right and only focus of theological
study is "the one true God and the one true man . . . The object of theology is, in fact, Jesus Christ."[23] Barth anticipates a dialogical metaphor
by describing theology as a *conversation* with scholars past and present, and with other students.[24] This perspective opens up an expansive
landscape for study: creation is the locus of the incarnation, in which
"Agape alone can be the dominant and formative prototype and principle
of theology."[25] This landscape has as its centrepiece a clear and unifying
purpose: Jesus, and the consequent "so what?" of trust in him. I think this
is precisely what the students I have surveyed want from their formation.

Banks's own educational model is *missional*, in which the focus of
education is the transformative kingdom, and in which the agents of
transformation are called to Christ-focused obedience (i.e., exemplary
discipleship). One of the periodic reflections of theological educators
must be to ask: is our focus church or kingdom? And is it the Christian
(or denominational) past, or the eschatological future, that shapes our
education? Goodliff asks, "What might ministry formation look like if it
took this wide theological horizon [of creation, salvation and eschatological culmination] seriously?"[26] In the same vein Joshua Searle suggests:
"Theological education must be concerned not only with the 'life of the

---

267–68. I have not been able to find another source for this lecture by Barth.

23. Barth, *Evangelical Theology*, 202.

24. Barth, *Evangelical Theology*, 172–73.

25. Barth, *Evangelical Theology*, 203.

26. Goodliff, *Shaped for Service*, 57.

mind,' but also with the formation of hopes and passions. Theological formation involves the transfiguration of the imagination in ways that correspond to the Kingdom values of the gospel."[27] One thing is clear: we must prepare those who are called to the ministry and leadership of churches to face a changing and uncertain future with the confidence of our ultimate end in Christ and with an appropriate competence.

Both Banks and Jennings identify something important in their analyses of the seminaries. This is the idea that the college or institution itself imposes a *shape* on the people who enter it. Banks argues that "What people tend to learn most is what the culture of an institution cultivates rather than what teachers teach,"[28] while Jennings challenges: "The question is not what they [students] should know. Too many educational institutions are lost in that question, looking obsessively at the commodities of learning. The question is, what should be the shape of the journey to know? What should be the character of the search?"[29] This seems to me to have the flavour of *metaphor* about it: the college/process is a metaphor for the kind of ministers and churches we help to shape.

Baptists have already partly grasped this question,[30] and we have already noted the purposeful shift in language away from education/ training and towards formation, which includes the shaping of the character as well as the mind. However, the underlying pressures of money and university accreditation still shadow the journey of a minister-in-training. Objectively this means that the world takes charge of the kingdom, through the necessities of survival. Baptists might well be anxious that the state has now "got us" through the demands of higher education. If students are formed under this narrative, what stories do they take into ministries?

THEOLOGY AS CAUGHT

The letter of 2 Timothy is full of warnings about poor doctrine, and these warnings are certainly transferable to today's culture of subjective

27. Searle, *Theology After Christendom*, 169.

28. Banks, *Reenvisioning*, 211.

29. Jennings, *After Whiteness*, 120.

30. Baptist Union, *Ignite Report*, 5, 20.

spirituality.[31] But how do we measure the validity of doctrine? Nigel Wright[32] and Stanley Grenz and Roger Olson[33] identify a "doughnut" model for theological thinking, comprising a non-negotiable centre of "dogma" (orthodox credal principles, etc); a surrounding level of "doctrine" (what we believe about sacramental practice, for example) and a wider outer ring of "opinion." How do we help students to identify the central core and to transmit it wisely in context? For if this were simple to establish, we would have no theological debate, no denominational diversity.

John of the Cross said: "The Father spoke one Word, which was his Son, and this Word he speaks always in eternal silence, and in silence must be heard by the soul."[34] Sound theology must always be referenced to Jesus, and this does not have to take the form of a traditional academic form of learning. Theology can be *caught* as well as taught, and the culture and structure of our institutions cannot therefore be (or be trying to be!) anything other than Jesus-shaped. In the Common Awards framework in which I teach,[35] reflective practice (RP) is compulsory, underpinning contextual learning. In practice, many students struggle with writing academic assignments on RP, yet in group discussions show that they can reflect well—biblically and theologically—on the issues that arise in their churches.[36] This indicates a robust intuitive theology that arises from a spirit and a life that are subordinated to Christ, and which can be developed by exploration with others who take the same journey—this is *caught* theology. Of course, caught theology is always deepened and refined by academic and systematic input, but it is also an outcome of faithful dialogue between fellow disciples in a framework that is shaped by Jesus, and a resource for formation.

I return to Banks's suggestion that "What people tend to learn most is what the culture of an institution cultivates rather than what teachers teach."[37] If he is right, the culture of the theological college is of paramount importance for the subliminal messages it delivers. If a college

31. See, for example, Heelas and Woodhead, *Spiritual Revolution*.

32. Wright, *How to Be a Church Minister*, 36.

33. Grenz and Olson, *Who Needs Theology?*, 73.

34. John of the Cross, *Collected Works*, 92.

35. Common Awards is a partnership between Durham University and the churches to offer awards in theology, ministry, and mission.

36. Collins analyses this problem in *Reordering Theological Reflection*.

37. Banks, *Reenvisioning*, 211.

places its focus on academic excellence and a fantastic library, then its student will at some level absorb the idea that academic excellence and achievement is the measure of ministry. If a college has a rigid and hierarchical culture that demarcates students and staff, then that is the culture students will imbibe. On the other hand, if a college understands students as learning partners, and allows students to see that tutors learn from them as well as teaching them, then that is the culture that students will take into their churches. Barth comments of doctoral recipients, "Only by his [sic] qualification as a learner can he show himself qualified to become a teacher."[38] I would call this kind of formation "dialogue," and dialogical interaction between student and college repositions education and formation.

I like the idea that college offers a liminal space in which students can be transformed. The term "liminal," building on the classical work of van Gennep[39] and Turner, is perhaps over-used today, but strictly means a threshold space ("betwixt and between"). One of the key characteristics of a liminal experience is a permanent transformation of the person who emerges. In the days of residential college it would have been easy to identify Turner's stages: withdrawal from the host culture (preliminal), the liminal time of separation and testing under a guide, and the post-liminal reintegration to society with a changed status (here, this means as an ordained minister).[40] We do not need to engage with a discussion of whether a Baptist understanding of ordination confers ontological change here, since a minister's *social* status (and the theory was originally developed from socio-anthropological data) is clearly changed from that of the student who enters college. However, most ministry education today is conducted very differently. Far fewer students leave their sending setting to come to college, and an increasingly common pattern is for student ministers to emerge from churches they are already leading or to start a pioneer project and then to seek education. Is college still a transformational space?

I think it can be argued that in contemporary Britain the fluid host culture represents the liminal space, and the college, together with other essential stakeholders—mentors, placement churches, and host associations—can function as a composite liminal guide. The classical liminal

38. Barth, *Evangelical Theology*, 172.

39. Gennep, *Rites of Passage*.

40. Turner, *Ritual Process*, ch. 3.

tests and challenges arise from the placement/church experience. Interestingly, this framing of the liminal space and guide raises the obvious question of whether transformation should be expected in the (corporate) liminal guide as well as the students: with a metaphor of dialogue, I think this is unavoidable, but very positive, since it continues the formation process in stakeholders as well as students.

Attendance at college on one or two days per week can no longer deliver this liminal experience *in situ*, and it is unhelpful to think that it can. For this reason I believe that the formational college is right to engage fully with the possibilities of the context to shape and form students for the ministry of God—even if this means relinquishing some control over the student's process, which can only be adequately accomplished through a partnership between student, context, and college, through a process of reflexive spiritual engagement. Dialogue is a very good metaphor for this process.

THEOLOGICAL EDUCATION AS DIALOGUE

Teaching and learning methods in higher education underwent a major change in the late twentieth century with a shift from "objectivist" to "constructivist" learning frameworks.[41] In objectivism, the underlying assumption is that knowledge exists independently of the knower and can be accessed and used independently of any set context. Teachers in this model acquire an expert body of knowledge about something and then pass it on to the learners, who are considered non-experts. On the other hand, constructivism is phenomenological in nature. Knowledge is not thought to have an independent existence but is created by the learning process. Certainly the Common Awards programme favours the constructivist approach and, appropriately for ministerial formation, constructivism is thought to promote deep learning—i.e. learning that is transformational to the person.[42] To be able to address the complexity of contemporary culture and pastoral work, ministers-in-training construct their learning in conversation with tutors, placements, and wider culture. Learning is a dynamic dialogical strategy for the rest of ministry.

---

41. See Biggs, "Enhancing Teaching through Constructive Alignment," 347–49.

42. Though there are criticisms of constructivism—especially that some students struggle to do it. See, for example, Haggis, "Constructing Images of Ourselves."

What does it mean to learn theologically in this way? Theology is frequently described as "talk about God"—but let us interrogate that idea for a moment. Here we see that formational learning really must have constructive elements. Can we ever truly talk *about* God in the way that we might talk *about* engineering? To talk *about* something is arguably to objectivize that something. I can talk *about* my car, or my laptop, and give you information of a certain kind *about* them which is entirely appropriate for objects. However, I will encounter more complexity when I talk to you *about* my friend or my sister. It becomes increasingly difficult to distinguish what Hannah Arendt[43] describes as "what" information from "who" information, when it refers to another person. If I simply give you details of someone's hair and eye colour, then you will feel I have given you nothing much. As soon as I give you more—i.e., some of that person's story—in the form of their relationship to me, their life journeys, their likes and dislikes, even their chosen occupations, then I have given you a great deal: but it is subjective information about another relatable being. The God of our Lord Jesus Christ is revealed as personal in Scripture; furthermore, God is revealed to us as ultimate Being: in which case God as Creator cannot be objectivized by God's creation, since that alternative is not available to us in our contingent status. Thus theology—talking about God—cannot be an objective academic exercise. It is loaded with the possibility of transformative power, although we must give permission for that power to be unleashed in and among us, just as we can choose to be open or indifferent to the call (or invitation to relationship) of another human person.

Alistair McFadyen explores the status of humans as those who are initiated into a primary (and involuntary) dialogue of call and response with God.[44] We exist because God calls us into dialogue with Godself—though God does not compel our affective response. We also exist in dialogue with other human beings who are invited into dialogue with God, although any person is free to refuse to respond to God's creative call. We thus inhabit a network of dialogues that can be empowering (if healthy) or oppressive (if distorted) and which shape our human experience. McFadyen argues that these dialogues shape and constitute not just our experience, but our personhood.[45]

43. Arendt, *Human Condition*, 244.

44. McFadyen, *Call to Personhood*.

45. This is controversial in some quarters: McFadyen has been challenged on the grounds that he confuses personality with personhood, relegates the personhood of

Let us now take this line of argument into theological education for formation. In this process we place ourselves under the potentially transformative influence of "talking about God." For many students this is (and should be) challenging: God may be revealed as less safe, less predictable, than previously imagined, and perceived certainties are traded for profound mystery. This is a key opportunity for educators, who face a choice: to collude with structural certainties or to allow and encourage (with the associated risks) a transformational dialogical space. This dialogue may be "undistorted" (i.e., conducted with mutual sharing, power, and respect) or "distorted" (when ideas and opinions are imposed in some manner through a false understanding of authority). For McFadyen, "monologue" is the domination of one dialogue partner by another and this is not the model of relational harmony for which we are created. Monologue may take various forms: we may drown another out (an overbearing or abusive attitude), we may be unable to hear the other (for example, by our internal bias), or we may simply misunderstand (the distortion of a broken world, the effect of Babel). We are called to none of this, but to seek and develop healthy dialogue, with God and with one another, in our education, our communities, and our interpersonal relationships.

In times of cultural upheaval and of marginalization of faith, when new horizons are constantly emerging, theological colleges can encourage students to deepen a healthy dialogue with Godself and with others, and to be open to the contexts, methods, and languages of such dialogue. This begins by understanding the educational formation process primarily as dialogue between tutors, students, and others. The journey undertaken is a shared one in which, ideally, tutors offer accumulated wisdom and knowledge, and students offer their contemporary experience and passion plus a necessary "second naïveté" of exposure to the task of hearing God's Word. However, both expose themselves to transformation by the other in the shared conversation with and about God.

In practice, what does this mean for theological education? I think it means approaching each teaching and learning moment humbly. Teachers are also learners and students are also teachers, recognizing one another as gift. For educators, it means listening and responding with integrity to student contributions and teaching evaluations. It means that

---

those who struggle with relationship, and elevates relationship (ontologically) above the persons who do the relating. See Harris, "Should We Say that Personhood Is Relational?" However, McFadyen's thesis is very useful pastorally.

the character of the college should be one of shared dialogue and desired transformation, of fellow conversationalists, without presumed hierarchy or status. For all, it means letting go of inappropriate judgements of others, so that everyone in the room has access to the conversation, for God calls whom God wills to the task of ministry. While all must be able to handle the Word well and exercise mature people-related skills within the body of Christ, academic prowess is not the sole measure of God's call. Recently I talked to two students who have dyslexia. Both are gifted student ministers and are clearly called by God. Both bring workplace skills and personal maturity into ministry. Both struggle with the requirements of a university diploma and ask why there is such an emphasis on formal academic work when there are other ways to acquire and assess the skills of ministry.

To use dialogue as a metaphor for formation also means to pay attention to the location of the conversation. If I go to France and speak only English, my experience and engagement will be diminished. To open myself to a new language and to new cultural influences will allow me to begin to absorb Frenchness until, eventually, I can inhabit both English and French cultures with ease—and transform my engagement with each.

I think we may identify two primary locations for the formational dialogue. First, we have already discussed the shift away from full-time residential education for formation towards placement-based or contextual and reflective models. Contextual students learn by doing the work of ministry and have the opportunity at college to be both reflective and reflexive. If this process is conducted prayerfully and respectfully on both sides, it is a highly fruitful example of mature dialogical practice, helping students to deepen their biblical and theological perspective, but it also brings the church's missional challenge directly into the dialogical classroom, so the classroom is open to transformation by engagement with culture. The second cultural location that shapes the dialogue is that of the college itself, remembering Banks's claim that students learn more from the culture of the college than from the teachers—the *caught* element of theology.

To consider dialogue as a metaphor for theological education as formation delivers another helpful perspective: that of process. To embrace one's personhood, to grow into exemplary discipleship, means to relinquish the anxiety of having to define what it is to achieve or to arrive, or to complete and finish a process of training that equips one for a professional role. Personhood is always about becoming, about continuing the journey deeper into Christ, until we are called fully into his presence. A minister embraces this journey explicitly and that is what sets her apart at ordination. The vows taken are to pursue that lifelong journey, and to repent of wrong turnings by making oneself accountable to others in the body of Christ: to continue in the habit of Christian dialogue that has been caught at college.

Finally, dialogue embraces a powerlessness appropriate to ministry, which could address the institutional power dynamics identified by Jennings in *After Whiteness*. In the many descriptions of leadership within the New Testament church there is a constant: the power of leadership is never power *over* and is never oppressive.[46] It is power *with*—an integrative power[47] that gives agency to the other within the parameters of the body of Christ.[48] This is the power of "undistorted" dialogue, in the terminology of McFadyen.

A college that can facilitate holy dialogue between tutors and students is a college where *all*, tutors and students, are formed in exemplary discipleship, because the culture is *caught* as well as taught. Students are neither infantilised nor idolised but are valued dialogue partners in the mutual development of discipleship. Their views are heard and weighed; their experience is valued and used; the rule of Christ is proclaimed over all.

46. Evans, "Powerless Leader," 91.

47. May, *Power and Innocence*, 109.

48. The ideal of the Baptist church meeting.

11

Ministry and Ecumenism

Ruth Bottoms

BY WAY OF INTRODUCTION

My own story in ministry is simultaneously a story of ecumenical involvement, engagement, and enrichment. It is also a story in which my and Paul Goodliff's ministries have overlapped and interrelated. He was the Area Superintendent, then Regional Minister Team Leader when I was in local pastorate in the Central Association. We have been colleagues in the Baptist Union of Great Britain whilst I chaired the Council and then Trustee Board and whilst he was head of the Ministry Department. We have swapped stories about our respective involvement as delegates to various committees of the World Council of Churches and in particular shared news of people we have both known in those settings. Then, in 2018, as Convenor of the Directors/Trustees of Churches Together in England, I steered the CTE Board through the appointment processes for a new General Secretary. Ultimately it was my privilege to ring Paul and offer him the post, and serve as line manager to him through his probationary period until my term of service finished.

Paul will have his own story to tell of what this overtly ecumenical role has meant for him personally, building as it did on his long ecumenical engagement throughout his ministry. All my ecumenical experience has moulded me in ways that I continue to discover. In this chapter I shall share a story from my ministry in an ecumenical context that I continue to return to since it continues to inspire me.

There are reasons for using a story. Both ministry and ecumenism are related to theology and spirituality. Story allows all of these to be partners in a conversation. Writing of the disciplines of theology and spirituality, Sheldrake argues that "the deeply experiential character of much late-twentieth century theology . . . is a remarkable shift given the centuries of abstract theological method."[1] He goes on to say that such a conversation is vital as it enables both theology to acknowledge that it is rooted in human experience and spirituality to establish itself as an area of academic study that, whilst not wholly theological, is yet interrelated with it. Thus the use of a story helps us gain an understanding of the lived experience of the reality of ministering in a particular ecumenical context. Beyond the documents and texts of ecumenical discourse, beyond any particular theology of ministry, is the practical outworking in a specific setting with particular personalities. Having recounted the story from my experience, I shall use it to reflect on the interplay between ministry and ecumenism.

A STORY

As I sought a move from my first pastorates, two rural village churches in Northamptonshire, I expressed an interest in moving to a Local Ecumenical Partnership (LEP). I wanted to see if what I met, talked about, and experienced at the international level on committees of the World Council of Churches could be embodied in the local in any meaningful way. In 1994 I was called to be the minister of Wendover Free Church,[2] a single congregation Baptist/URC LEP that shares premises with the Roman Catholic congregation, which were both also in covenant with the local Anglicans. We did a lot together in the village by way of shared worship, witness, and service.

Each Good Friday[3] you would find me, together with the vicar, the Roman Catholic priest, and three representative lay people from

1. Sheldrake, *Spirituality and Theology*, 95.

2. I was the Minister of Wendover Free Church from 1994 to 2004. Paul Goodliff has visited the shared premises in Wendover at times and reflects on this in "Annunciation," 128.

3. Since leaving Wendover, the various Holy Week liturgies have morphed and changed.

the congregations flat on the floor before an eight-foot rough wooden cross draped in purple cloth. There we would stay for two minutes, the ecumenical congregation standing silent, as we acknowledged again our total dependence upon the Christ of the cross for the salvation of the world. For me it became a profound part of my Good Friday observances.

We had our differences of course. Our monthly clergy lunches were about developing relationships between us. We tried to leave the majority of the discussions of practicalities about forthcoming events and joint initiatives to the Churches Together meetings. The clergy lunches became a place where we could share and also where we could debate: we had some challenging conversations.

For me sometimes, on days other than Good Friday, it was important to remember that corporate act of prostration. It was important to take myself back to that place in my prayer as I found myself frustrated by something or other for which we were struggling to agree on a way forward or to understand the other's point of view. Sometimes too I would take other sisters and brothers in Christ (including Baptists!) to that place in my mind's eye, needing to be metaphorically flat on the floor before the cross of Christ with them.

A MATTER OF DISAGREEMENT

In sharing the story of the Wendover Good Friday liturgy, I always feel the start sounds like the beginning of a joke: "Three people, a vicar, a priest and a minister, went into a church . . ." But of course, behind the different designations lie seriously different theologies about the nature of ministry, ordination, and oversight and the church. In our initial discussions about this symbolic act the Roman Catholic priest said it would be the clergy who prostrated themselves. It was me who suggested we needed to be joined by representative laity as well, and so we agreed there would be six of us on the floor.

Ecumenism is not about agreeing with one another in everything. We may seek to find areas of convergence, common ground, some things we can agree on, but the history of the church is one of disagreement. The weighty WCC report *Baptism, Eucharist and Ministry*, and its attendant volumes of responses from the churches, are testimony to just how much and how deeply we disagree with one another over some fairly fundamental issues. And that is before we start on any other matters around sexuality, colonialization and empire, missionary endeavours, abortion, divorce, birth control, and so on and so on. And it is not as though everyone within any one denomination would necessarily agree with one another either!

Sometimes our different understandings gave offence to one another. The act of prostration was followed by a further half hour of liturgy, which often included a short drama newly written each year by those of us in the Free Church. One time this took the form of several soliloquies of biblical characters talking about watching at the foot of the cross. I don't recall it in full: there was the soldier who was mostly concerned about whether he would win the cloak on the throw of the dice, but Mary the mother of Jesus also spoke. She talked of how Jesus, her eldest son, had always been different from his siblings. It was only weeks later, as we reviewed Lent, Holy Week, and Easter together, that I learnt this had offended our Roman Catholic friends. I had not understood until then that the idea of the Virgin Mary was that she was ever virginal and had no more children after Jesus and that biblical verses about his brothers and sisters were to be understood as extended family—cousins and the like. My Catholic colleague had been taken aback at the time, and had also faced questions from some of his parishioners about this. We all learnt.

My memory is that there was no stipulation that in the future the text of any drama we wrote should be passed by all the clergy first to check that we were all happy with it. That would have felt restrictive. Rather there was an acceptance that in seeking to do together what we could, we would at times inadvertently get it wrong and perhaps offend one another. But if we waited until we all agreed or were over-anxious about giving offence, then we would be the poorer for it.

There are those who seem to fear guilt by association, or that working together results in a watering down to some lowest common denominator, or that truth becomes subservient to unity.[4] The Wendover experience was one of learning together with generous hearts, growing in understanding of both what united us and what divided us.

---

4. Andy Goodliff charts the history of the Baptist Union of Great Britain's involvement in and debates about the Inter-Church Process, membership of Churches Together in England, and Churches Together in Britain and Ireland in *Renewing a Modern Denomination*, 135–56.

A MATTER OF HUMILITY

We used to rehearse our synchronized prostration for Good Friday! There is an art to it: you go down first on one knee, then the other, lean forwards with both arms to touch the floor, and walk your hands forward until your nose is on the carpet, stretching out your legs behind. Then reverse the process to get to your feet again. Though this may have made the action look more dignified and less messy, in the end there is not much that is dignified about being facedown on the carpet in front of a crowd!

But then, there was not anything dignified about a person hanging naked on a cross, dying by crucifixion. And we are exhorted in the Letter to the Philippians:

> Let the same mind be in you that was in Christ Jesus,
> who, though he was in the form of God,
> did not regard equality with God
> as something to be exploited,
> but emptied himself,
> taking the form of a slave,
> being born in human form,
> he humbled himself
> and became obedient to the
> point of death—even death on a cross. (2:5–8)

For me, the action of being prostrate with ecumenical colleagues was always a great leveller—literally and metaphorically. We all belonged there—all equally sinners, all equally beloved of God so that he gave his own Son, who endured the cross for each and every one of us. This is why when we faced challenges in our working and sharing together and I was frustrated over one thing or another, this was a place to return to in my prayer. Here all challenges are relativized. Humanity in need of God.

Now, I like to think I am Baptist by conviction! I have looked at our history, reflected on Scripture, explored our Baptist theology, been trained and formed at a Baptist college, and come to my own mind and nailed my colours to the Baptist ministry mast. But that does not mean I think that the Baptists, or more specifically, the Baptists of the Baptist Union of Great Britain, have got it all right, or even somehow have a fuller truth. And, let's face it, the Baptist tradition is not the oldest one around. We grew out of traditions that preceded us as our forebears came to new understandings in their context. I have sometimes used an activity in all-ages worship where we create a family tree of the Christian church, with people holding up cards to represent the different Christian traditions from Jesus and the first apostles through to today's mix. Like any family tree, it gets increasingly complicated with its break-ups and then its reunions, such as the formation of the United Reformed Church in 1972. The most common reactions to this activity are surprise at the sheer diversity of the Christian church and surprise at finding out whom their ancestors include.

Flat on the floor before the cross takes all of us back to the beginnings of the church of which Jesus Christ is the head. The two-thousand-year span of the history of the church between that event and today is a warning for all of us to not to elevate our own understandings.

In the twenty-first century "receptive ecumenism" has been developing as a concept. It is based on the idea of receiving Christ in the other. The Churches Together in England website says: "Receptive Ecumenism is both a way of thinking and a process that enables unity to be built up by receiving gifts from others. It challenges us to not think of what others might benefit from receiving from us, but instead invites us to recognize our needs and to put ourselves in the place of being a recipient."[5] The website further expresses the hope that such an approach would draw us closer together as a family in Christ, while also deepening our own respective identities.[6]

For me, our act of corporate prostration put us all in the position of being first and foremost recipients of the grace of God. From this place it becomes possible to humbly open ourselves and to be opened by the Spirit to receive Christ in and through the other.

A MATTER OF SPIRITUALITY

As a recipient, open to the other, I encounter God in spiritual practices that might once have seemed alien to me. In an article entitled "Baptists and Ecumenism Today," Paul Goodliff comments that "Spiritual Practices were once tightly policed by church traditions—evangelicals practised the quiet time, Catholics prayed the rosary and Orthodox the Jesus Prayer, and there was precious little overlap."[7] Having enumerated how

5. https://cte.org.uk/about/ecumenism-explained/receptive-ecumenism/.

6. For one Baptist response to receptive ecumenism, see Fiddes, "Learning from Others."

7. Goodliff, "Baptists and Ecumenism Today," 21.

spiritual practices are now much more widely shared, Paul comments, "And yes, it seems people from all shades of spirituality light candles these days, both in private prayers and in public worship."[8]

We could also add that Christians sing music from across many traditions too, with no concern for the denomination of the writer. So in the Wendover Good Friday liturgy the music of the day might include traditional hymns from various traditions, more modern worship songs, a Taizé chant, a more classical anthem by the Anglican choi,r and perhaps an Iona Community Wild Goose Worship Group song.

The reality is that many of us are sustained in our walk with God by a variety of traditions that have crossed denominational boundaries. Our Baptist colleges have regular quiet days, many ministers includes a pattern of regular retreat in their year, and spiritual direction is one of the suggested ways that ministers might sustain a habit of accountability in their continuing ministerial development.

In his work exploring the theology and spirituality of worship in Free Church traditions, Chris Ellis concludes by suggesting that Free Church worship might be an "ecumenical gift," presenting the convictions behind it as a model to be put alongside other models.[9] He calls it a "*discipleship* model of liturgical theology," to be put alongside the models of institutional, sacramental, and proclamational identified by James Empereur.[10] Ellis comments that "As different views of the same reality, they complement and enhance one another, while reminding us that they are views of the reality of worship and not the reality itself."[11]

The God we worship in spirit and in truth is far bigger than we can grasp or understand and our encounter with God is not constrained by human constructs. The joy of worshipping ecumenically, whether that be by joining in as a guest in another tradition or by sharing as we did in Wendover in an act of worship that has carefully blended different traditions together, is that our vision of God is enlarged.

For such a blending to have integrity and not simply be a hotch-potch of ideas required curiosity on everyone's part. Why was this action important to that tradition? What meaning lies behind it? What

8. Goodliff, "Baptists and Ecumenism Today," 21. See Goodliff, "Everyone Lights a Candle," for an extended exploration of ecumenical spirituality.

9. Ellis, *Gathering*, 255.

10. Ellis, *Gathering*, 255; referencing Empereur, "Models of Liturgical Theology," 263–66.

11. Ellis, *Gathering*, 255.

is the truth that we are trying to be conveyed? Deepened understanding enabled deepened appreciation, and allowed for meaningful participation and encounter with God in new ways, and growth in grace.

Having never prostrated myself before anything before, I am fascinated that over time this act of prostration publicly has become a regular place to go to in my personal prayer. I take with me in my imagination the sister or brother in Christ who for one reason or another at this moment is frustrating me! I might still return to robust debates with those people on whatever the matter is, but I would do so with a greater sense of the fellowship that already exists between us in the body of Christ.

A MATTER OF COMMUNICATION

An openness to receive implies that there will be sharing, listening, and talking. And there is always the possibility of miscommunication and misunderstanding. The first year we shared in this Good Friday liturgy, one of the members of the Free Church asked me to visit her later. She had been deeply disturbed by the act of prostration; for her it was idolatrous, worshipping the cross instead of God. I tried to explain that I saw it as a symbolic action.

In fact the joint prostration before the cross was only one of several symbolic acts in our shared Good Friday liturgy. Once we were all on our feet again, the cross would be unveiled from beneath the purple cloth with the declaration "Behold the wood of the cross." Purple, the colour of kings, and this cross would bear the King of the Jews. Purple, the liturgical colour of penitence and mourning. After hymns, readings, a short drama, and prayers, the wooden cross would then be shouldered by a number of the congregation, and we would all follow out in procession along the street to the "Manor Waste" (Wendover's term for a market square). En route, different people from all three congregations would take over the bearing of the cross. The procession symbolized that the condemned were forced to carry their own crosses to the place of execution. The pause for further hymns, readings, and prayers on the Manor Waste reminded us that our faith is that this act in history has consequences in every area of life today. The procession would then move on, finally arriving at St Mary's Anglican Church, where the cross was laid on the chancel step. As part of the liturgy that now took place, people were invited to come and venerate the cross by touching or kissing it. Here the invitation was to deep awe and wonder that God in Jesus would accept the cross. A final act with the cross was to the accompaniment of the hymn with the chorus:

> Lift high the cross the love of Christ proclaim.
> till all the world adore his sacred name![12]

Groups of six to eight people would come forward and together, holding its foot, head, and arms, literally lift high the cross. It might be a family or two doing this together. It might be a mix of people from all our congregations. Young and old, lifting it only as high as the smallest child or the person in the wheelchair. But lifting it together and acknowledging the mystery that somehow this instrument of torture was yet a sign of the salvation of the world. "I when I am lifted up from the world shall draw all people unto me" (John 12:32). Tears always pricked my eyes as I witnessed the cross born aloft time and time again.

With the exception of the person who had expressed her concerns about the act of prostration, members of the Free Church congregation participated happily in all the symbolic actions, although noticeably less came forward to touch or kiss the cross in veneration. After that first year, I used to write something each year about the symbolic meaning behind the actions for our shared Churches Together monthly magazine. Interestingly, I was often thanked by Anglicans and Catholic members for this article.

For me this all illustrates the importance of working at communication across our different church traditions. We need to be willing to explain why we do things. Our traditions have not come from nowhere, and often explaining ourselves to others renews the meaning for ourselves. The others may still disagree with us and choose not to participate, but understanding is deepened and the other's spirituality is respected, and our unity and fellowship deepened. Again, this is receptive ecumenism in action.

A MATTER OF WITNESS TO THE WORLD

Soon after I moved to Wendover, before my diary had become filled with churchy things, I attended a meeting of the village council. They

---

12. G. W. Kitchin and M. R. Newbolt, "Lift High the Cross," no. 575 in *Baptist Praise and Worship*.

were public meetings, though in the main people went when there was a particular item on the agenda that interested them. I was interested to see who were the elected councillors in the village and what sort of dynamics existed between them. At that time I was too recently arrived to be known as a community figure in the village. I can't remember what the topic under discussion was, but suddenly within the course of the debate someone said it would be a good idea to involve the churches. A councillor then pondered whom it would be best to approach. I was somewhat stunned when one of his colleagues responded with words to the effect that it didn't matter whom they approached as they would get all three churches anyway! Clearly the reputation of the three churches in the village was that they worked together. I don't think that public reputation has existed so strongly anywhere else I have ministered. But it was a significant witness in Wendover. Despite our differences, we could and did work together for the common good in the community and that was known.

The Wendover Good Friday liturgy, with its procession between church buildings and its pausing to pray on the Manor Waste, was overtly an act of witness to the people who were passing by. In that sense it was no different from many other open-air acts of witness that take place on Good Friday. What it seems to me the councillor was observing, though, was not just the result of occasional times when the churches worked together. It was known that this was in the very way of being in the churches of the village.

This found its expression in various ways: providing regular visits to the residential and nursing homes between us but without unnecessary duplication, shared communication in the monthly village newsletter, shared leadership of a course for people wanting to explore the Christian faith, combined support at Christmas for the local women's refuge, and so much more.

The debate about the relationship between unity and mission is long and continuing. The World Council of Churches brought together and continues to hold both the Faith and Order Commission and the Commission on Mission and Evangelism.

Jesus's prayer for the believers who were to come after the disciples in John 17:20–21 is that they "may all be one . . . so that the world may believe." Here unity and mission are intrinsically linked. Or, as the presidents of Churches Together in England (CTE) put it in their preface to the Theos report entitled *That They All May Be One*:

> Unity is not optional. It is built into the very heart of being Christian, for in Christ we become citizens of his kingdom, members together of his body, bound together with all our brothers and sisters across the world. "... [Y]ou are," Peter said, "a chosen race, a royal priesthood, a holy nation, God's own people, in order that you may proclaim the mighty acts of him who called you out of darkness into his marvellous light ..." (1 Pet 2:9). Mission and unity are therefore inseparable.[13]

The CTE board had commissioned the Theos report of 2017 as it recognized that the ecumenical landscape had altered considerably since its inception in 1990. Then it was comprised of sixteen member churches; by 2017 it was forty-four.[14] Many of the historic churches were in decline and churches were facing economic pressures and changing the priorities of what they funded. But new member churches were coming, variously linked to patterns of migration and new forms of spirituality and discipleship. It seemed the right moment to take stock and ask what sort of ecumenical instrument the churches wanted CTE to be. In the Executive Summary of the report, CTE's strengths as identified by its members include local engagement in mission:

> Indeed, this research shows that today ecumenism is most vibrant at the local level. Local churches cross denominational boundaries and work together on different aspects of mission, most notably social action.[15]

For me our walk of witness on Good Friday had integrity. This was not just an annual event when the churches came together but reflected and grew out of a commitment to be salt and light in the village.

BY WAY OF CONCLUSION

In drawing these reflections to some sort of conclusion, I want to look specifically at the significance of an ordained minister being committed to ecumenism. I am aware that ministry per se is not only exercized by people who are ordained. I am aware that the story and reflections above, whilst told from the perspective of myself as an ordained minister, could

---

13. Mladin, *That They All May Be One*, 7.

14. As of the beginning of 2022 there are fifty-two member churches.

15. Mladin, *That They All May Be One*, 8.

be replicated in large part by the congregation members who shared in the Good Friday liturgy.

Paul Goodliff, in writing in "Contemporary Models of Translocal Ministry: Ecumenical Landscapes,"[16] identifies the following four possible responses to ecumenism:

1. Resistance

2. Indifference

3. Affirmation with Distance

4. Enthusiasm

It will be clear from what I have written above that I come in the enthusiasts's camp, for whom Goodliff writes ecumenism is "an unavoidable corollary of the gospel, Scripture and dogmatic theology."[17] Though I am not sure that I think "enthusiast" is the best word. There have been too many ecumenical meetings that I have sat in that have felt as though they have become mired in treacle. I can be as frustrated as anyone else with what can feel like cumbersome structure and a focus on the minutiae. "Essentialist" would be for me a better word, picking up Goodliff's "unavoidable."

Early on in my ministry, Revd Dr Michael Taylor, then Director of Christian Aid, came to speak at the Central Area Baptist ministers' annual conference. I have forgotten what the title of his address was, and do not have the direct quote, but he said something to the effect that the task of ministry is to offer to the people of God in a particular place something of the understanding of God from the whole people of God. As a fledgling minister, but already being asked to represent Baptists in the World Council of Churches, it was a light bulb moment. I had understood that in my ordination I was being set apart by the Baptist church to be a minister of the gospel in the universal church. Yes, that ministry would find its locus in the specifics of the Baptist Union of Great Britain, but this was all but one small part of the whole.

Reflecting on the 1982 Lima document of the World Council of Churches, *Baptism, Eucharist and Ministry*, Roger Standing notes that it identified episcopal ministry as "personal, collegial and communal"[18]

---

16. Goodliff, "Contemporary Models of Translocal Ministry."

17. Goodliff, "Contemporary Models of Translocal Ministry," 48.

18. Standing, "Theological Issues," 29.

and further argued that all ordained ministry should be exercized in a personal, collegial, and communal manner:

> Personal, because the presence of Christ is most effectively mediated by the ordained person as an identified and representative figure; collegial because of the common shared task of representing the concerns of a community; and communal because it is rooted in the share life of a community under the guidance of the Spirit.[19]

Whatever one's theology of ordination (and there are a few with the Baptist family let alone beyond it), to be an ordained minister identifies one on the ground as a public, representative figure. Thus the signals one sends overtly and implicitly about how one views other Christian traditions is significant.

In a local setting, we are not going to resolve centuries of church history of division and debate. But how do we speak of one another? Do we seek to understand one another's theology and explain it, even whilst not agreeing with it, or do we just rubbish it? What example do we set in handling difference and disagreements between us? Are we willing to humbly receive from other traditions even as we offer our own tradition? Will we seek the God who is beyond our human constructs and worship in Spirit and in truth? Do we work at the communication between us, deepening understanding and relationships? And does all this offer a witness to a broken and hurting world and share hope of new possibilities?

Most of us are familiar with the reality on the ground that when people change, and new people come, other things change. It happens in work, in school, in politics. My ten years in Wendover saw two changes in both the Roman Catholic priest and the Anglican vicar. Each brought their own gifts and insights as well as past experiences, good and bad, of working ecumenically. The pattern of being ecumenical shifted and changed in turn both due to these personnel changes but also to responding to changes in the community around us.

I have since moved on from Wendover but I remain deeply ecumenical as an essential part of ministry. Paul Goodliff is retiring from his role as General Secretary of Churches Together in England and will have his own stories to tell as to why ministry and ecumenism belong together as we seek to be faithful disciples of Jesus Christ.

19. Standing, "Theological Issues," 29.

12

MINISTRY AND RESTORATIVE JUSTICE

Myra N. Blyth

I FIRST REMEMBER MEETING Paul Goodliff during my time as Deputy General Secretary of the Baptist Union of Great Britain (1999–2004). He was then a regional minister who distinguished himself on many levels but particularly, I recall, because for his attention to detail; in dress, he shunned the woolly jumpers favoured by many Baptists, in preference for meticulously coordinated ties, shirts, and suits; but also in worship. Whilst being a card-carrying charismatic, Paul demonstrated a thoughtful approach to the crafting of liturgy and sermons, which was not exactly the norm amongst his peers. His appointment to the position of General Secretary of Churches Together in England (CTE) was a fulsome recognition from across the national landscape that Paul is person who knows how to bring together and bridge, in his own person and ministry, diverse spiritual traditions and practices. He has, over several decades, been influenced and shaped both by the charismatic movement and by ecumenical spirituality, whilst maintaining throughout a keen sense of Baptist identity and ecclesiology. At every stage, Paul has been a reconciler, nurturing unity (as opposed to uniformity) and navigating difficult, often contentious discussions in a gracious and authentic way. This track record marks him out as a leader in Baptist life and in the wider ecumenical movement.

Paul has been a man of dialogue at the head of an ecumenical body, which exists to make it happen. It is the primary task of ecumenical organisations such as CTE to facilitate dialogue and deep listening on church-dividing issues. Prominent matters in recent decades have included the role of the churches combating apartheid in the 1970s and recognition of women in the 1980s and 90s. Most recently, issues of gender and sexuality have become increasingly prominent, and CTE has experienced its own storm. In 2021 the organisation's national gathering was meant to be the occasion when four new presidents were welcomed into their role; in CTE forty-nine members[1] are represented by six presidents, each one present on behalf of a different ecclesial family. On this occasion, the nominated person from the fourth presidency group was absent because the enabling body had voted, by a substantial majority, to request that "for the sake of ecumenical unity at present, the Fourth Presidency group show restraint by not exercising the office of their presidential appointment."[2] Put bluntly, the nomination of a woman, Hannah Brock Womack, was blocked on grounds of sexuality and specifically because she had entered into a same-sex marriage. While Brock Womack is still officially the fourth president of CTE, she is not able to take her place alongside the others.

Recounting this episode enables me to highlight Paul's gifts as a bridge-builder and prophetic reconciler; first, in seeing the need for dialogue. In his address to the assembled gathering, Paul drew attention to the vacant chair as a painful symbolic reminder of the urgent need for dialogue between the churches and the LGBT+ community. His remarks reminded me of another occasion, some years prior to this, when the former Archbishop of Canterbury, Rowan Williams, addressed an audience at the World Council of Churches, and opined that the question every ecumenical gathering must ask is: who is not yet at the table?[3] They have also prompted me to reflect further upon the aims and dynamics of ecumenism when the churches, some present and some absent, are confronted by apparently intractable obstacles to unity. In this chapter, in honour of Paul, I would like to present some thoughts on the latter, with

1. The membership has recently grown to fifty-two different church groupings, with the latest edition being the Vineyard Network.

2. https://cte.org.uk/churches-together-in-england-statement-on-the-fourth-presidency.

3. https://www.oikoumene.org/news/unity-is-gods-gift-to-the-church-says-archbishop-of-canterbury.

reference to debates concerning gender and sexuality. Recent events at CTE provide the backdrop to this reflection, but my purpose will not be to dwell upon the case. Instead, from the vantage point of my own academic interest in the principles and practices of restorative justice, I would like to encourage those with an interest in ecumenical progress—not only the professionals, but also ordinary believers—to cultivate a restorative culture and approach to their interactions.[4] In particular, this means embracing three principles which, I have argued persistently over the last decade, may be described as the pillars of restorative justice theory: (i) radical participation, (ii) moral seriousness, and (iii) reintegration.

Ecumenical discussions on the highly charged and contentious issues of gender and sexuality may find in these principles a roadmap towards genuinely constructive encounter. As a way of approaching ecumenical dialogue, in general—not to mention evaluating this or that dialogue, in particular—these principles hold together the ambition for engagement (*participation*) whilst also being respectful of difference (*seriousness*). They also imply an ambition for bringing back together or healing wounds (*reintegration*). In making this recommendation to those entering the debate on gender and sexuality, my overriding aim is, reflecting Paul's own example, to *encourage* dialogue. Yet, I am also genuinely confident in the model being proposed as a means of making progress together, since it has been shown to work elsewhere; namely, in a recent dialogue between the Vatican and the Baptist World Alliance concerning the historically divisive topic of Mariology, the identity and mission of Mary, the Mother of God. The latter resulted in a ground-breaking report, *The Word of God in the Life of the Church*,[5] which I have analysed for a forthcoming volume. In preparation for some closer application of the principles of restorative justice to the debate on gender and sexuality (part two of the present chapter), I would like to share some of my reflection on the Marian section of *The Word of God in the Life of the Church*. I am grateful to the coeditors of the volume in which this essay will appear in 2022, Ross Maidment and Matthew Mills, for permission to reproduce a selection from an early version as a case study here.[6]

---

4. For my work in this area, see Blyth, "Towards a Restorative Hermeneutic"; "Re-Imagining Restorative Justice"; and, with M. J. Mills and M. H. Taylor, *Forgiveness and Restorative Justice*.

5. See *Word of God in the Life of the Church*. For an overview of the whole report, see Blyth, "*Word of God in the Life of the Church*," a review article.

6. See Maidment and Mills, *Keeper of the Word*.

MARY: A CASE STUDY IN RESTORATIVE DIALOGUE
AND MUTUAL LEARNING

I consider the Baptist-Catholic conversations resulting in *The Word of God in the Life of the Church* to be an excellent example of restorative dialogue. Without intentionally doing so, they demonstrate the virtue of restorative principles. First, they demonstrate radical inclusion, because participants, representing communities that have been estranged for centuries, have embarked upon a journey together which is transforming relationships, turning one-time enemies into friends. Second, the conversations are morally serious because differences are not relativized or brushed under the carpet but acknowledged and respected despite a radical shift in tone and behaviour between the two communions. Violent and vitriolic rhetoric of the past has given way to listening and respectful conversation; monologue has been replaced by dialogue, and dogmatic statements by practical theology. Third, the goal of unity still lies in the future, but as hearts and minds are opened, perspectives challenged, and misunderstandings corrected, the path to reconciliation and unity is in the making. *The Word of God in the Life of the Church*, including in its reflections concerning Mary, leads me to propose that intentionally embedding restorative principles and practices into ecumenical dialogues may provide a vital clue for revitalising and reframing future conversations.

The Word of God in the Life of the Church is especially noteworthy because its drafters have attempted to present a methodology of "differentiated consensus." This is represented visually in the text itself by including in bold type what the partners could affirm together, whilst leaving space (light type) for elaboration or points of differentiation. Normally, dialogue reports adopt a different approach, speaking first about what divides and then moving on to points of agreement. According to Paul Fiddes (Baptist co-chair), this distinction is more than a question of style or semantics; it was an intentional way of speaking together (boldly) in the strongest possible way: "these bold statements manifest an excitement and an enthusiasm about having discovered what can be truly said together . . . the bold statements carry the resonances of a confession, jointly made, arising from common prayer, and gladly professed."[7] The part of the report dedicated to Mary (section 5) illustrates well-differentiated consensus in action. Together, in bold, the partners affirm that

7. Fiddes, "Conversation in Context," 8.

Mary is a representative figure—her faithfulness represents the faithfulness of the church—before going into light type to respectfully elaborate upon the view of Catholics that Mary is also the mother of the church.[8] The point to stress here is that the intention in the report is to affirm agreements in the strongest possible way. The result has been to achieve unprecedented consensus between Baptists and Catholics, which would have been inconceivable just fifty years ago.

First and foremost, the report begins with a common affirmation of the centrality of Scripture and the importance of its testimony: "Beliefs about Mary should be rooted in Scripture, warranted by Scripture, and not contradicted by Scripture."[9] This affirmation echoes *Dei Verbum*, the Second Vatican Council's "Dogmatic Constitution on Divine Revelation," where a renewed focus was given to the importance of Scripture in modern Catholicism.[10] It is a fitting starting point for these conversation partners, in order to establish the trust necessary to listen well. What emerges, however, is not only a common affirmation about the importance of Scripture but also a heightened appreciation for the differentiated ways in which each side engages and crucially finds scriptural warrant for what it says and believes concerning Mary.

The figurative or typological approach to biblical interpretation which has played a historic role in Catholicism resonates with Baptists, and indeed with evangelicals more generally, but views amongst Baptists are typically diverse. The most popular and conservative viewpoint regards only explicit "predictions" as scriptural, whilst others acknowledge more indirect allusions foreshadowing Christ; in turn, many are more cautious in this regard when it comes to Mary. For its part, *The Word of God in the Life of the Church* locates Mary among the holy women who kept alive the hope of Israel's salvation, and with reference to a number of Old Testament and Gospel texts the dialogue participants affirm together that there is scriptural warrant here for Mary to be called "Daughter of Israel": "she is the mother of the one called the Son of David and . . . she welcomes the Saviour with joy and he takes up his dwelling within her. [See Zeph 3:14–17; Joel 2:21–27; Zech 2:15, 9:9–10; Luke 1:28–33; Luke 3:31.]"[11] Whilst Baptist delegates stop short

8. See *Word of God in the Life of the Church*, 154–55.

9. *Word of God in the Life of the Church*, 133.

10. See *Dei Verbum* (1965) at https://www.vatican.va/archive/hist_councils/ii_vatican_council/documents/vat-ii_const_19651118_dei-verbum_en.html.

11. *Word of God in the Life of the Church*, 135.

of finding specific types or foreshadowing, there is also joint affirmation of a number of Old Testament passages which "may be interpreted as referring to Mary" (e.g., Isa 7:14; Gen 3:15).[12]

It was also significant and pleasing for the Baptist-Catholic dialogue to reach agreement concerning Mary's status as "Mother of God": "Mary is properly named the *Theotokos* or "God-bearer." The term indicates that she is the mother of the eternal Son of God according to his humanity."[13] Despite its patristic roots, the title *Theotokos* remains quite shocking to many Protestants and has been resisted by most Baptists till now, not because it does not express a profound truth or because it lacks scriptural warrant, but because it has been perceived as risking deifying Mary and elevating her above Christ. On this occasion, however, a combination of doctrinal and biblical considerations led to a ground-breaking decision. The significance of this deserves some reflection because, as Timothy Perry has argued, the title *Theotokos* is key to the formulation of an evangelical Mariology: "Mariology naturally arises out of Christology. What the church confesses about Mary stems from and is intended to clarify what it believes about Christ. And the point at which Mariology and Christology intersect is the confession of *Mary* as *Theotokos*, Mother of God."[14]

On the other hand, if titles like "Mother of God" challenged and enriched Baptist thinking in these dialogues, the same might be said to be true for the Catholic delegation when it came to the discussion of Mary as a model disciple.[15] The challenge in a tradition that appears to honour Mary most was to look again at the biblical testimony regarding Mary's humanity and to appreciate afresh the way Baptists and evangelicals generally may celebrate Mary for more than her humble obedience. The need to acknowledge Mary's humanity more fully is increasingly high-lighted in modern scholarship; for example, Luke's account weaves an intriguing and complex account of Mary which is not so much subservient as subversive. Through the annunciation and birth stories and in Mary's song, *Magnificat*, Luke presents a young, poor Jewish woman in the line of biblical prophet-liberators. Her response to Gabriel's announcement, "here am I, servant of the Lord, let it be with me according to your word"

---

12. *Word of God in the Life of the Church*, 137; also 138.

13. *Word of God in the Life of the Church*, 143.

14. Perry, *Mary for Evangelicals*, 269.

15. See *Word of God in the Life of the Church*, 150–51.

(Luke 1:38), places Mary in the company of powerful liberators of God's people, such as Shiphrah and Puah, Deborah, Jael, Esther and Judith.[16] The image of humble compliance, so strong in Catholic devotional practice, does not reflect what Scot McKnight has called "the real Mary": "The real Mary was a dangerous woman. She was dangerous to the powers *that be* because she predicted the powers *that will be*. She was dangerous to the likes of Herod and Augustus, emperor of Rome, because she claimed that her son was born to be king. And, instead of sitting back hoping good things would happen for Israel, Mary turned the wheel of history to make things happen for Israel."[17]

In short, by their methodology (of "differentiated consensus"), their frankness and honesty, and the extent of new ground broken, the Baptist-Catholic dialogue on Mary certainly pushed the boundaries of unity. It challenges Baptists to think afresh about their reading of Scripture, and to appreciate more how and why Catholics find reasons for honouring Mary with many titles. In turn, it encourages Catholics to look afresh at their own Marian teaching, including the dangers of excess in Marion piety, and to consider how Mary might be yet more honoured by a fuller appreciation of her human discipleship. The manner in which deep listening has been made possible has adhered to key restorative principles: firstly, participation has been expanded to include the voiceless by revisiting Scripture and articulating afresh the place of Mary in salvation history; second, the conversation has been morally serious by facing up to the historic division and harmful consequences of past Marion debate. The participants have made themselves vulnerable—risking criticism and rejection by some of their own—by permitting the changing cultural and theological landscape to influence their reading of history and Scripture. And thirdly, they have prioritized a pastoral and missiological perspective which seeks to find points of common ground that not only repair past harm, but which seek to reconcile and restore the body of Christ for the sake of her witness in the midst of the life of the world.

Given the significance of these discussions both for their content and restorative methodology, it is regrettable that they have received scant attention in the life of the Union.[18] Most Baptist ministers and congregations have no knowledge of this work. The report, which has

16. Perry, *Mary for Evangelicals*, 67–81, 95–96.

17. McKnight, *Real Mary*, 25.

18. See also my comments in Blyth, "Meaning and Function of 'Dynamic Equivalence,'" 171.

so much insight to offer when it comes to engaging constructively and restoratively with difficult issues in the life of the Baptist Union, is largely hidden and undervalued.

LESSONS ON RESTORATIVE DIALOGUE FOR THE GENDER-AND-SEXUALITY DEBATE

I have suggested that ecumenical dialogue needs to embrace restorative principles in order to provide space for deep listening: (i) radical partici-pation, (ii) moral seriousness, and (iii) reintegration. I would now like to develop this thesis, bearing in mind the Marian case study just outlined, with specific reference to issues of gender and sexuality currently divid-ing Christians, including Churches Together in England.

(i) *Radical participation* ensures that whenever harm has been done, all stakeholders have a place at the table. Dialogue on human sexuality needs to be radically reframed so that there is room at the table for all. It is counterproductive, indeed harmful, for institutional leaders and theologians to talk amongst themselves *about* rather than *with* the people most affected by their decisions. There must be a genuine place at the table for those who are harmed, disenfranchised, and disillusioned by the church on account of their gender or sexuality. Marian discussions are a timely reminder that division is not eradicated by vitriolic arguments. Rather than repeating the mistakes of the past, dialogue on sexuality needs to be reframed—but how? The starting point some have argued is to recognize and own our vulnerability. Inherent in the principle of radical participation is, I would suggest, a challenge to all—victims and offenders alike—to embrace their vulnerability.

The case for the life-enhancing potential of vulnerability has been made by pioneering philosophers such as Pamela Sue Anderson. As Matthew Mills writes, drawing on the work of Anderson:

> True "neighbour love" ... is only actualised when it is "performed openly and creatively." When it is open to the risk of hurt—vul-nerability and wound-ability—and has faith in the creative po-tential of encounters of love to make the future better than the past. Such vulnerability acts as a "provocation for enhancing life by creating a space for transformation." Referring to geopoliti-cal conflict Anderson called for the transformation of a "dark myth" of vulnerability on the part of nation states which "creates a pattern for human relations where vulnerability generates fear,

which in turn generates violent forms of self-protection and/or self-other control." In short a pathological yearning and search for *in*vulnerability.[19]

Contrary to this myth, Anderson argues that "in the embrace of vulnerability . . . there is the life-enhancing potential of 'openness to mutual affection.'"[20] Vulnerability is a virtue or disposition—one which restorative justice and Christian spirituality share. Only when we recognize and own our vulnerability (our need of the other to be fully ourselves) will we find the reason and the courage to risk all in relation to the other. Vulnerability needs to be nurtured and practiced in the church if the discussion on human sexuality is to become a mutual and life-giving process. Perhaps fearful of the vulnerability that open dialogue requires, many in the church choose to avoid difficult conversations, and remain ignorant of the harmful consequences.

(ii) *Moral seriousness* means not making light of harm and injury but rather addressing division and disagreement through a process of mutual dialogue and deep listening. The method of "differentiated consensus" that emerged in the recent the Marian dialogues and the common ground achieved was little short of remarkable. It offers hope that wherever rhetoric gives way to listening, empathy and understanding can grow. It shows how centuries of hatred can be overcome by opening a space to listen to the other, to read Scripture through the other's eyes, and to feel how they experience God's Word shaping the world. Such deep listening relies on shared stories, entering respectfully and non-judgementally into the other's experience. There is nothing cheap about the grace that flows from deep listening, and this is the approach that is followed in the Creating Sanctuary project.[21] Five personal stories form a powerful narrative about rejection by the church on account of sexuality. In the congregations where this study was piloted, congregants have been challenged in diverse ways by the stories. Not surprisingly, opinions on sexuality ranged across a spectrum and will continue to do so, but the pain participants felt about the damage done to the individuals had a unifying impact, creating a collective desire and will to repair the harm done to sexual minorities and to find a way forward in their own congregations

19. Blyth et al., *Forgiveness and Restorative Justice*, 23; citing Anderson and Fiddes, "Creating a New Imaginary," 48, 49.

20. Blyth et al., *Forgiveness and Restorative Justice*, 23.

21. https://www.creatingsanctuary.org.uk. I am a core team member of this project.

that will restore fellowship within Christ's body. "Fellowship," derived from the Greek word *koinonia*, has come to be understood as a unity in diversity, or as it was once described to me, it means being "a communion of disagreement." In other words, the nature and calling of the church is not to strive for uniformity but to embrace a more costly unity: *koinonia*, unity in diversity. A morally serious dialogue does not seek to minimize disagreement but, in a sense, to amplify it, to give credence to the historical, theological, and spiritual experience of the other, so that all feel valued in the dialogue. Disagreement is amplified, but (at the same time) vitriol is taken away. In the book *Good Disagreement?*, conservative evangelicals respond to Archbishop Justin Welby's questions: "Can we transform bad disagreement into good disagreement? What would that look like in practice?" The range of topics of disagreement highlighted in this book is very limited and the glaring absence of dialogue or disagreement on sexuality is regrettable, though unsurprising. Same-sex relations seemingly rank amongst the editors non-negotiable areas, yet the general argument put forward in the book points to the obvious conclusion that sexuality—as a church dividing issue—deserves serious attention and in the manner that is put forward for disagreeing well.

In the chapter where two women (Liz and Clare) discuss the topic of women in leadership, Liz vividly describes the highs and lows of disagreeing well:

> This sort of conversation about disagreements is tiring on every level: emotionally, physically, and spiritually. There is something exhausting about ensuring that you are doing justice to your own arguments and reasoning and those of the person you are talking to. That means a discipline of listening well to get inside their thinking, to engage with their scriptural hermeneutic, and to understand how they relate to God in prayer, worship, and Bible study. It is exhausting to allow oneself to be challenged and to take the challenge well and seriously, particularly when the subject goes to the very heart of one's calling and self-understanding in God, and yet not allow it to be personal.
>
> There were several points where I had to think, pray and study very hard to allow God to work with me, to allow myself to be in the place of uncertainty. If I am honest the work of disagreeing well with Clare was made harder because some people didn't understand why I was doing it; why it was important to get out of the castle and stop lobbing rocks [or ducking them! my insert]. Some challenged me hard that there were people

whom you should just not talk to, that it was selling the pass, that if you disagree, you disagree and that is it. That was very hard. I completely understood where they were coming from, but I believe we always have to talk to try to understand the other, if only so that we can disagree well. I will always hold that we have to be godly in our disagreement and that means listening and getting to know the other. I can anticipate situations where I may conclude that someone is profoundly wrong, but I cannot anticipate circumstances where I would regret getting to know them, spending time listening, allowing myself to be challenged to return to scripture and to my knees.[22]

(iii) The third principle, *reintegration*, signals that restoration is not simply looking backward, analysing what went wrong, but looks to a future where one-time enemies will be reconciled, and the rejected will be reintegrated into the community as equal members. Crucially, it points to the inherently social nature of restoration and reconciliation bringing together people and communities into a network of social relationships where true healing and reconciliation is realized. This is significant because restorative justice has often been criticized as overly individualistic, concerned only with the restoring of relations between individuals and unrelated to the social and collective identity and destiny of human community. But contrary to this, the principle of reintegration goes further than personal and interpersonal relations: it is not sufficient for an individual or even for harmer and harmed to address harm and repair the damage; there is a collective dimension whereby the wider community shares responsibility for harm done and for righting wrong. There is embedded within the principle of reintegration a social dimension which seeks not only to repair harm, but to transform situations and to create a better more just world.[23]

Theology—like restorative justice—has sometimes been criticized for an overly personal and individualistic understanding of sin and salvation; but as a corrective to this, twentieth-century atonement theology has revived an ancient more corporate and social understanding of sin

22. Goddard and Hendry, "From Castles to Conversations," 160–61.

23. On discussion about how to bring about a better world, Michael Taylor opines that restorative justice might be described as incremental, indirect, or gradualist; that is, it does not seek through direct action to reform the social and economic order but rather, by way of education, persuasion, and example, uses strategies such as embedding restorative principles into public life. See Blyth et al., *Forgiveness and Restorative Justice*, 100.

and atonement. A rereading of Irenaeus's theology of the cross (*Christus victor*)[24] resonates strongly with the restorative principle of reintegration.[25] First, it highlights that sin is an all-pervasive corrupting power (structural and systemic) and atonement means both liberation from social and political oppression and the restoration of broken relationships. The drama of Christ's life, death, and resurrection is a staggering demonstration of how, by walking the way of vulnerability, weakness, and persuasion, Christ righted wrong and overcame death. Second, salvation is conceived as a progressive movement of all creation into the wholeness and likeness of Christ. It invites our participation in the drama of redemption through a life of committed discipleship. That "the one died for the many" (2 Cor 5:14) witnesses to how the victimhood of Christ can transform any situation and affirms that we are saved not alone, but together. That "we are one body but many members" (1 Cor 12:14) affirms an integrationist understanding of human community: together, not alone, we become Christ's body, a community knit together in love. Understood in reintegrationist terms, the cross points to the hope and promise that all creation is in the process of being changed and transformed into the image and likeness of Christ.

I have argued that the conversations between Baptists and Romans Catholics adopted a forward-looking restorative model. They started from a place of trust and respect: celebrating what is shared, acknowledging difference, and being open/vulnerable to the other and to change how the other is perceived. The process was reintegrative because one-time enemies gradually became travelling companions. Of course, there is still a long way to travel and some of the yet-uncharted areas of disagreement include conversations on gender and sexuality. But these conversations illustrate the redemptive power of the reintegration principle; that when we welcome "others" as equals before God to sit around the table, deep listening can begin. A similar approach in other urgent conversations holds out the promise that we will all surely be changed and grow, in and through Christ, into that fuller *koinonia* which is communion with God.

---

24. Irenaeus, *Against Heresies*, V.1.i.

25. See Blyth, *Toward a Restorative Hermeneutic*, 103–9.

CONCLUSION

When Paul was the head of ministry at the Baptist Union, he enabled fruitful discussion in the Baptist Union's Council and Assembly on same-sex relations. He showed great wisdom and courage at that time. The Baptist Union continues to engage with these issues, but over time the possibility to engage in an open way has become strained. Recent discussions and statements in the Baptist Union and in CTE suggest that relationships are raw. The hope is that a restorative approach will win through this impasse: expanding the space so that all can safely come to the table (*radical participation*), embracing vulnerability as the means to reach to the other in mutual affection (*moral seriousness*); and journeying forward together into the wholeness and likeness of Christ (*reintegration into the community*).

These principles can help to navigate a way forward where harm can be addressed and in the longer term the kingdom imperative of *koinonia*, unity in diversity, might be realized. In the current global context where the church in the United Kingdom and Europe is more challenged than ever to maintain its presence and mission, there must surely be common ground found and reciprocal commitment within the body of the church.[26]

---

26. Here I commend the ecumenical resource *Creating Sanctuary*, which seeks to model this principle and to approach the subject of human sexuality through a restorative lens. The resource has been produced to help congregations think and reflect on issues relating to human sexuality and same-sex relationships. It does not assume all will think the same way but it seeks to encourage good dialogue and to ensure that the harm done by the church to the LGBT community does not continue.

13

MINISTRY AND COUNSELLING[1]

Alistair Ross

THERE WAS A SHOCKED silence. I had just stated Freud did not invent psychotherapy or counselling, which was clearly news to the trainee therapists present. Henri Ellenberger located counselling as part of centuries-old healing traditions found in faith and tribal communities.[2] These communities' central roles were played by religious or spiritual leaders, elders, gurus, shaman, wise women, and the like. So counselling has deep roots as one part of Christian ministry, although these are often overlooked. Recovering these roots is important given the trend for ministers to become therapist-pastors more engaged in understanding and interpreting the intricacies of the psyche rather than the cure of souls. Yet we need to be alert to the danger of setting up a false dichotomy of either-or, rather than both-and. Adopting an autoethnographic approach, I am both a Baptist minister of religion and a psychodynamic therapist drawing on my identity as a non-identical twin. Part of who I am exists as a person alone, with a unique identity as a self, and as a person-with-another involving a unique identity as a twin. Using Ricoeur's "willingness to suspect, willingness to listen,"[3] I adopt a "naïve" approach (also advocated by Ricoeur) of asking the questions: In what ways does a metaphorical use of the term "counselling," or the broader term "therapy," make connections

1. Due to the nature of confidentiality any clinical material presented here, other than my own, is composite in nature and does not refer to any one individual.

2. Ellenberger, *Discovery of the Unconscious.*

3. Ricoeur, *Freud and Philosophy,* 27.

with ministry? And what unexpected connections can be discovered? I am also adopting a "therapeutic" approach of attending to the emotional resonances metaphors generate in the reader. These differ from person to person but, like reading poetry, there is always something new. In the words of Alice Oswald, "a whisper of darkness, a shiver of not-knowing that passes under the surface of the poem but if you miss its movement then you are left with only small, personal sealed up poetry, poetry of what has been rather than might be."[4]

WHAT IS MINISTRY?

This apparently simple question is deceptive, if not controversial, so it requires the complex answers which Paul Goodliff skilfully addresses.[5] I cannot replicate such a breadth and depth of thinking, so my response is as a minister in a secular context using autoethnographic reflection involving my prejudices and experiences. I view ministry as a professional role within a faith community that involves training and affirmation through recognition by, and the service of, others. My understanding of ministry is that it also needs to be accompanied by a matching integrity, or struggle for such an integrity, that can be shaped into something indefinably more. This view of ministry reflects the embodied sinking feelings in my stomach, and my spirit, which I experienced as a minister in pastoral charge when someone told me about their newly found, self-appointed "ministry." They always expected me to be excited. I recall one person whose "ministry" was not endorsed by the local church, and which required him to be away from home many months a year, leaving behind a young wife with three children under the age of five with no local family support. Struggling on "widow's mite" finances, she was kept going by practical support from the church, which she could not tell her husband about because he was so angry that the church had not recognized his "ministry." For the sake of balance, I experience that same sinking feeling when I encounter people who occupy a ministerial role but without an apparent matching commitment to an inner world of transformation or forms of continuing ministerial development. They seem to view their role in terms of status, but as I encounter them I am left with an aching emptiness as if I have encountered form without

4. Oswald, "Art of Erosion."
5. Goodliff, *Shaped for Service.*

substance. This sounds horribly judgemental, as we all struggle to meet ideals, but it alerts me to how much I value and believe in ministry. It is too important not to be passionate about. What is also important is that there is no one-size-fits-all for ministry. Each person has their unique identity and experience where the training offers foundations to build on but not a blueprint of the finished building. One of the key foundations is a depth of theological understanding and a desire to apply this in pastoral practice. Even though I work professionally as an academic, researcher, writer, and trainer of psychodynamic therapists, I still read as much theology as I do psychotherapy. I feel I have so much to learn from both.

THE LANDSCAPE OF MINISTRY

In this analogy ministry is located within an ever-shifting social and cultural landscape.[6] While some trends or fashions fade, others remain despite becoming unfashionable, and some irrevocable. A first challenge for ministry is to find unfashionable wisdom in past theological and philosophical traditions, such as in the work of the American theologian Tom Oden.[7] There is one caveat, which is the danger of living as a church community in a set-apart Christian world which retreats into the past, a mythical past seen through rose-tinted spectacles. The minister's thinking may exist in the period of early Protestant Reformation thought. He (in this tradition ministers are male) largely ignores the contributions of many women to that Reformation. Neither would he want to live in such times dispensing with electricity, drugs and antibiotics, accessible transport, radio and television, and the like. While I was part of a chaplain's department in a large psychiatric hospital, searching for ways to relate faith to fragile patients suffering with challenging mental health, I found no help or succour in Donald Macleod's article "Counselling and Biblical Psychology." In a journal recommended by my former Baptist College theological tutor, I read:

> Every pastor's library should contain standard reference works on psychiatry as well as basic guides on common counselling problems (such as depression and marital breakdown). In any normal ministry today, these will be well used. But all must lie

6. Hodson, "Landscapes of practice."

7. See Oden, *Pastoral Theology*, with its chapter "Anticipations of Psychotherapy"; and his *Systematic Theology*.

under the regime of Scripture. Supposing this to be so, what guidance does Scripture give? The most important thing, probably, is a biblical psychology . . . First, the fact that man bears the image of God. No matter how degraded the individual appears to be . . . Secondly, the emphasis that man is a psycho-somatic unity . . . The proper management of the body thus becomes a primary Christian duty and the discovery that chemical therapy and physical therapy have benign effect on the mind cause no surprise. Thirdly, the insistence that man is sinful. He is totally depraved. His whole nature is corrupt—his intellect, his emotions, his will, even his conscience. Sin affects his opinions, his moods, his priorities and his relationships. He suppresses revelation. He is hostile to God. He is blind to the gospel. He is self-centred and deceitful. He lives behind a façade, wearing a mask and frequently making real identification and diagnosis almost impossible.[8]

While Macleod might be viewed as extreme, there is a resurgence of the explicit and implicit assumption of uncritical, unreformed Reformed theology and biblical counselling. The real challenge is to move from the apparently secure and calm seas of monologue and inhabiting a secure bubble dominated by prescribed Christian tradition. The experience of ministry and the expectations and demands on ministers has changed out of all recognition, so there can be no retreat solely to the wisdom or practices of the past. Fresh thinking and engagement are required.

The second challenge for ministry is to find wisdom in the present with its acute awareness of difference, diversity, power, the need for liberation, and the need for understanding of the self and community. Establishing such a dialogue is found in the arena of pastoral and practical theology,[9] with rich resources contained in the journal *Practical Theology* (full disclosure, I am on the editorial board), the British and Irish Association of Practical Theology, and in the writings of Stephen Pattison, Elaine Graham, Pamela Cooper-White, Anthony Reddie, Nicola Slee, Zöe Bennett, and many others. The particular challenge for ministers is to engage with the richness and diversity of such thinking and practice. It is a discipline that is uncomfortable—none of us like having our beliefs, values, and assumptions challenged, if not changed. It is equally enriching as ministry best exists in dialogue: within the minister herself through her inner and outer worlds, within the faith

8. Macleod, "Counselling and Biblical Psychology," 15.

9. See Goodliff, *Care in a Confused Climate*.

community itself, and between the faith community and the social and cultural worlds it is part of. This involves the stormy waves of dialogue, where ministry is driven forward by the Spirit towards new horizons despite the nagging feeling the ship might sink.[10] Valuable as this is, it is a parallel but different task from working with metaphors.

THERAPEUTIC SIMILES AND NEW CONNECTIONS

How does therapy act as a metaphor for ministry and vice versa? Therapy, like ministry, is a multilayered discipline with its own convergences and divergences. The term "therapy" is used here to cover counselling, pastoral counselling, counselling psychology, psychotherapy, and psychoanalysis whilst recognising each has a distinctive and valuable history. In contemporary use "therapy" has become an inclusive term conveying the essence of these helping and healing professions.[11] An important place to begin is by describing what therapists do,[12] and in this regard I am shaped by a psychodynamic approach,[13] while Paul Goodliff's counselling training adopted a broader, more eclectic approach. We used to work together teaching pastoral counselling with Ruth Layzell for St John's College, Nottingham (sadly now closed). It was a great fun and a real joy to work together. We combined aspects of ministry and counselling as reflected in the following sections.

Ideally therapy offers: a place to talk and listen; a context without judgement; a secure, confidential space offering a supportive but not unchallenging relationship; the opportunity of making sense of complex issues both with the individual and their family/social system; the possibility of new thoughts and actions; an understanding of the present in the light of the past; attending to unconscious processes and repeating patterns; and working creatively with silence (the latter three being specific features of a psychodynamic approach). To this can be added ongoing professional and ethical development through supervision by therapists of their work. There are clear overlaps with many aspects of ministry, yet therapy is not ministry and vice versa, although there are

---

10. Hodgson, *Winds of the Spirit*.

11. See Reeves, *Introduction to Counselling and Psychotherapy*.

12. See McLeod, *Introduction to Counselling and Psychotherapy*.

13. Ross, *Introducing Contemporary Psychodynamic Counselling and Psychotherapy*.

skills that can be used.[14] As these categories are explored, what will emerge are metaphorical connections to ministry, and differences from ministry.

A Place to Talk and Listen

The client (to use counselling language) is encouraged to talk freely, while the counsellor listens. Listening has long been a hallmark of wisdom and healing traditions down through the centuries. It took a new direction with the emergence with Freud listening to his early women patients,[15] which formed the basis of psychoanalysis and expanded into a key feature of all therapy. By contrast, ministers are often professional talkers. They are expected to speak, lead, and pronounce in religious, personal, and social contexts. Before people talk and share deeply personal and often shame-filled thoughts and feelings, they often test out to see whether the person is actually listening to them. Like throwing a pebble into a pond, they drop in a thought or feeling, and wait to see if the therapist notices the ripples. I see clients from all faith backgrounds (not necessarily Christian) who, knowing I have a ministerial background, might ask a faith- or religious-type question. In that moment I suspect they are testing out if I am going to adopt a ministerial persona and offer a solution before I have really heard their real issue. I usually say, "That sounds an important question/issue for you. Could we park it for the moment?—as before we explore that I need to get a real sense of who you are as a person. Tell me about how you came to be here?" "Tell me about growing up and what that was like?" Rarely do we ever return to their original question. The ability to listen requires a discipline in the therapist not to talk, to wait, to be present and silent when need be. Or in Bonhoeffer's words, "the 'beginning of love for [others] is learning to listen to them.'"[16]

A Context without Judgement

Often the clients I see who come from a faith background arrive with the additional burden of being judged, by their internal superegos and by external parental and/or authority figures. They long for the warm sun

14. Ross, *Counselling Skills.*
15. See Ross, *Freud.*
16. Khalid, "At the Bedside," 150.

and cool breeze of not being judged, again. There is a place of recognition that they have made mistakes, but not with the scalpel-sharp words that cut to the bone. A feature of all therapies is the creation of a relationship in which a person is enabled to find their own way through, even if they report feeling suicidal. What is right for one person is rarely right for another. It is not that therapists don't make judgements; it is rather that they contain thoughts or feelings in a discipline that puts the client's thoughts and feelings before their own. Judgement is suspended. As I reflect on my mistrial past, I am saddened by times when, in my desire to uphold a definitive biblical interpretation (as I regarded it then) within a conservative evangelical tradition, as a consequence I missed the person and left them feeling judged. If you are one of those people, judged by me or any other, I apologize. So what are the questions therapy poses? Is a central part of ministry to uphold religious beliefs and practices, with a clear understanding of what constitutes right and wrong? If so, there are always going to be challenges, but what is important is how we act in those challenges. In meeting people, ministers need to encounter them as they are, and offer an empathic way of being that matches the vulnerableness of the moment. Rushing to an answer, a solution, or a judgement shuts down the other person and can leave them feeling imposed upon. Underpinning this are sets of beliefs and values about what constitutes authority and how this should be exercized. Hidden power is a dark side of ministry rarely addressed until something goes badly wrong.

Secure and Confidential Space

The therapy profession has changed the way people understand confidentiality. It is essential in therapy but comes at a cost, the burden of knowing but not speaking. Ian was part of a small group of like-minded evangelical Christian friends which had been together for many years. They had worked through an affair, divorce, depression, bereavement, and cancer (in remission), and then one member became open about his sexual orientation. While working through this as a group, someone broke confidentiality because it was a "point of principle" and reported this to the Ian's church, denomination, and the national organization he was part of. As a consequence, Ian was dismissed by the church, disciplined by his denomination, and became a pariah in the wider organization. The group of friends split, Ian hurt by the betrayal and the loss of a secure, confidential space that had been such a lifeline for many years. Thankfully, many in ministry have acquired the ability of holding the pain, sadness, flaws, and mistakes of others and many have received a depth of pastoral care as a consequence. The challenge is to put the other first. Indeed the French Jewish philosopher Emmanuel Levinas would say that attending to the other, participating in the immanence and transcendence of God, is the whole purpose of living.

Making Sense and Meaning Making

That the whole is more than the sum of the parts is an idea taken from the Austrian and German Gestalt philosophical and psychology traditions, made popular through Gestalt therapy pioneered by Fritz and Laura Perls. We make sense first by identifying the constituent parts in order to see the whole, but the whole is often more than we imagined. This principle applies to therapy and ministry. People come to therapy looking to discover how it all makes sense and sometimes discover it doesn't; it is what it is in all its pain and complexity. A rush to meaning never helps. A well-meaning person once visited me while I was recovering from serious injury and asked me, "So what is God teaching you in this?" I later wrote about my experience, but in that moment it was deeply unhelpful for them to impose their view of God on my experience as if this was my view of God.[17] A view that everything has to make sense and be part of God's plan avoids the careful reconstruction that is required and which therapy allows. Decorating a room needs more than a few rolls of wallpaper to cover the cracks. Having bought a Victorian terraced house, we discovered that in removing the wallpaper most of the crumbling plaster came with it, revealing the original lath-and-horsehair construction. Once uncovered, this wall could have its cracks dealt with and be built up with a skimmed-plaster finish.

Several therapeutic skills are captured by the term "not-knowing." This is difficult to do and needs continual practice because our natural curiosity means we always want to know. It also exposes therapists' feelings as being the person looked too for an answer, insight, or help. Behind it lies the idea of not making assumptions. The British psychoanalyst Wilfred Bion introduced the term "K" to mean both knowledge, coming

17. See Ross, "An Experience of Falling" and "On Learning from (Being) the Patient."

to know something not previously known which emerges through relationship, and allowing new discoveries. This has important implications for ministry. In building a pastoral relationship with church members when they need support, they are not looking for a religious professional with knowledge; rather they are seeking someone with whom they can discover what they need to know in the moment.

New Thoughts and Actions

The opportunity to offer space to think differently is an important aspect of therapy. This has become an aspect of cognitive-based therapies helping replace unhealthy for healthy cognitive thought processes, which can replace entrenched patterns. Yet therapy needs to do much more than this as people are far more complex that the sum total of their cognitions. Like making meaning, experiences can be reframed, memories explored, emotions identified and expressed, a previously unheard voice speak, prohibitions faced and overcome. Psychological (and spiritual) damage can be halted, repairs undertaken, memories archived (accessible when required), and permission given for new thinking. I went into therapy thinking I was one kind of person and came out knowing I was another, with a greater awareness of what I could be for others, but also how I could harm. I thought differently and felt able to be more of the person I wanted to be, whilst working within the limitations of a complex relational heritage. Ministry, individually and collectively, needs to grasp opportunities to think and act differently. Health can be seen in an ongoing search for new expressions of enduring beliefs and values while offering forms of creative engagement. It also needs to hold in mind that people are complex and no one pattern, process, worship style, or eucharistic or evangelistic pattern fits everyone. Ministry can learn from therapy the value of adopting a holistic approach of valuing each person's body, mind, and spirit.

Understanding the Present in the Light of the Past

Freud used an archaeological metaphor to advance his idea that we understand the present by excavating the past. This can be expanded with the idea of French philosopher Merleau-Ponty. "Every present includes in the end through its horizons of immediate past and nearest future the whole of possible time."[18] The past in each person needs a voice and this is why clients seek me out as a psychodynamic therapist. Am I shaped by growing up in a tenement in inner-city Glasgow? Is my self-identity shaped by being a fraternal twin? The list could be long but the answer is clearly "yes." In many ways this process should be familiar to ministers through their preaching. This involves an engagement with biblical texts in which the challenge is to interpret them in the light of an original context (where known) and the current context (where we live now). In this sense each person needs the same interpretive care as if they are a "living human document,"[19] or in Bonnie Miller-McLemore's contemporary term, a "living human web."[20] So why does this fail to happen? In part it is to do with being alongside a person in crisis who is focussing on the here and now and implying, "I am in pain; take it away, now. Who cares about the past?" Or, "I can't get out of bed because of depression. Who cares about its origins?" Therapy is also a developmental process, which begins in crisis focussed on a presenting problem but then moves through to the careful process of excavation. It also relates to the complex nature of memory and how we reconstruct narratives often fragmented by trauma. The relational containment of therapy allows the parts to be identified, detraumatized, and added into the mosaic of who we are and how we want to live, emotionally and spiritually.

Attending to Unconscious Processes and Repeating Patterns

Not everyone believes there is such a thing as the unconscious, either as an entity or a philosophy or aspect of the mind. Neuroscience has demonstrated brain mechanisms involving unconscious processes but not necessarily evidence of the unconscious itself, although there is evidence pointing in that direction. Not all therapies acknowledge the unconscious, yet it forms a unique and central part of Freud and Jung's thinking, followed by all subsequent psychoanalytic thinkers and practitioners.[21] From my days working in a psychiatric hospital, I explored this idea in depth for the first time. I had already read Jung's *Memories, Dreams and Reflections*, listened to a series of L'Abri cassette

18. Merleau-Ponty, *Phenomenology of Perception*, 109.

19. Gerkin, *Living Human Document*.

20. Miller-McLenmore. "Living Human Web."

21. Ross, *Introducing Contemporary Psychodynamic Counselling and Psychotherapy*.

tapes (remember those!) by Richard Winter on Freud, and dived into the depths of Frank Lake's *Clinical Theology* (1966), which I subsequently researched.[22] Unconscious processes can be seen in repeating patterns. As a minister and therapist, I once worked with Jan, a younger woman married to Dan, an older man. Their difficulties were deeply entrenched and, like many Christians, they delayed seeking help until too much damage had been done. Her concerns focussed on his ageing, as she looked younger than her age and he looked even older than the already large age gap. Feeling trapped, Jan left the marriage, and I left the area. Several years later I was visiting and did a comical double-take as I saw Jan walking on the other side of the street with her new partner, who was physically almost an exact double of her first. Jan still looked young, and her partner looked similarly old. I never knew the details of the story but the past appeared to be repeating itself and I have always wondered what unconscious processes were at work in her life.

Working Creatively with Silence

Silence is a rare commodity in a noise-saturated society. I long for it because I no longer have it since developing tinnitus in my early forties, and I miss the opportunity to wait in silent prayer. Many people are unfamiliar and uncomfortable with silence. Therapists need to be attentive to the quality of silence because it can be experienced as punitive or shaming for the client.[23] Such silence can be like a parental figure who used it as a means of control or punishment, leaving a child feeling abandoned. For someone with a Christian faith, it can be deeply distressing when their God has become silent. People may read about Job's experience but they certainly don't want to go through it. This has often been called a "dark night of the soul," although St. John of the Cross's meaning is much deeper and more complex. Silence becomes equated with abandonment. A warm summer's day turns to a cold endless winter's night. Therapists attend to how clients experience silence by a depth of listening, of not rushing to talk, patient waiting, allowing new truths to emerge, and allowing thoughts and feelings to emerge from the depths of the psyche/ soul. Yet not all silence is pathological. Rachel Muers[24] and Hina

22. See Ross, *Evaluation of Clinical Theology.*
23. Goodliff, *With Unveiled Face.*
24. Muers, *Keeping God's Silence.*

Khalid[25] identify silence as a reflection of the creative power of God that can be recreated into the silence (and touch) of a human encounter. Alice Oswald's inaugural lecture as Professor of Poetry at Oxford University observed that "a poem is a way of speaking into the silence to see what speaks back."[26] This offers a creative way of working with this silence. It is a craft with a long apprenticeship served by those who themselves have been silent, waiting in the silent presence of another.

MINISTRY THROUGH THE LENS OF THERAPEUTIC METAPHOR

Ministry is challenging and my reflection is that the demands faced have increased exponentially. Black lives matter and racism needs challenging. Woman's lives matter and so much still needs addressing in terms of identity, safety, and domestic and sexual violence. Mental health matters and stigma needs challenging. Poverty matters with the ongoing challenge of addressing economic justice and social exclusion. It is so easy to feel overwhelmed and I have no desire to add even more to this load. Yet, standing outside ministry and looking in, I can see the danger of getting so involved in the urgent demands that we miss the strategic and wider picture. My regret is that early on I did exactly that, thinking that ministry was everything, until a spiritual encounter with a group of minsters where I experienced a calling to be a psychotherapist alongside ministry. One of my companions on this journey, then and now, has been Paul Goodliff. So, this chapter is part of the book's wider reflective process to help us see how ministry could be enhanced depending on each person's skills and abilities. There is always so much to learn and it is an encouragement to continue to grow, whether in ministry, in psychotherapy, or both. It begins by nurturing that capacity to listen in a way that encompasses spoken and unspoken words and emotions, staying with and bearing witness to a story, avoiding the easy answers, hearing echoes of the past, being alert to promptings of the spirit/psyche, not feeling the need to rush, and nurturing fragile hope for the future.

25. Khalid, "At the Bedside."
26. Oswald, 'Art of Erosion."

14

MINISTRY AND PREACHING

Wale Hudson-Roberts

THE EVENT WAS SCHEDULED for August 28, 1963. It was a mile-long march from the Washington Monument to the Lincoln Memorial, built in honour of the president who had signed the Emancipation Proclamation a century earlier. The March called for the desegregation of public accommodation and public schools, the redress of violations of constitutional rights, and an expansive federal program to train employees. Its demands were just. It produced a bigger turnout than expected. An estimated 250,000 people arrived at the largest event in the history of America. It was graced by many celebrities, including Bob Dylan and the soul singer Mahalia Jackson.

The significance of this event was not lost on Martin Luther King Jr. His preparation had been meticulous, but it is the extemporaneous section of his speech that history remembers.[1] The inclusion of the "I Have a Dream" passage was a spontaneous addition, which may or may not have been prompted by Mahalia Jackson. She had heard him employ this refrain at a demonstration in Detroit a few months earlier. Jackson and King had a good relationship, he often turning to her when in need of a musical uplift. Now standing next to him, when he began struggling with his prepared text, she shouted, "Tell 'em about the dream, Martin."[2]

---

1. Younge, *Speech*, 95. In what follows I am indebted to Younge's account.
2. Younge, *Speech*, 95–96.

And so, King kicked off. He took the listening crowd to church, as they say. This "Baptist preacher"[3] began slowly, a combination of what Gary Younge calls "powerful pauses" with clear and exaggerated diction. In his first minute King uttered only seventy-seven words.[4]

"But one hundred years later the Negro is not free . . ."[5] is the first of King's many phrases he repeats to emphasize his point.[6] Each time King returns to the phrase, he says it with greater speed and louder, "so that its effect is more rousing."[7]

Four minutes in, King was finding his rhythm and stride. He was reading less, speaking more, "redirecting his attention from the words on paper to the audience with the words."[8]

> We have come to this hallowed spot to remind America of the fierce urgency of now.

The "I Have a Dream" speech remains one of the "defining moments in the history of American civic rhetoric."[9] How can one forget King's delivery? It was nothing less than "majestic." Dyson says of King, "his lilting cadences stretched along a spiral of intermittent sonic crescendos."[10] His rhythms were varied as he intersected "blues and gospel."[11] Lifted by the crowd's momentum, King reflected his peoples struggle, pain, suffering, and the yearning for a resurrected black community. Black enslavement, historical and present, is rehearsed in nineteen minutes. Dyson remarks, "brevity is the servant of justice."[12]

King, the preaching performer, drunk from the roots of the best of American preachers. These included Gardner Taylor, King's preaching

---

3. King said of himself, "I am fundamentally a clergyman, a Baptist preacher"; cited in Lischer, *Preacher King*, 3.

4. Younge, *Speech*, 106.

5. All references to King's "I Have a Dream Speech" come from https://www.npr.org/2010/01/18/122701268/i-have-a-dream-speech-in-its-entirety. See also Younge, *Speech*, xi–xvii.

6. Younge, *Speech*, 107.

7. Younge, *Speech*, 107.

8. Younge, *Speech*, 110.

9. Dyson, *I May Not Get There with You*, 16. In what follows I am dependent on Dyson's argument.

10. Dyson, *I May Not Get There with You*, 17.

11. Dyson, *I May Not Get There with You*, 17.

12. Dyson, *I May Not Get There with You*, 17.

idol and the poet laureate of the American pulpit.[13] King did not use, during his "Dream" speech, hiccups, gyrations, or rapid rhythmic shifts to assist his crescendo. His rich baritone voice with its ominous tone did the trick. As a vocal magician, his Southern cadences, booming baritone voice, and gravitas helped his listeners to their feet during the closing parts of his addresses. This delivery style, honed through years of practice, is repeated in his "Dream" speech. Commencing with his normal slow delivery, his thunderous voice casually moved through his composition. His voice assisted his virtuoso performance to reach its pinnacle towards the end and with the words—now known around the world as among the most famous in history—"I have a dream that one day this nation will rise up and live out the true meaning of its creed." Such was King's style that the latter part of his dream speech appeared to be even more powerful than his introduction.

Confident of his delivery, if not fully confident of his speech, King came to the packed crowd to speak not just about his dream for America but also his foreboding nightmare. With striking and "forceful" metaphors[14] he named the situation of black people as "crippled by the manacles of segregation and the chains of discrimination." It is Dyson's view that "King penetrated the national conscience and sutured black suffering to America's identity as the wealthiest country on the globe."[15] Despite America's vast resources and commitment to justice, it had issued blacks a bad check. Inscribed on the returned check, says King, were the words: "insufficient funds." The purpose of the march was to "cash the check" and "collect on the promises that had been made."[16]

As the challenge continued, he repudiated the many white Americans who thought that blacks should be comfortable with gradualism, an eerily slow pace towards possible transformation.[17] He said "no!" to it. He confronted this strategy head on, declaring "the fierce urgency of now" and reminding America that the "sweltering summer of the Negro's legitimate discontent would not pass until the coming of the autumn of freedom and equality." To the powerful in Washington, King issued a fiery warning:

13. Dyson, *I May Not Get There with You*, 179; cf. Lischer, *Preacher King*, 51.

14. Dyson, *I May Not Get There with You*, 18.

15. Dyson, *I May Not Get There with You*, 18.

16. Dyson, *I May Not Get There with You*, 18.

17. Dyson, *I May Not Get There with You*, 18.

> There will be neither rest nor tranquility in America until the
> Negro is granted his citizenship rights. The whirlwinds of revolt
> will continue to shake the foundations of our nation until the
> bright day of justice emerges.

This passage is often used to discourage black people from revolt, but this
is to misinterpret its message. King urged his allies not "to quench the
revolutionary thirst for justice."[18] So, in answer to the rhetorical question
of when black civil rights devotees would be satisfied, King "thundered
a string of resolute 'nevers.'"[19] King ended this section with the words of
the prophet Amos: ". . . justice rolls down like waters and righteousness
like a mighty stream."

Both Paul Goodliff and I attended, at different times, "The Preacher's
College," as Spurgeon's has in the past been known.[20] Paul has always
been a thoughtful and justice-orientated preacher. His commitment to
advocacy and racial justice, reflected in his role as General Secretary of
Churches Together in England, fits well with this chapter, which seeks
to honour one Baptist preacher by examining the preaching of another
Baptist, Martin Luther King Jr. King, like my colleague Paul, was unable
to divorce justice from his preaching. King's preaching overflowed with
the justice theme. He was no ordinary preacher; his probing questions
helped America question its societal conscience, eventually confessing it's
racism. In this chapter I will explore how the prophetic and theological
can and must intersect in every preaching experience. It is very much an
exercise in theology through biography.[21] The chapter will also consider
how King's Baptist roots and theology informed and shaped his peach-
ing, contributing to the content of his iconic "I Have a Dream" speech.
It will also investigate the question "If King were alive today, what global
themes might he explore?," concluding with a challenge to take seriously
the theology and preaching of King.

King's "I Have a Dream" speech is one of the most misinterpreted
speeches in history. It is not a benign speech promoting a colour-blind
theology, an idea happily peddled by many white Americans. On the
contrary, a careful analysis of King's words should enable the reader to

18. Dyson, *I May Not Get There with You*, 19.

19. Dyson, *I May Not Get There with You*, 19.

20. See Goodliff, *Shaped for Service*, 244.

21. In James McClendon's *Biography as Theology*, Martin Luther King Jr. is the
focus of one of the chapters.

appreciate its audacious and revolutionary content. The words uttered on August the 28ᵗʰ captured the suffering of centuries of oppression. This was a speech that encapsulated white racism, privilege, and brutality. It called it out on the international stage for what it was, and demanded reparatory justice, and for black people to be judged not by their ethnicity but their character.

"I Have a Dream" has been identified as King's definitive and prophetic statement on racial justice. For those who read accurately the text and its subtext, he became an enemy of the state.[22] King's intention, lest we forget, was not to narrate a dream but to present an impending nightmare. In Dyson's words again, "while the phrases that expose racial horror are as beautiful as the phrases that clarify hope, they are obscured because they are not as frequently quoted."[23] There is a need to pay full attention to the whole speech, because, like the biblical prophets, King speaks judgement as well as hope.

THE PREACHER AND JUSTICE

The "I Have a Dream" speech was an impassioned call for justice. King was becoming tired of the abuse that back people experienced. His dream for America was haunted by concerns of an impending nightmare. As for change, it had to be in the now. The March on Washington was King's *kairos* moment. It is no wonder he dreamt that one day America would live out the true meaning of its creed, that the state of Mississippi would be transformed into an oasis of freedom and justice, that his four little children would be judged by the content of their character, that the black children in Alabama would be able to join hands with white children, and that the glory of the Lord would be revealed on all flesh, not just some.

According to James Cone, King's theological understanding of justice was influenced by his black church roots as well as by white Protestant liberalism.[24] King grew up among black Baptist churches, but through his time in seminary it was "liberal Protestantism [which] provided the

22. The Assistant Director of the FBI at the time of the speech, James Sullivan, said King was "the most dangerous Negro of the future of the nation"; cited in Younge, *Speech*, 126.

23. Dyson, *I May Not Get There with You*, 17.

24. Cone, *Martin and Malcolm*, 121. In what follows I am dependent on Cone's argument.

intellectual framework for the public expression of his faith."[25] With
some enthusiasm, King "embraced liberal theology's accent on the social
gospel" and its commitment to the kingdom of God.[26] Cone argues that
King used liberal Protestant theology to articulate his religious convictions about America, knowing that his liberal God-talk would be more
easily absorbed by a white audience than the spirituality of black people.
The more "black" elements of his speech were more "emotional," their
meaning and symbolism largely lost on those who had not experienced
slavery and segregation.[27] His American dream for justice, as well as his
"I Have a Dream" speech, were significantly derived from his liberal faith.
If there was continuing tension between his liberal and black church
influences, it was the centrality of the cross that separated him from
liberal theology and placed him in the black religious tradition.

Building on the foundation of his namesake, the reformer Martin
Luther, the cross was God's way of condemning segregation and embracing integration.[28] It signalled the "no!" to alienation between blacks
and whites and the "yes!" to their reconciliation. In the mind of King,
the cross became an eternal expression of God's commitment towards
justice. It also reflected the suffering and pain that untold numbers of
black Americans were forced to experience, the resurrection symbolizing
the hope of an unquenchable dream. King's theological understanding
of the cross and of the suffering of Jesus was the catalyst that energized
his "absolute commitment to non-violence,"[29] a praxis he regarded as
just. He was convinced that "oppressed people must use moral means
to achieve just ends."[30] Nothing was more important to King than his
faith in "a God of justice, love and hope—a faith centred on the cross of
Jesus."[31]

The "I Have a Dream" speech is deeply rooted in the justice theme.
It displays a commitment to incarnational preaching—the exegeting of
the Scriptures and the public square. It demonstrates a commitment to
the oppressed and is grounded in the promises of the Hebrew prophets.

25. Cone, *Martin and Malcolm*, 122.

26. Cone, *Martin and Malcolm*, 132.

27. Cone, *Martin and Malcolm*, 132.

28. Cone, *Martin and Malcolm*, 127.

29. Cone, *Martin and Malcolm*, 128.

30. Cone, *Martin and Malcolm*, 129.

31. Cone, *Martin and Malcolm*, 129.

King had clearly stood with Moses and shared his vision on Sinai, and he knew for himself the dream of Moses imagining the land of promise in Deuteronomy 34.[32] "I have been to the mountaintop" said King in his final speech, and the experience of Moses came alive again in an entirely new context.

King's understanding of justice, like many good preachers, evolved over time. Justice meant white people treating black people with equity and ensuring a level economic and political playing field. In many of his speeches after the Montgomery bus boycott, he implored black people to stand up for their rights. He encouraged black people to boycott the bus and to stand up for justice, not love alone.

When King began to view the Montgomery movement through a global lens, his vision found its roots in the idea of the "beloved community."[33] He became acutely aware that the beloved community could only be achieved through justice and so he began to develop a theology that was informed less by the local and more by the global. Cone argues that "the oneness of humanity, informed by creative divine love began to move to the centre of his thinking."[34] Love and justice were combined in King's thinking, love being the means of establishing justice, of which the goal was the beloved community.[35]

A theology of justice belongs at the front and centre of preaching, no less today than it was for King. Preaching is an empty shell if it is not underpinned by a commitment to advocacy.[36] God's work of advocacy started with the commitment of God's own self. Beginning with God, then, guarantees that we will not be tempted to rush towards overly simplistic, subjective interpretations of advocacy. If preachers begin by looking at God's own historical commitment to advocacy, God's active love for the world, they will continue to give priority to God and not merely human reflections. It is crucial that today's preachers learn to engage with social political issues, and to move beyond the temptation to stay on seemingly safe ground. This gets right to the heart of the matter. Based on their understanding of God, preachers should look at the world

32. Brueggemann, *Practice of Prophetic Imagination*, 24.

33. For more on King's language of the "beloved community," see Baldwin, *Voice of Conscience*, 81–84.

34. Cone, *Martin and Malcolm*, 64.

35. See Cone, *Martin and Malcolm*, 64, 126.

36. In the next couple of paragraphs I am developing thoughts from my chapter "Preaching on Intercultural Issues."

through a liberation lens. This is what the "I Have a Dream" address does remarkably well. It is in no sense myopic. It is global in its reach and influence, and global in its depth, width, and height.

The prerequisite for any theology of justice is listening. Clearly preachers must listen to God, both in Scripture and through their understanding of the societies they live in. From the Exodus story onwards, the God of the Bible is repeatedly presented as liberator. The God of Exodus is the God of the slaves, longing for their freedom from slavery. God's clear hatred of political oppression, corruption, and bloodshed is everywhere in the Law, the Prophets, and all the Hebrew writings. God consistently hears and responds to the cries of oppressed people and is evidently committed to their deliverance. Sarah Travis has some wise words for preachers committed to applying the recurring themes from the "I Have a Dream" speech:

> Preaching on justice involves a desire to disengage from empire, to disrupt and reorient colonising discourse toward a more life-giving discourse. It recognizes the world is not what it should be and begins to construct a new way of interpreting both the past and present. To decolonise preaching is to imagine a human community no longer shaped by a discourse of captivity. Such preaching aims at the transformation of an unjust and oppressive world.[37]

THE PREACHER AND REPARATIONS

For good reasons, reparatory justice was an important theme in King's vision. The history of African Americans had been steeped in enslavement; loss of life, dignity, land, and family followed the enslaved for centuries. Each life stolen by their oppressors. Even the new American laws supposedly providing a semblance of parity for African Americans were disappointing because of their inability to create a just America for African Americans.

In the "I Have a Dream" address, King's demand for reparations was very clear: "In a sense we have come to our nation's capital to cash a check." The metaphor starts from "the jail cells of Alabama and ends in a New York bank vault."[38] Many young black people were arrested during

37. Travis, *Decolonizing Preaching*, 90.
38. Younge, *Speech*, 108.

the Birmingham marches. The movement quickly needed to generate large sums of money, leading to the release of the young men.[39] King made the point that American banks hold trillions of dollars, amounts far exceeding the bail money demanded by the courts. It was locked in American vaults and should be released to compensate the millions of African Americans who attempted to live their lives under the curse of enslavement, those whose economic opportunities had been drastically curtailed because of history's cruel past. King was adamant. Reparations, alongside other concrete expressions of justice, needed to happen now. Such urgency was not at all surprising. Remedying the inherited inequalities would ultimately only happen through reparations. Reparations, for King, would entail America, blighted by exploitation, taking its own history seriously, a concrete acknowledgement of the effects that harmful policies have had on black bodies. Reparation was a way of making the country whole and providing African Americans with the opportunities to become somebodies. Allen Dwight Callahan puts it aptly when he writes:

> Reparations, therefore, redress not only the ravages of slavery, but its continuing effects. American racism did not instantaneously vanish after 1863. Kidnapping, terror, rape, torture, murder, "every drop of blood drawn with the lash": all these heinous crimes were perpetuated as a matter of course under a slave regime constituted by them. But just as important, these crimes continued to be perpetrated in new ways long after the disestablishment of the slave regime and its replacement by another regime just as dependent on the disenfranchisement of African Americans . . . Reparations necessarily redress the persistent effects of racial discrimination that have perpetuated the exploitation of black labor, black products, black culture, and black bodies from the Industrial Age to the Information Age.[40]

Demanding that America should repair its damage was a bold invitation. It certainly presented a powerful challenge to the structures that linked privilege with whiteness. It forcibly challenged the inheritance of European colonialism, the Atlantic slave trade, and the heritage of British colonial power. King's "I Have a Dream" speech put all these issues more firmly on America's political agenda. King's clarion call for reparations was typical of his theological response to injustice, and of

39. Younge, *Speech*, 108.
40. Callahan, *Embassy of Onesimus*, 59–60.

his determination to challenge the church's historical preference for supporting the status quo. King consistently made connections between the good news of Jesus and his call to black people everywhere to imitate Jesus in actions and words. King's challenge to America to make urgent repair revealed a man fearlessly navigating theological tensions between the personal and the political. Aware of the consequences, the possibility that such strident words would accelerate his death were not lost on King, yet, undeterred, King demanded financial recompense. King was willing to address challenging issues in the public square. He was a prophetic preacher, inhabiting a broken world.

Societal challenges continue in abundance: climate injustice, poverty, war, famine, environmental degradation, and social and economic inequality are just a few of the global issues that today's preachers are invited to address.

To preach prophetically requires preachers to listen acutely to the pain in the world in its many guises, and to address the world both in its present and future realities. The preacher, then, is immediately cast in the role of a prophet.[41] The task of interpreting ancient texts becomes inseparably fused with issues of justice in the public square. Walter Brueggemann has compared the preacher to a traditional Hebrew scribe, one who works carefully with ancient texts, enabling them to shed fresh light and wisdom on the big issues of the moment.[42] The preacher, then, is not someone peddling ideas of their own making, but someone whose inspiration is grounded in an ancient biblical tradition, bringing it to life for a new time. As a prophetic preacher, King's emphasis on reparations demonstrates his commitment to the oppressed and the cause of deconstructing every surviving manifestation of evil. It also speaks of King's ability, as a naturally prophetic preacher, to grapple theologically with complex and controversial issues, and not retreat from them. King was cognisant, as all mature preachers should be, to imagine a human community shaped by discourses of love and freedom, dominance and captivity. Such preaching aims at the transformation of an unjust and oppressive world.

Lewis Baldwin writes that "King felt that every minister of the Gospel becomes a prophetic preacher by virtue of their calling."[43] Aware,

41. Brueggemann, *Practice of Prophetic Imagination*, 1.

42. Brueggemann, *Practice of Prophetic Imagination*, 2.

43. Baldwin, *Voice of Conscience*, 79.

in his words, that "the church of his day was increasingly becoming 'an irrelevant social club with no moral or spiritual authority,"[44] King was hopeful that the church would rekindle its ancient tradition and dissenting voice. He cherished the image of the church as a prophetic voice and witness. This is powerfully reflected in his "I Have a Dream" address with the theme of reparations playing a critical part in it.

THE PREACHER AND CONTEXT

Preachers never live in a vacuum, but always in a context. Therefore, the murder of George Floyd in 2020 must inevitably impact our preaching today. I am not suggesting the preacher must only privilege issues of race, although the dehumanisation of the black people, as a global disease, cannot help but become a theological matter for the preacher, and not a mere intellectual exercise. Relevance was important to King along with context. Even though he had the intellectual ability to explore the most erudite of themes, he remained a grounded preacher, sticking closely to themes on militarism, poverty, and class, issues that impacted the masses. All preaching should be grounded in the reality of the oppressed, absorbing and listening to the relevant issues from the community and reflecting them in proclamation.

In his "Autobiography of Religious Development," written when he was only twenty-one years of age, King interpreted his Baptist world as one that shaped, informed, and influenced his theology, ecclesiology, and indeed his entire identity. It appears the sanctuary of Ebenezer Baptist Church in Atlanta, the church pastored by his father, played a pivotal role in his formation. King said, "The church has always been a second home for me as far back as I can remember I was in church every Sunday."[45]

For King, Ebenezer Baptist Church was a sacred space and King was comfortable enough in that space to internalise the richness of the church's theology and spiritual values. The intrinsic dignity of all humanity and the necessity of its proclamation by the preacher with either a focus on "sustainers" or "reformers" were just some of the important lessons King absorbed during his ministerial formation at Ebenezer

---

44. Baldwin, *Voice of Conscience*, 79; citing King, *Where Did We Go?*, 96.

45. King, "Autobiography of Religious Development"; cited in Lischer, *Preacher King*, 15.

Baptist Church.[46] Who were the sustainers? They included people like King's great grandfather, A. D. Williams, who was deeply committed to preaching about the spiritual needs of the enslaved and refused to challenge the causes behind enslavement. The reformers assumed a different position. They were described as "race men" and they knew how to speak truth to power; they dreamt of a new world order, with just conditions for black people; they employed the mastery of their words to capture their vision and bring about radical change.[47] In his preaching, King was committed to both traditions. In the "I Have a Dream" speech we see this most forcibly in his words:

> We can never be satisfied as long as the Negro is the victim of the unspeakable horrors of police brutality. We can never be satisfied as long as our bodies heavy with the fatigue of travel cannot gain lodging in the motels of the highways and the hotels of the cities. We cannot be satisfied as long as the Negro's basic mobility is from a smaller ghetto to a large one. No, no, no we are not satisfied, and we will not be satisfied until justice rolls down like waters and righteousness like a mighty stream.

I am sure King aligned himself to African American preachers, those dedicated to reform such as Edward Blyden, Harriet Tubman, Frederick Douglass, and Nat Turner. No doubt King's greatest exposure to the ideal of reformist Christianity occurred at Ebenezer, where highly respected preachers regularly patronised the pulpit. They were living proponents of the linkage between religion and racial justice. Through such greats King learnt how to preach a reformist theology to the white supremacist. This was but another context that informed King's preaching, and an important one at that. Indeed, his reformist position is reinforced in his "I Have a Dream" speech. Though white commentators tend to interpret this speech through a rather gentle lens, the truth is that for its time this was a radical interpretation of racial justice which severely critiqued the white establishment. All this reminds the Baptist preacher of the importance of context within the drama of preaching.

I wonder, if King were alive today, what contemporary concerns he would be encouraging preachers to wrestle with? Misogyny would likely be on his list of priorities. In the aftermath of the brutal murder of Sarah Everard (in March 2021), it seems the British public have woken up to

46. Lischer, *Preacher King*, 28.
47. Lischer, *Preacher King*, 28.

the horrors of misogyny.[48] The gravity of this issue confirms why the preacher needs to engage with a womanist and feminist theology and ground it in his or her sermons. This is an issue of our time to which women and men, black and white need to give serious attention, and to engage our congregations.

I would also expect that King would encourage preachers to address issues of climate injustice. This is an issue that is not going to disappear anytime soon. When you think that the continent of Africa contributes the least to the earth's environmental dangers, yet it is the most vulnerable to their impact, this highlights why this challenge will be with us for many years to come. Africa's environmental challenges threaten not only the continent's public health but also its economy and social fabric. This is a global injustice. Swathes of Africans may be forced to leave their beloved continent, which will be drained of their skills and talents because of climate injustice. With King's passion and commitment for global justice, climate injustice might be the second issue to feature on King's list of contemporary matters for preachers.

A third concern would be poverty. The March on Washington, often described as the "Poor People's Campaign" or the "Poor People's March on Washington," illuminated King's commitment to this concern. The Poor People's Campaign was motivated by a desire for economic justice, the idea that every person should have what they need to live. King shifted his focus to these issues after observing that gains on civil rights had not improved the material conditions for African Americans. Yet decades after the death of King, economic injustice remains firmly on the global map, with masses of people migrating from poverty to countries that promise something like survival. Indeed, a critical function of the preacher is to tell powerful stories of the oppressed and poor and to reason why God stands firmly on their side. King did this well. He not only lambasted those in power for their rapacious quest for more power, but the content of his sermons also reinforced his commitment to be with and for the poor.

As a public theologian, King was committed to the intersect between God-talk and societal injustice. King's theological commitment to a new dawn and a new day, one laced with justice for all, was reflected in his "I Have a Dream" speech.

48. See for example the article by Gaby Hinsliff in *The Guardian*, March 15, 2021, https://www.theguardian.com/commentisfree/2021/mar/15/vigils-sarah-everard-women.

Finally, the task of the preacher includes commitment to a postcolonial biblical interpretation, taking seriously the reality of empires in the ancient and contemporary worlds. By remembering and acknowledging projects that have dehumanised the other, postcolonial interpreters can bring a new and fresh perspective to the text and the drama of preaching. Themes around racism and justice explored in his "I Have a Dream" speech and its challenge to white America demonstrate King's commitment to decolonised preaching.[49] King knew that this type of preaching does not attempt to offer easy answers to the problem of evil, nor does it easily untangle the complex threads that make up postcolonial life. Rather, what this type of theologically reflective and truth-telling preaching can do is to imagine and proclaim a new and just formation of human relationship that is more reflective of God's own life and God's desire for a flourishing and beloved creation.

Numerous books and essays have explored King's enduring legacy. Nearly all of them have commented on his brilliance as a civil rights leader and social activist. Regrettably, a paucity of historians and theologians celebrate him as a Baptist preacher and theologian. He was both. King is an unsung Baptist theologian and preacher.

King had given much thought and care to theodicy; listening to the cries of the broken. He gave careful attention to the ways in which evil impacts black lives: the oppressive structures and systems that destroy the black American soul. The venerable James Cone believed that King's teachings were fundamental to the development of black theology. He encouraged black theologians to learn from the feet of the Baptist theologian who worked within the tradition of the black church. From what I can gather, King's real theological genius relates to his ability to appeal to white intellectual sources which provide a framework for his discourse on love and non-violence. This he did without compromising his theological integrity within the black tradition.

But King was more than a theologian. He was also a Baptist preacher from beginning to end. His preaching was rooted in personalism,[50] the idea that God is personal, and every human being is created in the image of God and in possession of inviolable dignity. His theological vision influenced his preaching and further propelled his commitment to envision what he described as "the triple evils of poverty, racism, and

---

49. For some further reflections, see Hudson-Roberts, "De-Colonizing Theology."
50. See Lischer, *Preacher King*, 57–60.

militarism."[51] King came to believe that racism, economic exploitation, and war were crippling America's ability to create a beloved community defined by love and non-violence. In his preaching King baulked against such evils. King's most memorable speeches—"Our God Is Marching On," "Beyond Vietnam: A Time to Break the Silence," "The Other America," "I've Been to the Mountaintop," and of course "I Have a Dream"—each share a golden thread: they all speak truth to power.

There are reasons why King is my preaching hero, and I am guessing one of Paul Goodliff's too. Before Christine (my wife) introduced me, in 1995, to the radical King, I like many of my Baptist colleagues regarded King as an internationally revered civil rights leader, thrust onto the international landscape mainly because of his "Dream" speech. It took a while for me to recognise that King was more than an exceptionally gifted civil rights leader. He was also a maestro with words, able to convey his insights (theological and otherwise) with unprecedented eloquence and a depth of conviction. Presentation remained one part of his preaching tapestry. King's commitment to dismantling the triple evils confirms him as a prophetic preacher able and willing to preach in the public square. This required gift and courage.

History has not been kind to King's character and that might be because King's character has not always been kind to history. What is, however, incontrovertible is that black Baptist America has left, not a saint of the Baptist world, but one of the greatest preachers of any decade, whose preaching style and content, on this side of history, remain forever etched in preaching memorabilia. Professor Anthony Reddie hits the nail on the head when he says, as he often does to me, "Baptists have not only produced one of the finest theologians in the world, but the finest preacher of all time." He is a black man. His name is King, Dr. Martin Luther King, and we Baptists should celebrate and learn from his preaching achievements more than we currently do.[52]

---

51. Reddie, "Preaching of Martin Luther King, Jr," 179.

52. For another recent British Baptist engagement with King and preaching, see Woodman, "'I Have a Vision.'" See also, Gotobed, "Rediscovering Justice"; Hopkins, "Martin Luther King, Jr," in Reddie, *Journeying to Justice*; and Reddie, "Preaching of Martin Luther King, Jr," in Reddie, *Intercultural Preaching*.

15

MINISTRY AS PRAYER

John Colwell

In those days when the number of the disciples was increasing, the Grecian Jews among them complained against the Hebraic Jews because their widows were being overlooked in the daily distribution of food. So the Twelve gathered all the disciples together and said, "It would not be right for us to neglect the ministry of the word of God in order to wait on tables. Brothers and sisters, choose seven men from among you who are known to be full of the Spirit and wisdom. We will turn this responsibility over to them and will give our attention to prayer and the ministry of the word." (Acts 6:1–4)

ONE CAN BUT BE bemused by the common notion that this incident in Acts represents the appointing of the first diaconate. Of course it is always tempting to read current practice back into the New Testament in order to promote such practice as "biblical" (in this instance, to make such a claim for that form of diaconate that has been common in Baptist churches), but the assertion is weakly founded. It may be that the word "deacon" (διάκονος) is en route within the New Testament to the naming of a specific office within the church (as might be the case in Rom 16:1; Phil 1:1; 1 Tim 3:8–13), but the office of "deacon" that emerged over the first hundred years of the church's existence was a junior order of ministry bearing little resemblance to a Baptist diaconate. However, and more fundamentally, one should note that the word in this passage that gives us our word "deacon" and here is translated "ministry" (διακονία) refers both to the responsibility to which "the seven" were appointed and also to the continuing responsibility of the apostles. Now we may, of course, compare the responsibilities of Baptist deacons to the social and administrative responsibilities identified here—but this is no justification for identifying such as "biblical" deacons, anymore than it is ground for naming as "deacons" those commissioned in this passage—they were more simply those set aside for a particular responsibility in order to liberate the apostles to continue with their specific responsibility. And both responsibilities are identified as ministry, as service, as *diakonia* (διακονία).

That this common word so often translated as "ministry" is a general word for *service*, that a "minister" is a *servant*, should not be overlooked or underplayed. It has become fashionable in recent years, both in and beyond the church, to promote the idea of "servant leadership," but, as I have argued elsewhere,[1] one should be suspicious of a noun when used as an adjective. Which is the qualifier here: is one primarily a servant who serves by leading, or a leader who leads by serving? Does one who ministers self-identify primarily as a servant or primarily as a leader? And one ought also to remember that the notion of leadership within the New Testament is overwhelmingly the leadership of example rather than the leadership of telling other people what to do (Heb 13:7). Stephen, Philip, and the others were set aside to serve the church in the fair distribution of food to those in need; the apostles were to continue to serve the church through the Word and through prayer.

Now, that the apostles were to devote themselves to the ministry of the Word is, surely, unsurprising. Eleven of them, at least, had comprised Jesus' intimate circle: they had seen his miracles; they had heard his teaching; they were witnesses of his resurrection. Moreover (and perhaps more especially), Jesus had promised that the Holy Spirit would teach them "all things," would "remind" them of everything he had said to them, would "guide" them "into all truth" (John 14:26; 16:13). In the days well before the writing of any of that which we know as the New Testament, it was the living and personal testimony of the apostles that was foundational in the life of the church in every sense. Luke tells us that the first church "devoted themselves to the apostles' teaching" (Acts 2:42), and the word rendered "devoted" (προσκαρτεροῦντες) should signify to us that we are

1. Colwell, "Integrity and Relatedness," 18.

not dealing here with detached and abstracted doctrine, with credal box-ticking. As Stanley Hauerwas and others have repeatedly affirmed, it is not that Christian doctrine has ethical implications; rather the claim that Jesus is Lord is itself an ethical (and doxological) commitment.[2] The apostles' teaching, not to mention the example of their lives, gave shape to those first communities of disciples: both in the lives of the apostles and in those growing communities of disciples, doctrine was embodied.

But what perhaps is surprising is the addition of prayer to this ministry of the Word as descriptive of the distinctive responsibility of the apostles. Luke clearly was not implying that prayer was the exclusive prerogative of the apostles—he had previously described the first church as devoted to prayer just as they were devoted to the apostles' teaching, to fellowship, to the breaking of bread—but he was surely implying (or rather, he was recording the apostles themselves as implying) that prayer was a particular responsibility of the apostles alongside the ministry of the Word: they were separated to prayer just as they were separated to the Word. We are accustomed to thinking of ordained ministry in terms of a ministry of Word and sacrament, but I am unaware (or perhaps just ignorant) of any liturgy for ordination that, beyond a promise to remain faithful in prayer, explicitly separates an ordinand for a ministry of Word and prayer. I can certainly conceive of an understanding of sacrament that identifies such as a form of prayer—a sacrament can be understood as an enacted prayer in response to a specific promise—but I would struggle to think of an understanding of prayer that identifies it as sacrament (without so broadening an understanding of sacrament as to empty it of any specific significance). Moreover, the sheer number of baptisms noted in the Acts of the Apostles, together with the references to the breaking of bread "in their homes" (Acts 2:46), would strongly suggest that neither celebration was presided over exclusively by the apostles. So, without prejudice to the appropriateness of an understanding of ordained minis-try as a ministry of Word and sacrament, we are compelled to contend with the significance of the apostles' self-understanding as being sepa-rated to a ministry of the Word and prayer.

2. So for instance "[w]e Christians ought not to search for the 'behavioral implica-tions' of our beliefs. Our moral life is not comprised of beliefs plus decisions; our moral life is the process in which our convictions form our character to be truthful"; Hauerwas, *Peaceable Kingdom*, 16.

David Bebbington identifies activism as one of the key characteristics of evangelicalism[3] and, to my shame, I recall almost fifty years ago being robustly rebuked by a Franciscan Sister when I, with the arrogance characteristic of youth, questioned the point of contemplative monastic orders. I suspect that most of us instinctively would sit more comfortably with being separated to a ministry of Word and leadership, a ministry of Word and management, a ministry of Word and pastoral care, a ministry of Word and social involvement, a ministry of Word and political engagement—but a call to a ministry of Word and prayer comes as a rather discomforting challenge. All too easily we embrace more obviously productive activities to consume our time: there are books to read, sermons to prepare, people to visit, meetings to arrange or attend, strategies to form, programmes to devise—of course we would hope to do all these things prayerfully (whatever that means), but to deprioritize all such activity in favour of prayer itself would strike many of us as an excuse for idleness.

I suspect, however, that the truth of the matter is rather the other way around: it is not that a commitment to prayer is a pretext for limiting such activism but rather that such activism is a pretext for evading a commitment to prayer. Though instinctively suspicious of statistics, the questionnaires on which they are based, and the unqualified candour of our responses to such questionnaires, it is hard not to conclude that many (if not most) in ordained ministry struggle with any disciplined life of prayer. And while a disposition to activism, alongside pressures to conform to the expectations of deacons, church members, and wider society, may underlie such struggles, I suspect a deeper root lies in our struggles with the dynamic of prayer itself.

> Little Boy kneels at the foot of the bed,
> Droops on the little hands little gold head.
> Hush! Hush! Whisper who dares!
> Christopher Robin is saying his prayers.[4]

I am deeply grateful for parents who taught me to pray, both morning and evening, and who themselves set an example of prayerfulness, themselves praying always at the beginning and ending of the day and pausing to pray whenever anything significant arose in the course of the day. I recollect (though I have no reference for it) Christopher Milne

3. Bebbington, *Evangelicalism in Modern Britain*, 10–12.
4. Milne, "Vespers."

commenting on his father's poem that if one left it beyond the age of six to teach a child to pray, one had probably left it too late. But one should also recollect Christopher Milne's somewhat ambivalent appreciation of the stories and poems his father wrote of his childhood and recollect also the slightly tongue-in-cheek but all-too-realistically believable manner in which the poem continues:

> God bless Mummy. I know that's right.
> Wasn't it fun in the bath tonight?
> The cold's so cold and the hot's so hot.
> Oh! God bless Daddy - I quite forgot.
>
> If I open my fingers a little bit more,
> I can see Nanny's dressing-gown on the door.
> It's a beautiful blue, but it hasn't a hood.
> Oh! God bless Nanny and make her good . . .

Now there's nothing wrong, and quite a lot right, in naming people and situations before God—this, for instance, is the essence of so-called bidding prayer. The problem is that, for very many of us, the practice of prayer doesn't progress much beyond the "God bless Mummy; God bless Daddy" stage, possibly expanding on the descriptions of Mummy, Daddy, or whatever as if the Omniscient One might be ignorant of their particular situation and needs. Moreover, and more fundamentally, we tend to continue to think of prayer as something we are doing or offering to God—a human dynamic, a human (and perhaps meritorious) work. I'm hesitant to name anything as the "secret" of prayer, but perhaps the most profound insight into the dynamic of Christian prayer is that it is participatory: the Christian prays *in* Christ and together with all the saints—never in isolation.

Merely the recognition that the ascended Jesus prays for us is a most comforting reassurance in and of itself: when I am too tired to pray, too preoccupied to pray, too lazy to pray, too aware of my own guilt and shame to pray, wholly confused as to how to pray—Jesus prays.[5] With others I suspect that the prayer of Jesus witnessed in John 17 is rightly termed his "High Priestly Prayer" rather than merely his "Prayer of Consecration." The passage is not merely a witness to how Jesus prayed, then, but is rather given to us as an insight into how Jesus prays now: he continually prays that we may be kept, that we may be made holy,

---

5. See Rom 8:34; Heb 7:25; 1 John 2:1.

that we may be one, that we may be with him to see his glory. And with others I suspect also that when Jesus teaches his disciples to pray "*Our Father* . . . ," he is encouraging them and us to pray with him, to realize that we now are joined to his unique sonship before the Father, to realize that to pray is to share in his praying. To suffix a prayer with the phrase "in the name of Jesus" is not an empty mantra: it identifies our praying with Jesus's praying; it identifies us as not praying on our own behalf but on his.[6] And, following the tradition of the *munus triplex* (the threefold office of Christ), we can perhaps identify three interrelated aspects of our participatory praying, of what it means to pray in Christ and together with all the saints.

In the first place, our praying is a participation in and outworking of Christ's sovereign rule, and this in (at least) two respects. To begin with, the Son and the Father, together with the Spirit, are of one undivided essence: "God was reconciling the world to himself in Christ" (2 Cor 5:19); the Son is not pleading our cause with a reluctant or antagonistic Father—and neither are we. In prayer we are no more attempting to bend God's will to ours than we are informing God of that of which God might be unaware or persuading God to care about a person or situation as deeply as we do. There is nothing of which God is unaware, nor could God possibly care more deeply than he does.[7] Prayer may "change things" (see below), and prayer certainly changes us, but prayer does not change God: God could not be more knowing, more loving, more compassionate, or more caring than he is eternally.

I first met Paul Goodliff in the early 1980s. We had attended the same school in Brighton in the 1960s but some six years apart and only met when Douglas McBain, then the senior minister at Lewin Road Baptist Church, Streatham, asked me to teach Paul New Testament Greek.[8] At the time both Paul and I were enthusiastically involved in various manifestations of the charismatic movement; in that and in other contexts, I have been present in many prayer meetings where the participants seemed to think that the Almighty was hard of hearing and could be moved by our manifest enthusiasm, passion, and persistence. By different routes and perhaps for differing reasons, I, Paul, and one

6. ". . . it is not a picture of Jesus as a successful lawyer in court pleading our case before the Judge of heaven and earth, but a picture of Jesus making a prayer for our prayers to ride upon"; Fiddes, *Participating in God*, 90.

7. See Matt 6:8.

8. See Paul's reflections in Goodliff, "Becoming Present to God," 3.

or two others among the contributors to this volume came to embrace a more contemplative and peaceable pattern of prayer. Over the years Paul and I became firm friends and it was through our discussions, along with others, concerning the nature of ministry and the cruciality of a rhythm of prayer to sustain such that the Order for Baptist Ministry was conceived and formed.

To pray with Jesus and with all the saints is certainly to pray the prayer that he gives to us as his disciples, whether as a prayer in itself or as a pattern for prayer, but maybe more profoundly to pray with Jesus is to pray with him in Gethsemane. Now this could easily issue in a major diversion within this article: the prayer of Jesus in Gethsemane brings into sharpest focus the christological implications of his humanity and his deity, of the will of the Son and the will of the Father. Here Christian history too often has stumbled over the temptation to divide what ought never to be divided: to divide the will of the Son from the will of the Father (contrary to the Council of Nicaea), to divide the humanity of Christ from the divinity of Christ (contrary to the Council of Chalcedon). But at its simplest the narrative of Gethsemane presents us with the one who is truly and fully God submitting himself as one who is truly and fully human to the will of the Father. Such submission is certainly agonizing; it may even in some sense be reluctant and faltering (if we take the narrative seriously), but it is finally trustful.[9] What may appear in Gethsemane and at Golgotha as tragedy is in fact triumph; it is the one who submits to betrayal, abuse, and crucifixion who reigns; the kingship of Jesus is cruciform. According to the Synoptic Gospels, only a few days previously Jesus had cleared the temple courts of money changers and traders: it is always God's will that we oppose human injustice, exploitation, and the misuse of power, but to pray with Jesus is to be ready to submit ourselves trustfully to what we know to be God's will for us no matter how painful, no matter how apparently incomprehensible. To follow Jesus is to take up a cross. In prayer we participate in the reign of Jesus by trustful submission to purposes we cannot comprehend or express. The kingly reign of Jesus is witnessed and furthered through our trustful and submissive praying, through our identification with his Gethsemane prayer. I am highly suspicious of those who claim to find prayer easy: the primary reason for prayer being far from easy is that, in most respects, we simply do not know how to pray; we can only come

9. For a compelling reflection on the significance of the Gethsemane prayer, see Judson, "Awake with Christ in Gethsemane."

before God in agonizing and tearful, yet trustful silence. Such prayer is a Trinitarian event: the Holy Spirit takes our agonizing yet trustful and submissive silences and includes those agonizing silences in the praying of the Son before the Father:

> . . . the Spirit helps us in our weakness. We do not know what we ought to pray for, but the Spirit himself intercedes for us with groans that words cannot express. And he who searches our hearts knows the mind of the Spirit, because the Spirit intercedes for the saints in accordance with God's will. (Rom 8:26–27)

But this leads us to the second respect in which prayer may be a participation in the sovereign office of Christ. As the conundrum has often been expressed: If prayer is, in this regard, no more than a submission to the sovereign will of God, then why pray? If God is sovereign, why pray? If God isn't sovereign, why pray? God either will do what he will do anyway or, if God isn't sovereign, he is impotent to respond. But what if the one who effected his will through the agony of Gethsemane and the cross chooses similarly to effect his will through the struggles and silences of our praying? Jesus first tells Peter (Matt 16:19) and then all his disciples (Matt 18:18) that whatever they bind on earth will have been bound in heaven: if prayer represents the reign of Jesus through submission to God's will, might it not also represent the reign of Jesus as a means of effecting that will, on earth as in heaven? The true dignity of prayer is not that our praying is an attempt to bend God to our will, but rather that our praying is an expression and effecting of God's will on earth, or as Enda McDonagh has put it, prayer is "the way we let God loose in the world."[10] Through our praying, as through our lives and every form of humble and unassuming service, Jesus is effecting his sovereign rule in the world and in our lives.[11] I can conceive of no greater responsibility or privilege.

And just as prayer is a participation in Christ's office as sovereign, so also it is a participation in his office as priest. Revelation depicts the saints surrounding the throne rejoicing in their given identity as kings and

10. McDonagh, *Doing the Truth*, 40–57; cited in Hauerwas, *Peaceable Kingdom*, 108.

11. ". . . prayer is a God-ordained means of fulfilling what God wills. Intercessory prayer is not one means of settling God's mind on a course of action, but one of the ways in which the already settled mind of God effects what he has decreed"; Helm, *Providence of God*, 159.

priests; as the saints who surround the throne, they pray and their prayer rises as incense before God.[12] Jesus alone and uniquely has entered the true holy of holies both as sacrifice and priest on our behalf, but just as he brings us by the Spirit to share in his kingship, so also he brings us by the same Spirit to share in his priesthood. The notion of the priesthood of all believers, much trumpeted by Baptists, has an unfortunate tendency to default to a notion of the priesthood of each believer and a preoccupation with what might (or might not) be "my" ministry. This is almost the converse of the insight that we all share together in the single and unique priesthood of Jesus. At the Lord's Supper we re-present the once-for-all sacrifice of Jesus under the signs of bread and wine; we are present in him before the Father, participating in his priesthood and sacrifice, and through our eating and drinking we are feeding and drinking again of him, renewing our dwelling in him and his dwelling in us by the Spirit. But what it means for us to participate in Christ's priesthood, though supremely expressed and focused at the Lord's Supper, is not exhausted here. A priest is a mediator, one who mediates the creature to the Creator and the Creator to the creature; one who, by the Spirit, mediates the presence of God to the neighbour and to the world and, correspondingly, holds the neighbour and the world before God.

In the first sense, then, to participate in the priesthood of Jesus is simply to be consciously and actively part of the church as his body; to live coherently as one whose life only makes sense because Jesus was crucified and rose from the dead; to live meekly, peaceably, faithfully; and by such living (mostly unconsciously) to be a means of the presence of Christ to the neighbour and to the world. There may be a particular sense in which those separated to ordained ministry are so separated as living sacraments both to the church and to the world, but such separation is without prejudice to the church itself as a whole being in the form of a living sacrament, a promised presence of God to the world through the mediating presence of the Spirit.[13] And this, perhaps, is what it means to live prayerfully—not in the sense of continuous petition but rather in a continuous expectation of the Spirit's presence in us and through us. I am

12. See Rev 5:10; 8:3–4; cf. 1 Pet 2:9.

13. ". . . the Church, in Christ, is in the nature of sacrament—a sign and instrument, that is, of communion with God and of unity among all men"; *Lumen Gentium*, in Baum, *De Ecclesia*, I 1. Cf.: ". . . God has gathered together and established as the Church, that it may be for each and everyone the visible sacrament of this saving unity" (II 9).

not primarily implying here a felt presence—though such feelings may be welcome and encouraging—but rather a trustful resting in the promise of Christ's presence in and through us by the Spirit. And as thus mediating the presence of God to the neighbour and to the world, we participate in the priestly ministry of Jesus.

And those called to pastoral ministry may participate in this priestly ministry of Jesus in a quite specific sense. Baptists among others rightly reject sacerdotalism, an assumption of agential authority on the part of those separated through ordination to Christian ministry. We may not be called to be agents with the authority in and of ourselves to manipulate God's grace in the lives of men and women, but we are separated in a specific manner to be instruments and thereby bearers of this grace. In Christian ministry we are wholly impotent and incompetent to effect anything that truly and eternally matters, but we minister in the wake of a promise that the Holy Spirit will breathe and act through our weakness and vulnerability, that we may be bearers of the presence of God to those for whom we have pastoral responsibility, that by grace those who receive us will receive him, that those who hear us will in reality hear him. As participating in this particular manner in the priestly ministry of Jesus, we are bearers of the presence of God.

But we participate also in the priesthood of Jesus by representing the neighbour and the world before God. Here is the right place (and the right understanding) of the "God bless Mummy, God bless Daddy" prayer. In prayer we hold people and situations before God, interceding on behalf of those who can and do pray for themselves and similarly for those who can't or won't, interceding on behalf of a world that is God-forsaking but never God-forsaken. But here especially the simple bidding prayer, naming a person or situation before God, is to be encouraged. Our God does not need a situation explained or elaborated. God does not need to be persuaded by our passion, compassion, or enthusiasm. More particularly (and recalling what has previously been said), though we may cherish our desires and hopes for those people and situations we bear before God, it is God's will that we seek for those people and situations, knowing that God's ultimate good may not be furthered by our perception of a penultimate good. Our first prayer always is that God's name should be hallowed. Our concluding prayer always is that God should be glorified.

Moreover, there is surely a particular sense in which such petitionary prayer is a quite specific responsibility of those separated to pastoral ministry. Time and again throughout the Old Testament we find Moses, the psalmists, and the prophets pleading with God on behalf of the people, holding them before God in their prayers, acting as mediators on behalf of the people before God, and thereby fulfilling a priestly ministry. Jack Hair, who was the minister of the Baptist church in which I spent my teenage years and which recommended me for ordained ministry, shared with me his habit of regularly praying for every church member, generally simply naming them before God but sometimes naming specific situations and circumstances and holding them in moments of quietness before him. It is a habit I embraced and followed throughout the years of pastoral ministry, both in the churches I have pastored and in the college for the students for whom I had some pastoral care. And even now in retirement I endeavour to follow a disciplined pattern of regular prayer for these from my past and for the members of the church of which I am presently a member. Of course I am quite unaware of the specific circumstances of the majority of those that I hold in prayer in this way—that isn't the point; I continue to assume (or perhaps presume) a responsibility for them before God. This may strike some as a minimal exercise of pastoral responsibility—but what could be less minimal than prayer when that prayer is offered on behalf of the Son before the Father?

And just as in prayer we participate in the kingly and priestly offices of Christ, so also we participate in his prophetic office, and this again in (at least) two respects. As those who pray we are, with all the saints of the present and the past, signs of things to come. Some while ago I was expressing to a friend how grateful I was for life itself and for so much that life for me has entailed. This friend (relation) would identify himself as an atheist and, as I talked in this way, it slowly dawned on me that he had no idea what I was talking about: for him everything simply just is; there is no one to whom ultimately to be grateful. Too easily we can overlook just how strange is our everyday language and behaviour to those who do not share our faith and commitment. When my grandmother first became a Christian as a widow and single parent in the 1920s, the first change her children (my mother and my uncle) noticed was her pausing to pray whenever there was cause for specific gratitude or specific concern. For those who do not know God, prayer is the oddest thing, gratitude to God is the oddest thing, trust in this God against all that is apparent is the oddest thing, and hopefulness is perhaps the oddest thing of all. Most of us go through our Christian lives without realizing just how incomprehensibly odd we are. To live faithfully, hopefully, and lovingly within the world is prophetic in and of itself—and we will live thus if our praying is bounded by gratitude and trustful expectation. Perhaps the most immediate manner in which prayer can change a situation is by changing us within that situation and, through our witness, challenging the manner in which others view that situation. A disciplined rhythm of prayer, whether we realize it or not, changes us and renders us a prophetic presence within the world. I write this in the second year that the world has been groaning under the COVID-19 pandemic: there could not be a more appropriate moment for grateful, hopeful, trustful, charitable living to be a prophetic witness to the one who is the source of that gratitude, hopefulness, trust, and love.

But here again there is surely a quite specific manner in which those separated to a ministry of the Word, through being separated also to prayer, participate in the prophetic office of Christ. One of the effects of the Enlightenment on Protestantism (and to a lesser extent also Catholicism) was to reduce the Scriptures to the givenness of the purely objective. For both biblical liberalism and biblical fundamentalism the text of Scripture is perceived as objectively accessible; the testimony of prophets and apostles is reduced to dead letters on a page to be unpacked critically and "scientifically." The place of prayer in this interpretative task is entirely secondary to literary critical theory or evangelical dogmatic tradition. Precritical interpretations of Scripture, not to mention the interpretations of Old Testament texts by New Testament writers, are dismissed as unwarranted and wholly subjective. So perhaps here supremely we should pause to ponder the significance of the apostles being separated to prayer alongside the ministry of the Word. If we perceive the Scriptures as an object at our disposal, then prayer is superfluous in their interpretation and exposition. But if we receive the Scriptures as a means of grace with the promise that the Spirit who inspired its human authors will speak through these texts, rendering them a living word to and through us, then prayer is surely foundational to this dynamic. The Scriptures are given to us not merely that we should be informed but that we should be transformed through our hearing of them being read and expounded. And here supremely we are wholly incompetent. We might be competent to inform, to lecture on the Scriptures, but we are wholly incompetent to effect transformation; we are wholly dependent upon the Spirit, we are wholly dependent upon prayer. The Middle Ages witnessed the institution of universities and the consequent gradual disjoining of a separation to study from a separation to prayer. The Enlightenment confirmed and reinforced that disjunction. I was formerly Tutor in Christian Doctrine and Ethics at Spurgeon's College and I made it my mission to abolish the "and" linking doctrine and ethics as if they could be separate and separable disciplines:

> ... for the searching and right understanding of the Scriptures there is need of a good life and a pure soul, and for Christian virtue to guide the mind to grasp, so far as human nature can, the truth concerning God the Word. One cannot possibly understand the teaching of the saints unless one has a pure mind and is trying to imitate their life.[14]

And correspondingly I would seek to repudiate the "and" linking prayer and the ministry of the Word. Such a disjunction would have been unthinkable for the apostles, remained unthinkable for the first thousand years of the church's existence, and should be reaffirmed as unthinkable for us.[15] Theological language that is not at the same time doxological language is ultimately inauthentic. The language of doctrine is the language of prayer and praise. To be separated to a ministry of the Word is to be separated to prayer—where this is not the case, one simply isn't separated to an authentic ministry of the Word.

To pray in the name of Jesus, then, is to participate on earth in his continuing kingly, priestly, and prophetic ministry. I can conceive of no greater privilege or responsibility. Such praying should be the rhythm of my life that orders and precedes every other activity, not least the ministry of the Word.

---

14. Athanasius, *On the Incarnation*, 96 (57).

15. For a recent reflection on the gradual disjunction of theology and prayer, see Cocksworth, *Prayer*.

Bibliography of the Writings of Paul W. Goodliff

———. "Annunciation: Behold a Virgin Shall Conceive." In *Rhythms of Faithfulness: Essays in Honor of John E. Colwell*, edited by Andy Goodliff and Paul Goodliff, 128–39. Eugene, OR: Pickwick, 2018.

———. "Anyone Still for Ordination?" *Ministry Today* 50 (November 2010) 4–11.

———. "Approaching Retirement." *Ministry Today* 57 (April 2013) 23–28.

———. "Baptists and Ecumenism." *Baptist Ministers' Journal* 346 (April 2020) 17–23.

———. "Baptist Church Polity." In *Church Laws and Ecumenism: New Paths for Christian Unity*, edited by Norman Doe, 188–207. New York: Routledge, 2020.

———. "Baptist Church Polity and Practice." *Law & Justice* 168 (2012) 5–21.

———. "Baptist Theology Reconsidered: A Review Article." *Baptist Quarterly* 46.3 (July 2015) 113–19.

———. "Becoming Present to God." In *Rhythms of Faithfulness: Essays in Honor of John E. Colwell* edited by Andy Goodliff and Paul Goodliff, 3–15. Eugene, OR: Pickwick, 2018.

———. "Capability and Competence." *Baptist Ministers' Journal* 320 (October 2013) 3–6.

———. *Care in a Confused Climate: Pastoral Care and Postmodern Culture.* London: Darton, Longman & Todd, 1998.

———. "The Church as Sign and Agent of the Kingdom." In *On Earth as in Heaven: A Theology of Social Action for Baptist Churches*, edited by Stephen Finamore, 34–42. Didcot: Baptist Union, 1996.

———. "Capability and Competence." *Baptist Ministers' Journal* 320 (October 2013) 3–6.

———. "Conscience and Natural Law: A Calvinist Perspective." In *The Legal Legacy of the Reformation: Catholic and Protestant Approaches Then and Today*, edited by John Duddington. Forthcoming.

———. "Contemporary Models of Translocal Ministry: Ecumenical Landscapes." In *Episcope: The Theory and Practice of Translocal Oversight*, edited by Paul Goodliff and Roger Standing, 44–58. London: SCM, 2020.

———. "Contemporary Models of Translocal Ministry." In *Translocal Ministry: Equipping the Churches for Mission*, edited by Stuart Murray, 55–63. Didcot: Baptist Union, 2004.

———. "Diversity of Ministries." In *A Dictionary of European Baptist Life and Thought*, edited by John H. Y. Briggs et al., 325–26. Milton Keynes: Paternoster, 2009.

———. "Doing or Being: An Old Chestnut Revisited." *Baptist Minister's Journal* 228 (October 2004) 3–12.

———, and Roger Standing, eds. *Episcope: The Theory and Practice of Translocal Oversight*. London: SCM, 2020.

———. "Episkope and Supervision." In *Episcope: The Theory and Practice of Translocal Oversight*, edited by Paul Goodliff and Roger Standing, 244–53. London: SCM, 2020.

———, with Andy Goodliff. "Gunton on Theology, Ministry and the Christian Life." In *T & T Clark Handbook of Colin Gunton*, edited by Andrew Picard, Myk Habets, and Murray Rae, 221–35. London: T & T Clark, 2021.

———. "In Obedient Living Find Your Home: Reflections on Baptists and Discipleship." In *Gathering Disciples: Essays in Honor of Christopher J. Ellis*, edited by Myra Blyth and Andy Goodliff, 60–72. Eugene, OR: Pickwick, 2017.

———. "Inclusive Representation Revisited." *Challenging to Change: Dialogues with a Radical Baptist Theologian. Essays Presented to Dr Nigel G Wright on His Sixtieth Birthday*, edited by in Pieter J. Lalleman, 105–16. London: Spurgeon's College, 2009.

———. *Ministry, Sacrament and Representation: Ministry and Ordination in Contemporary Baptist Theology and the Rise of Sacramentalism*. Centre for Baptist History and Heritage Studies 2. Oxford: Regent's Park College, 2010.

———. "Ministry Today UK: A Personal Baptist Reflection." *Ministry Today* 72 (February 2018) 4–9.

———. "Natural Law in the Baptist Tradition." In *Christianity and Natural Law: An Introduction*, edited by Norman Doe, 140–61. Cambridge: Cambridge University Press, 2017.

———. "Networks." Paper presented as part of Baptist Futures Process, Baptist Union of Great Britain, 2012.

———. "On Eagles' Wings: Exploring the Hinterlands of the Order for Baptist Ministry." Paper written for the tenth anniversary of the Order for Baptist Ministry, December 2020. https://www.orderforbaptistministry.co.uk/?wpfb_dl=240.

———. "Ordination." In *A Dictionary of European Baptist Life and Thought*, edited by John H. Y. Briggs et al., 367–69. Milton Keynes: Paternoster, 2009.

———. "The Pastoral Care of Pastoral Counsellors." *Ministry Today* 23 (October 2001) 26–28.

———. "Pastoral Call." In *A Dictionary of European Baptist Life and Thought.*, edited by John H. Y. Briggs et al., 377–78. Milton Keynes: Paternoster, 2009.

———. "The Power and the Glory." *Ministry Today* 3 (February 1995) 6–12.

———, and Andy Goodliff, eds. *Rhythms of Faithfulness: Essays in Honor of John E. Colwell*. Eugene, OR: Pickwick, 2018.

———. *Shaped for Service: Ministerial Formation and Virtue Ethics*. Eugene, OR: Pickwick, 2017.

———. "Surviving and Thriving in Ministry." *Ministry Today* 19 (June 2000) 7–10.

———. "Training Ministerial Students in Spirituality." *Ministry Today* 33 (Spring 2005) 203–13.

———. "Translocal Ministry and Scholarship." In *Episcope: The Theory and Practice of Translocal Oversight*, edited by Paul Goodliff and Roger Standing, 225–31. London: SCM, 2020.

———. "We Want It All, and We Want It Now?" *Ministry Today* 39 (March 2007) 111–18.

———. *With Unveiled Face: A Pastoral and Theological Exploration of Shame*. London: Darton, Longman & Todd, 2005.

———. "Women's Ministry: An Exploration at a Historic Moment." *Baptist Quarterly* 45.8 (October 2014) 485–99.

———. "The Word Made Flesh, Lent, Good Friday." *Theology* 121.2 (2018) 122–23.

General Bibliography

Adair, John. *Effective Leadership: How to be a Successful Leader.* Rev. ed. London: Pan, 1990.

Aelred of Rievaulx. *Spiritual Friendship.* Cistercian Fathers 5. Kalamazoo, MI: Cistercian, 1977.

Alvesson, Mats, and Andre Spicer, eds. *Metaphors We Lead By: Understanding Leadership in the Real World.* New York: Routledge, 2011.

Anderson, Pamela Sue, and Paul S. Fiddes. "Creating a New Imaginary for Love in Religion." *Angelaki* 25.1–2 (2020) 46–53.

Arendt, Hannah. *The Human Condition.* 2nd ed. Chicago: University of Chicago Press, 2018.

Athanasius. *St. Athanasius on the Incarnation: The Treatise De Incarnatione Verbi Dei.* Translated and edited by a Religious of CSMV. London: Mowbray, 1953.

Baldwin, Lewis V. *The Voice of Conscience: The Church in the Mind of Martin Luther King, Jr.* Oxford: Oxford University Press, 2010.

Banks, Robert. *Reenvisioning Theological Education: Exploring a Missional Alternative to Current Models.* Grand Rapids: Eerdmans, 1999.

The Baptist Hymn Book. London: Psalms and Hymns Trust, 1962.

Baptist Praise and Worship. Oxford: Oxford University Press, 1991.

Baptist Union of Great Britain. *Ignite Report.* Didcot: Baptist Union, 2015.

Barbour, Reid. *Literature and Religious Culture in Seventeenth-Century England.* Cambridge: Cambridge University Press, 2002.

Barenboim, Daniel. *Everything Is Connected: The Power of Music.* London: Verso, 2008.

Barth, Karl. *Evangelical Theology: An Introduction.* Translated by Grover Foley. London: Weidenfeld & Nicolson, 1963.

Baum, Gregory. *De Ecclesia: The Constitution on the Church of Vatican Council II with Commentary.* London: Darton, Longman & Todd, 1965.

Baxter, Richard Baxter. *The Reformed Pastor.* Abridged 5th ed. Edinburgh: Banner of Truth, 1974 (1656).

Bear, Bethany Joy. "Fantastical Faith: John Bunyan and the Sanctification of Fancy." *Studies in Philology* 109.5 (Fall 2012) 671–701.

Beasley-Murray Paul. *A Call to Excellence.* London: Hodder & Stoughton, 1995.

———. *Dynamic Leadership.* Eastbourne: Marc, 1990.

———. *Living Out the Call,* book 2, *Leading God's People.* 2nd ed. Feed-a-Read, 2016.

———. *Make the Most of Retirement.* London: DLT, 2020.

———. "Ministers' Reading Habits." *Baptist Quarterly* 49.1 (January 2018) 23–44.

————. *Retirement Matters for Ministers*. Chelmsford: College of Baptist Ministers, 2018.

————. *This Is My Story: A Story of Life, Faith, and Ministry*. Eugene, OR: Wipf & Stock, 2018.

Bebbington, David W. *Evangelicalism in Modern Britain: A History from the 1730s to the 1980s*. London: Unwin Hyman, 1989.

Begbie, Jeremy. "Play It (Again): Music, Theology and Divine Communication." In *Creative Chords: Studies in Music, Theology and Christian Formation*, edited by Jeff Astley, Timothy Hone, and Mark Savage, 45–75. Leominster: Gracewing, 2000.

————. *Resounding Truth: Christian Wisdom in the World of Music*. London: SPCK, 2008.

Berry, Wendell. *The Art of the Common Place: The Agrarian Essays of Wendell Berry*. Edited and introduced by Norman Wirzba. Berkeley, CA: Counterpoint, 2002.

Bevans, Stephen. *An Introduction to Theology in a Global Perspective*. Maryknoll, NY: Orbis, 2009.

Bevans, Stephen, and Roger Schroeder. *Constants in Context: A Theology of Mission for Today*. Maryknoll, NY: Orbis, 2004.

Biggs, J. "Enhancing Teaching through Constructive Alignment." *Higher Education* 32 (1996) 347–64.

Billingsley, Naomi. *The Visionary Art of William Blake*. London: I. B. Tauris, 2018.

Blake, William. *The Marriage of Heaven and Hell*. Oxford: Oxford University Press, 1975.

Blyth, Myra N. "The Meaning and Function of 'Dynamic Equivalence' in Ecumenical Dialogues." In *For the Sake of the Church: Essays in Honour of Paul S. Fiddes*, edited by Anthony J. Clarke, 163–72. Oxford: Regent's Park College, 2014.

————. "Re-Imagining Restorative Justice: The Value of Forgiveness." *Oxford Journal of Law and Religion* 5.1 (2016): 66–78.

————. "Towards a Restorative Hermeneutic: Local Christian Communities Responding to Crime and Wrongdoing." PhD thesis, University of Birmingham, 2012.

————. "*The Word of God in the Life of the Church*: A Review Article." *Baptist Quarterly* 45 (October 2013) 248–53.

Blyth, Myra, Matthew Mills, and Michael H. Taylor. *Forgiveness and Restorative Justice: Perspectives from Christian Theology*. London: Palgrave Macmillan, 2021.

Boff, Leonardo, and Clodovis Boff. *Introducing Liberation Theology*. Maryknoll, NY: Orbis, 1987.

Bonhoeffer, Dietrich. *Life Together*. Translated by John W. Doberstein. London: SCM, 1954.

Britannica. "Temperance Movement." https://www.britannica.com/topic/temperance-movement.

Brown, Thomas Edward. "My Garden." In *The Oxford Book of English Verse, 1250–1900*, edited by Arthur Qiuller-Couch, 1063. Oxford: Clarendon, 1912.

Browne, John. *A History of Congregationalism and the Memorials of the Churches in Norfolk and Suffolk*. London, Jarrold & Sons, 1877.

Brueggemann, Walter. *The Practice of Prophetic Imagination*. Minneapolis: Fortress, 2012.

Burnett, Francis Hodgson. *The Secret Garden*. London: Arcturus, 2018.

Callahan, Allen Dwight. *Embassy of Onesimus: The Letter of Paul to Philemon*. Valley Forge, PA: Trinity, 1997.

Calvin, John. *Institutes of the Christian Religion*. 2 vols. Translated by Henry Beveridge. London: James Clarke, 1949.

Campbell, Charles L. *The Scandal of the Gospel: Preaching and the Grotesque*. Louisville: Westminster John Knox, 2021.

Carey, Hilary M. *God's Empire: Religion and Colonialism in the British World, c. 1801–1908*. Cambridge: Cambridge University Press, 2011.

Challoner, Richard. *The Garden of the Soul, or, A Manual of Spiritual Exercises and Instructions for Christians Who, Living in the World, Aspire to Devotion*. Richardson and Son, 1843.

Childress, Kyle. "Proper Work: Wendell Berry and the Practice of Ministry." In *Wendell Berry and Religion: Heaven's Earthly Life*, edited by Joel James Shuman and L. Roger Owens, 71–82. Lexington: University Press of Kentucky, 2009.

Clarke, Anthony J. *Forming Ministers or Training Leaders?: An Exploration of Practice in Theological Colleges*. Eugene, OR: Resource, 2021.

Clarke, Anthony J., and Paul S. Fiddes. *Dissenting Spirit: A History of Regent's Park College, 1752–2019*. Oxford: Regent's Park College, 2017.

Clayton, Paul C. *Called for Life: Finding Meaning in Retirement*. Herndon, VA: Alban, 2008.

Cocksworth, Ashley. *Prayer: A Guide for the Perplexed*. London: T. & T. Clark, 2018.

Coggan, Donald. *On Preaching*. London: SPCK, 1978.

Collier, Winn. *A Burning in my Bones: The Authorised Biography of Eugene Peterson*. Milton Keynes: Authentic, 2021.

Collins, Helen. *Reordering Theological Reflection: Starting with Scripture*. London: SCM, 2020.

Colwell, John E. "Integrity and Relatedness: Some Critical Reflections on Congregationalism and Connexionalism." *Baptist Quarterly* 48.1 (2017) 11–22.

———. *Living the Christian Story: The Distinctiveness of Christian Ethics*. Edinburgh: T. & T. Clark, 2001.

———. *The Rhythm of Doctrine: A Liturgical Sketch of Christian Faith and Faithfulness*. Milton Keynes: Paternoster, 2007.

Cone, James. *Martin and Malcolm and America: A Dream or a Nightmare?* Maryknoll, NY: Orbis, 1991.

Copenhaver, Martin B. "The Vow of Stability." In *Pastoral Work: Engagements with the Vision of Eugene Peterson*, edited by Jason Byassee and L. Roger Owens, 157–65. Eugene, OR: Cascade, 2014.

Cortez, Marc. *Theological Anthropology: A Guide for the Perplexed*. London: T. & T. Clark, 2010.

Cross, Anthony R. *"To Communicate Simply You Must Understand Profoundly": Preparation for Ministry Among British Baptists*. Didcot: Baptist Historical Society, 2016.

Davies, Jason W., ed. *R. S. Thomas: Autobiographies*. London: J. M. Dent, 1997.

Day, Christopher. *Places of the Soul*. London: Thorsons, 1990.

Drury, John. *Music at Midnight: The Life and Poetry of George Herbert*. London: Allen Lane, 2013.

Dyrness, William. *Reformed Theology and Visual Culture*. Cambridge: Cambridge University Press, 2004.

Dyson, Michael Eric. *I May Not Get There with You: The True Martin Luther King, Jr.* New York: Free Press, 2000.

Edgington, David. "Hope UK — A Walk Through History." https://www.hopeuk.org/wp-content/uploads/Walk-Through-History-PDF.pdf

Ellenberger, Henri. *The Discovery of the Unconscious.* New York: Basic Books, 1970.

Ellis, Christopher. "Being a Minister: Spirituality and the Pastor." In *Challenging to Change: Dialogues with a Radial Baptist Theologian*, edited by Pieter J. Lalleman, 55–70. London: Spurgeon's College, 2009.

———. *Gathering: A Theology and Spirituality of Worship in Free Church Tradition.* London: SCM, 2004.

Ellis, Robert. "Sporting Space, Sacred Space: A Theology of Sporting Place." *Religions* 19.8 (2019). https://doi.org/10.3390/rel10080473.

Elven, Cornelius. *Report of the Associated Churches of the Particular Baptist Denomination Assembled at Wortwell, in the County of Norfolk, on . . . the 7th and 8th . . . of June, 1831. With an Address on the Subject of Spiritual Reform.* Ipswich: S. H. Cowell, [1831].

Empeurer, James. "Models of Liturgical Theology." In *Twenty Centuries of Christian Worship*, edited by Robert E. Webber, 263–66. The Complete Library of Christian Worship. Nashville: Star Song, 1994.

Essick, John Inscore, and Mark Medley. "Local Catholicity: The Bodies and Places Where Jesus Is (Found)." *Review and Expositor* 112.1 (February 2015) 47–59.

Evans, Mary. "The Powerless Leader." In *On Eagles' Wings: An Exploration of Strength in the Midst of Weakness*, edited by Michael Parsons and David J. Cohen, 78–92. Eugene, OR: Wipf & Stock, 2008.

Farely, Edward. *Theologia: The Fragmentation and Unity of Theological Education.* Philadelphia: Fortress, 1994.

Fiddes, Paul S. "A Conversation in Context: An Introduction to the Report, *The Word of God in the Life of the Church*." *American Baptist Quarterly* 31.1 (2012) 7–27.

———. "Learning from Others: Baptists and Receptive Ecumenism." *Louvain Studies* 33 (2008) 54–73.

———. *Participating in God: A Pastoral Doctrine of the Trinity.* London: DLT, 2000.

———. "Spirituality as Attentiveness: Stillness and Journey." In *Under the Rule of Christ*, edited by Paul S. Fiddes, 25–57. Macon, GA: Smyth & Helwys, 2008.

———. *Tracks and Traces: Baptist Identity in Church and Theology.* Carlisle: Paternoster, 2003.

Freeman, Curtis. *Contesting Catholicity: Theology for Other Baptists.* Waco, TX: Baylor University Press, 2014.

Freire, Paulo. *Pedagogy of the Oppressed.* Translated by Myra Bergman. New York: Herder, 1972.

Gardner, W. H. *Gerard Manley Hopkins (1844–1889): A Study of Poetic Idiosyncrasy in Relation to Poetic Tradition.* 2 vols. London: Oxford University Press, 1958.

Geertz, Clifford. *The Interpretation of Cultures.* New York: Basic Books, 1973.

Gennep, Arnold van. *The Rites of Passage.* Chicago: University of Chicago Press, 1960.

Gerkin, Charles. *An Introduction to Pastoral Care.* Nashville: Abingdon, 1997.

———. *Living Human Document: Re-Visioning Pastoral Counselling in a Hermeneutical Mode.* Nashville: Abingdon, 1984.

Goddard, Liz and Clare Hendry. "From Castles to Conversations: Reflections on How to Disagree Well." In *Good Disagreement?: Grace and Truth in a Divided Church*, edited by Andrew Atherstone and Andrew Goddard, 151–70. Oxford: Lion Hudson, 2015.

Goldstein, David, "Introduction." In *The Song of Songs*, a translation by Peter Jay. London: Anvil Press Poetry, 1975.

Goodhart, David. *The Road to Somewhere: The Populist Revolt and the Future of Politics.* London: Hurst, 2017.

Goodliff, Andy. *Renewing a Modern Denomination.* Eugene, OR: Pickwick, 2020.

Gorringe, Timothy J. "Climate Change: A Confessional Issue for the Churches?" Operation Noah lecture, 2011. http://operationnoah.org/wp-content/uploads/2014/06/Tim_Gorringe_lecture_0.pdf.

———. *The Common Good and the Global Emergency.* Cambridge: Cambridge University Press, 2011.

———. "Salvation by Bricks: Theological Reflections on the Planning Process." *International Journal of Public Theology* 2.1 (2008) 98–118.

———. *The Theology of the Built Environment.* Cambridge: Cambridge University Press, 2002.

Gorringe, Timothy, and Rosie Beckham. *Transition Movement for Churches.* Norwich: Canterbury, 2013.

Gotobed, Julian. "Rediscovering Justice." *Baptist Ministers' Journal* 340 (October 2018) 20–27.

Grass, Tim. *"There My Friends and Kindred Dwell": Strict and Particular Baptist Chapels of Suffolk and Norfolk.* Ramsey: Thornhill, 2012.

Green, Laurie. *Let's Do Theology: Resources for Contextual Theology.* Rev. ed. London: Mowbray, 2009.

Grenz, Stanley J., Roger E. Olson. *Who Needs Theology?: An Invitation to the Study of God.* Downers Grove, IL: InterVarsity, 1996.

Haggis, T. "Constructing Images of Ourselves: A Critical Investigation into 'Approaches to Learning' Research in Higher Education." *British Educational Research Journal* 29.1 (2003) 89–104.

Harris, Harriet. "Should We Say That Personhood Is Relational?" *Scottish Journal of Theology* 51.2 (1998) 214–34.

Harrison, Brian. *Drink and the Victorians: the Temperance Question in England, 1815–1872.* 2nd ed. Staffordshire: Keele University Press, 1992.

Hart, Trevor. *Between the Image and the Word.* Farnham: Ashgate, 2013.

Hauerwas, Stanley. *The Peaceable Kingdom: A Primer in Christian Ethics.* Notre Dame: Notre Dame University Press, 1983.

Hayes, Nick. *The Book of Trespass: Crossing the Lines That Divide Us.* London: Bloomsbury, 2020.

Heelas, Paul, Linda Woodhead, *The Spiritual Revolution: Why Religion Is Giving Way to Spirituality.* Oxford: Blackwell, 2005.

Helm, Paul, *The Providence of God.* Leicester: InterVarsity, 1993.

Herbert, Edward Lord, of Cherbury. *Autobiography.* Edited by Sidney Lee. 2nd ed., rev. London: George Routledge, 1906.

Herbert, George, *The English Poems of George Herbert.* Edited by Helen Wilcox. Cambridge: Cambridge University Press, 2011.

———. *The Priest to the Temple.* In *The Works of George Herbert*, edited by F. E. Hutchinson, 224–90. Oxford: Clarendon, 1941.

Hexter, J. H. *The History Primer.* London: Penguin, 1972.

Hodgson, Peter. *Winds of the Spirit*. London: SCM, 1994.

Hodson, Martin. "Landscapes of Practice: A Model to Enrich our Understanding of Christian Ministry?" *Practical Theology* 13.5 (2020) 504–16.

Holloway, Richard. *Godless Morality: Keeping Religion Out of Ethics*. Edinburgh: Canongate, 2000.

Holmes, Stephen R. *Baptist Theology*. London: T. & T. Clark, 2012.

———. "Knowing Together the Mind of Christ: Congregational Government and the Church Meeting." In *Questions of Identity: Studies in Honour of Brian Haymes*, edited by Anthony R. Cross and Ruth Gouldbourne, 172–88. Oxford: Regent's Park College, 2011.

———. "The Radical Ecclesiology of Nigel Wright." In *Challenging to Change: Dialogues with a Radical Baptist Theologian*, edited by Pieter Lalleman, 117–28. London: Spurgeon's College, 2009.

Hopkins, Dwight N. "Martin Luther King, Jr." In *Journeying to Justice: Contributions to the Baptist Tradition across the Black Atlantic*, edited by Anthony G. Reddie with Wale Hudson-Roberts and Gale Richards, 167–76. Milton Keynes: Paternoster, 2017.

Hopkins, Gerard Manley. *Correspondence*, vol. 1, 1852–1881. Edited by K. K. R. Thornton and Catherine Philips. The Collected Works of Gerard Manley Hopkins 1. Oxford: Oxford University Press, 2013.

———. *The Journals and Papers of Gerard Manley Hopkins*. Edited by Humphrey House and Graham Storey. 2nd ed. Oxford: Oxford University Press, 1959.

———. *The Poems of Gerard Manley Hopkins*. Edited by W. H. Gardner and N. H. MacKenzie. 4th ed. London; Oxford University Press, 1967.

———. *The Sermons and Devotional Writings of Gerard Manley Hopkins*. Edited by Christopher Devlin. London: Oxford University Press, 1959.

Hudson-Roberts, Wale. "De-Colonising Theology—A Continuing Challenge for the 21st Century." In *Being Attentive: Explorations in Practical Theology in Honour of Robert Ellis*, edited by Anthony Clarke, 28–44. Oxford: Centre for Baptist Studies in Oxford, 2021.

———. "Preaching on Intercultural Issues." In *Intercultural Preaching*, edited by Anthony G. Reddie and Seidel Abel Boanerges with Pamela Searle, 149–66. Oxford: Centre for Baptist Studies in Oxford, 2021.

Hughes, Gerard W. *God of Surprises*. London: Darton, Longman & Todd, 1985.

Jacobsen, Eric O. Jacobsen. *Sidewalks in the Kingdom: New Urbanism and the Christian Faith*. Grand Rapids: Baker, 2003.

Jennings, Willie James. *Acts*. Belief: A Theology Commentary on the Bible. Louisville: Westminster/John Knox, 2017.

———. *After Whiteness: An Education in Belonging*. Grand Rapids: Eerdmans, 2020.

———. "Being Baptized: Race." In *The Wiley-Blackwell Companion to Christian Ethics*, edited by Stanley Hauerwas and Samuel Wells, 277–89. 2nd ed. Oxford: Wiley-Blackwell, 2011.

———. "Can White People Be Saved?: Reflections on the Relationship between Missions and Whiteness." In *Can 'White' People Be Saved?: Triangulating Race, Theology, and Mission*, edited by Love L. Sechrest, Johnny Ramirez-Johnson, and Amos Yong, 27–43. Downers Grove, IL: InterVarsity, 2018.

———. *The Christian Imagination: Theology and the Origins of Race*. New Haven, CT: Yale, 2010.

———. "The Christian Story of God's Work: An African American Response." In *T & T Clark Handbook of Christian Theology and Climate Change*, edited by Ernst M. Conradie and Hilda P. Koster, 474–79. London: T. & T. Clark, 2020.

———. "Disfigurations of Christian Identity: Performing Identity as Theological Method." In *Lived Theology*, edited by Charles Marsh, Peter Slade, and Sarah Azaransky, 67–83. Oxford: Oxford University Press, 2016.

———. "Eco-Theology and Zoning Meetings: An Interview with Willie Jennings." *Reflections*, Spring 2019. https://reflections.yale.edu/article/crucified-creation-green-faith-rising/eco-theology-and-zoning-meetings-interview-willie.

———. "Foreword." In *Healing Our Broken Humanity*, by Grace Ji-Sun Kim and Graham Hill. Downers Grove, IL: InterVarsity, 2018.

———. "Overcoming Racial Faith." *Duke Divinity Magazine*, Spring 2015, 4–9.

———. "A Place of Redemption: Putting Church on the Ground." Lecture at the Slow Church Conference, Englewood Christian Church, 2014. https://englewoodreview.org/willie-jennings-slow-church-conference-audio/.

———. "Protestantism." In *The Cambridge Companion to Literature and Religion*, edited by Susan Felch, 249–61. Cambridge: Cambridge University Press, 2016.

———. "Reframing the World: Toward an Actual Christian Doctrine of Creation." *International Journal of Systematic Theology* 21.4 (October 2019) 388–407.

John, Eeva, Naomi Nixon, and Nick Shepherd. "Life-Changing Learning for Christian Discipleship and Ministry: A Practical Exploration." *Practical Theology* 11.4 (2018) 300–14.

John of the Cross, Saint. *The Collected Works of Saint John of the Cross*. Translated by Kieran Kavanaugh and Otilio Rodriguez. Rev. ed. Washington: Institute of Carmelite Studies, 2017 (1991).

Johnson, Hugh. *The Story of Wine: From Noah to Now*. London: Mitchell Beazley, 1989.

Judson, Timothy R. "Awake with Christ in Gethsemane: Lament in Dietrich Bonhoeffer's Christological Ecclesiology." PhD diss., University of Aberdeen, 2021.

Klaiber, A. J. *The Story of the Suffolk Baptists*. London: Carey Kingsgate, 1931.

Khalid, Hina. "At the Bedside: A Theological Consideration of the Role of Silence and Touch in the Accompaniment of the Dying." *Scottish Journal of Theology* 73.2 (May 2020) 150–59.

Kreslinger, Gisela H. *The Soul of Wine*. Downers Grove, IL: InterVarsity, 2019.

———. *The Spirituality of Wine*. Grand Rapids: Eerdmans, 2016.

Ladonne, Jennifer. "A Taste of the Divine: Monks and Nuns making Wine in France." *France Today*, November 8, 2019. https://www.francetoday.com/food-drink/wine_and_spirits/monks-and-nuns-making-wine-in-france/.

Larousse Wine: The Definitive Guide for Wine Lovers. London: Hamlyn, 2011.

Lischer, Richard. *The Preacher King: Martin Luther King, Jr. and the Word That Moved America*. 2nd ed. Oxford: Oxford University Press, 2020.

Lohfink, Gerhard. *Jesus and Community*. Minneapolis: Fortress, 1984.

Lovett, Ashley. "'To Become the Future Now': Baptists Being Shaped by the Table." In *Gathering Disciples: Essays in Honor of Christopher J. Ellis*, edited by Myra Blyth and Andy Goodliff, 153–71. Eugene, OR: Pickwick, 2017.

Luther, Martin. "Christ Dwells Only with Sinners." In *The Minister's Prayer Book*, edited by John W. Doberstein. Rev. ed. London: Collins, 1986.

Macleod, Donald. "Counselling and Biblical Psychology." *EVANGEL* 1.3 (July 1983) 15.

Maidment, Ross J., and Matthew J. Mills, eds. *Keeper of the Word: The Virgin Mary in Recent Encounters between Anglicans, Baptists and Catholics.* Oxford: Regent's Park College, forthcoming (2022).

Maltmann, Alex. "The Role of Vineyard Geology in Wine Typicity." *Journal of Wine Research* 19.1 (January 2008) 1–17.

Marlow, Jon J. *Thriving in Curacy: Overcoming Problems in the Placement and Training of Curates.* Cambridge: Grove, 2021.

Martin Luther, Calvin. *The Way of Being Human.* New Haven, CT: Yale University Press, 1999.

Marvell, Andrew. "Thoughts in a Garden." In *The Golden Treasury*, selected by Francis Turner Palgrave. London: Collins, 1954.

May, Rollo. *Power and Innocence: A Search for the Sources of Violence.* New York: Norton, 1972.

McBeath, Clare, and Tim Presswood. *Crumbs of Hope: Prayers from the City.* Peterbourgh: Inspire, 2006.

McClendon, James Wm. *Biography as Theology.* Philadelphia: Trinity, 1990 (1974).

McDonagh, Enda, *Doing the Truth: The Quest for Moral Theology.* Notre Dame: Notre Dame University Press, 1979.

McFadyen, Alistair I. *The Call to Personhood: A Christian Theory of the Individual in Social Relationships.* Cambridge: Cambridge University Press, 1990.

McGill, William J. "The Calling: George Herbert, R. S. Thomas and the Vocations of Priest and Poet." *Anglican Theological Review* 82.2 (2000) 371–89.

McKenzie, Timothy A. "Torn in Two: Vocation and Wholeness in the Poetry of George Herbert, Gerard Manley Hopkins and R. S. Thomas." PhD thesis, University of Glasgow, 1999.

McKnight, Scot. *The Real Mary: Why Evangelical Christians Can Embrace the Mother of Jesus.* Brewster, MA: Paraclete, 2007.

McLeod, John. *An Introduction to Counselling and Psychotherapy.* 6th ed. London: Open University Press, 2019.

Medley, Mark. "Stewards, Interrogators, and Inventors: Toward Practice of Tradition." In *Tradition and the Baptist Academy*, edited by Roger A. Ward and Philip E. Thompson, 67–89. Milton Keynes: Paternoster, 2011.

Merleau-Ponty, M. *Phenomenology of Perception.* London: RKP, 1962.

Mignolo, Walter. *The Idea of Latin America.* Oxford: Blackwell, 2005.

Miller-McLemore, Bonnie. "The Living Human Web: A Twenty-Five-Year Retrospective."
Pastoral Psychology 67.2 (2018) 305–21.

Milne, A. A. "Vespers." In *When We Were Very Young.* London: Methuen, 1924.

Mladin, Natan, Rache Fidler, and Ben Ryan. *That They All May Be One: Insights into Churches Together in England and Contemporary Ecumenism.* London: Theos, 2017.

Muers, Rachel. *Keeping God's Silence: Towards a Theological Ethics of Communication.* Oxford: Blackwell, 2004.

Northcott, Michael. *Place, Ecology and the Sacred.* London: Bloomsbury, 2015.

Nuttall, Geoffrey. *The Holy Spirit in Puritan Faith and Experience.* Oxford: Blackwell, 1946.

Oden, Thomas C. *Ministry Through Word and Sacrament.* Grand Rapids, Baker, 1988.

———. *Pastoral Counsel.* Crossroad, 1989.

————. *Pastoral Theology*. New York: Harper Collins, 1983.

————. *Systematic Theology*. 3 vols. New York: Harper Collins, 1987–1993.

Oswald, Alice. "The Art of Erosion." Inaugural lecture as Professor of Poetry, University of Oxford, 2019. http://podcasts.ox.ac.uk/art-erosion.

Panayi, Panikos. "Immigration, Multiculturalism and Racism." In *20th Century Britain: Economic, Cultural and Social Change*, edited by Francesca Carneval et al., 247–61. Abingdon: Routledge, 2014.

Pattison, Stephen, and James Woodward. "An Introduction to Pastoral and Practical Theology." In *The Blackwell Reader in Pastoral and Practical Theology*, edited by James Woodward and Stephen Pattison, 1–19. Oxford: Blackwell, 2000.

Percy, Martyn. *The Ecclesial Canopy: Faith, Hope, Charity*. Farnham: Ashgate, 2012.

————. *Shaping the Church: The Promise of Implicit Theology*. Farnham: Ashgate, 2010.

Perry, Tim. *Mary for Evangelicals: Toward an Understanding of the Mother of Our Lord*. Downers Grove, IL: InterVarsity, 2006.

Peterson, Eugene. *Subversive Spirituality*. Grand Rapids: Eerdmans, 1997.

————. *Under the Unpredictable Plant*. Grand Rapids: Eerdmans, 1992.

Radcliffe, Timothy. *Alive in God: A Christian Imagination*. London: Bloomsbury 2019.

Reader, John. *Local Theology: Church and Community in Dialogue*. London: SPCK, 1994.

Reddie, Anthony G. *Theologising Brexit: A Liberationist and Postcolonial Critique*. Abingdon: Routledge, 2019.

Reddie, Richard. "'The Preaching of Martin Luther King, Jr." In *Intercultural Preaching*, edited by Anthony G. Reddie and Seidel Abel Boanerges with Pamela Searle, 167–82. Oxford: Centre for Baptist Studies in Oxford, 2021.

Reeves, Andrew, ed.. *An Introduction to Counselling and Psychotherapy*. 2nd. ed. London: Sage, 2018.

Ricoeur, Paul. *Freud and Philosophy: An Essay in Interpretation*. New Haven, CT: Yale University Press, 1970.

Richards, Kent Harold. "Psalm 34." *Interpretation* 40.1 (January 1986) 175–80.

Ridley, M. S. *"In Memoriam," Containing a Brief Sketch of the Ministerial Life and Labours . . . Cornelius Elven. To Which Is Added an Account of the Services Held in Connection with the Funeral, with the Sermon Preaching on the Following Lord's Day*. Bury St. Edmunds, 1873.

Rix, Robert. *William Blake and the Cultures of Radical Christianity*. Aldershot: Ashgate, 2007.

Roach, David. "Baptists and Alcohol: Is the Consensus Shifting?" Baptist Press, November 2, 2018. https://www.baptistpress.com/resource-library/news/baptists-alcohol-is-the-consensus-shifting/.

Ross, Alistair. *Counselling Skills for Church and Faith Community Workers*. Buckingham: Open University Press, 2003.

————. *An Evaluation of Clinical Theology, 1958–1969*. Oxford: CTA, 1993.

————. "An Experience of Falling." *Therapy Today* (October 2014) n.p.

————. *Introducing Contemporary Psychodynamic Counselling and Psychotherapy*. London: Open University Press, 2019.

————. "On Learning from (Being) the Patient." *Psychodynamic Practice* 22.3 (2016) 273–77.

————. *Sigmund Freud*. Stroud: History Press, 2016.

Rowland, Christopher. *Blake and the Bible*. New Haven, CT: Yale University Press, 2011.

———. "Christology, Controversy and Apocalypse: New Testament Exegesis in the Light of the Work of William Blake." In *Christology, Controversy and Community: New Testament Essays in Honour of David R. Catchpole*, edited by David G. Horrell and Christopher. M. Tuckett, 355–78. Leiden: Brill, 2000.

Ryle, Gilbert. "Jane Austen and the Moralists." In *Collected Papers*, vol. 1, *Critical Essays*, 286–301. London: Routledge, 2009.

———. "The Thinking of Thoughts: What Is 'Le Penseur' Doing?." In *Collected Papers*, vol. 2, *Collected Essays, 1929–1968*, 494–510. London: Routledge, 2009.

Sands, Justin. "Introducing Cardinal Cardijn's See–Judge–Act as an Interdisciplinary Method to Move Theory into Practice." *Religions* 9.4 (2018). https://doi.org/10.3390/rel9040129.

Schreiter, Robert J. *Constructing Local Theologies*. London: SCM, 1895.

Searle, Joshua T. *Theology after Christendom: Forming Prophets for a Post-Christendom World*. Eugene, OR: Cascade, 2018.

Sedmak, Clemens. *Doing Local Theology*. Maryknoll, NY: Orbis, 2002.

Shaw, Shona. "God of Love We Praise You." In *Gathering Disciples: Essays in Honor of Christopher J. Ellis*, edited by Myra Blyth and Andy Goodliff, 47–58. Eugene, OR: Pickwick, 2017.

Sheldrake, Philip. *Spirituality and Theology: Christian Living and the Doctrine of God*. London: Darton, Longman and Todd, 1998.

Simkin, John. "Temperance Society." https://web.archive.org/web/20120520013722/ http://www.spartacus.schoolnet.co.uk/REtemperance.htm.

Smith, C. Christopher, and John Pattison. *Slow Church*. Downers Grove, IL: InterVarsity, 2014.

Soskice, Janet Martin. *Metaphor and Religious Language*. Oxford: Oxford University Press, 1985.

Standing, Roger. "Theological Issues: Constants in Context." In *Episkope: The Theory and Practice of Translocal Oversight*, edited by Roger Standing and Paul Goodliff, 14–43. London: SCM, 2020.

Stanley, Brian. *The Bible and the Flag: Protestant Missions and British Imperialism in the Nineteenth and Twentieth Centuries*. Leicester: Apollos, 1990.

Stanton, Graham D. "A Theology of Complexity for Christian Leadership in an Uncertain Future." *Practical Theology* 12.2 (2019) 147–57.

"Statement from the Baptist World Alliance Symposium on Baptist Identity and Ecclesiology." *American Baptist Quarterly* 38.1 (Spring 2019) 109–11.

Taylor, Charles. *The Ethics of Authenticity*. Cambridge, MA: Harvard University Press, 1991.

Teresa of Avila. *The Life of Saint Teresa*. Translated with an introduction by J. M. Cohen. London: Penguin, 1957.

Thomas, R. S., ed. *A Choice of George Herbert's Verse*. London: Faber, 1981.

———. *Collected Poems 1945–1990*. London: J. M. Dent, 1993.

———. *The Echoes Return Slow*. London: MacMillan, 1988.

———. *Laboratories of the Spirit*. London: MacMillan, 1976.

———. "The Making of a Poem." In *R. S. Thomas: Selected Prose*, edited by Sandra Anstey, 107–18. Bridgend: Poetry Wales Press, 1986.

———. *No Truce with the Furies*. Newcastle upon Tyne: Bloodaxe, 1995.

Tournier, Paul. *Learning to Grow Old*. London: SCM, 1960.

———. *Seasons of Life*. London: SCM, 1964.

Travis, Sarah. *Decolonizing Preaching: The Pulpit as Postcolonial Space.* Eugene, OR: Cascade, 2014.

Turner, Victor. *The Ritual Process: Structure and Anti-Structure.* Ithaca, NY: Cornell University Press, 1977.

Tyrell, Terry. *The History of Garland Street Baptist Church, Bury St Edmunds.* Privately printed, 2020.

Volf, Miroslav. *After Our Likeness: The Church as the Image of the Trinity.* Grand Rapids: Eerdmans, 1998.

Walton, Izaak. *The Lives of Dr. John Donne, Sir Henry Wotton, Mr. Richard Hooker, Mr. George Herbert.* 4th ed. London: printed by Tho. Roycroft for Richard Marriot, 1675.

Wayman, Benjamin. "Imagining the Future of Theological Education." *Christian Century,* February 10, 2021. https://www.christiancentury.org/article/features/imagining-future-theological-education.

Weaver, John. "Spirituality in Everyday Life: The View from the Table." In *Under the Rule of Christ: Dimensions of Baptist Spirituality* edited by Paul S. Fiddes, 135–67. Macon, GA: Smyth & Helwys, 2008.

Wells, Samuel. "Changing the Moral Climate." Sermon preached at St Martin-in-the-Fields, August 8, 2021. https://www.stmartin-in-the-fields.org/changing-the-moral-climate/.

———. *Improvisation: The Drama of Christian Ethics.* London: SPCK, 2004.

———. *Incarnational Ministry.* Norwich: Canterbury, 2017.

West, Shearer. *Portraiture.* Oxford: Oxford University Press, 2004.

White, Norman. *Hopkins: A Literary Biography.* Oxford: Oxford University Press, 1995.

Williams, Anne. "Gracious Accommodations: Herbert's 'Love (III).'" *Modern Philology* 22.1 (1984) 13–22.

Williams, Raymond. "Culture in Ordinary." In *Resources of Hope: Culture, Democracy, Socialism.* London: Verso, 1989.

Wirzba, Norman. *From Nature to Creation: A Christian Vision for Understanding and Loving Our World.* Grand Rapids: Brazos, 2015.

———. *This Sacred Life.* Cambridge: Cambridge University Press, 2021.

Wolff, H. G. D. *Joel and Amos.* Hermeneia. Philadelphia: Fortress, 1977.

Wolterstorff, Nicholas. *Art in Action: Toward a Christian Aesthetic.* Carlisle: Solway, 1997.

Woodman, Simon. "'I Have a Vision': Assessing the Impact of Martin Luther King Preaching at Bloomsbury Central Baptist Church." In *Re-Membering the Body: The Witness of History, Theology, and the Arts in Honour of Ruth M. B. Gouldbourne,* edited by Anthony R. Cross and Brian Haymes, 237–56. Eugene, OR: Pickwick, 2021.

Woodward, James, and Stephen Pattison, eds. *The Blackwell Reader in Pastoral and Practical Theology.* Oxford: Blackwell, 2000.

The Word of God in the Life of the Church: A Report of International Conversations between the Catholic Church and the Baptist World Alliance, 2006–2010. American Baptist Quarterly 31.1 (2012) 28–122.

World Council of Churches. *Baptist, Eucharist and Ministry.* Faith and Order Paper 111. Geneva: World Council of Churches, 1982.

Wright, Nigel. *How to Be a Church Minister.* Abingdon: Bible Reading Fellowship, 2018.

————. *The Radical Kingdom: Restoration in Theory and Practice.* Eastbourne: Kingsway, 1986.

Wright, N. T. "How Can the Bible be Authoritative? (The Laing Lecture for 1989)." *Vox Evangelica* 21 (1991) 7–32.

Yoder, John Howard. *Body Politics: Five Practices of the Christian Community before the Watching World.* Scottdale, PA: Herald, 1992.

Lightning Source UK Ltd.
Milton Keynes UK
UKHW021121120622
404294UK00006B/575